GREG CHAPPELL

Not Out

FROM INDIA TO BALL TAMPERING TO AUSTRALIAN CRICKET'S FUTURE

Greg Chappell with Daniel Brettig

Hardie Grant

BOOKS

Published in 2021 by Hardie Grant Books, an imprint of Hardie Grant Publishing

Hardie Grant Books (Melbourne)
Wurundjeri Country
Building 1, 658 Church Street
Richmond, Victoria 3121

Hardie Grant Books (London)
5th & 6th Floors
52–54 Southwark Street
London SE1 1UN

hardiegrantbooks.com

 A catalogue record for this
book is available from the
National Library of Australia

Greg Chappell
ISBN 978 1 74379 723 5

10 9 8 7 6 5 4 3 2 1

Cover design by Luke Causby
Typeset in 10.75/15 pt Minion Pro by Cannon Typesetting
Cover image courtesy of Greg Chappell Cricket Centre

The iconic Greg Chappell hat is available through www.cricketcentre.com.au

Printed in Australia by Griffin Press, part of Ovato, an Accredited
ISO AS/NZS 14001 Environmental Management System printer.

 The paper this book is printed on is certified against the
Forest Stewardship Council® Standards. Griffin Press holds
chain of custody certification SGSHK-COC-005088. FSC®
promotes environmentally responsible, socially beneficial and
economically viable management of the world's forests.

Hardie Grant acknowledges the Traditional Owners of the country on which we
work, the Wurundjeri people of the Kulin nation and the Gadigal people of the
Eora nation, and recognises their continuing connection to the land, waters and
culture. We pay our respects to their Elders past, present and emerging.

CONTENTS

Preface		v
1	A participant, not an observer	1
2	Allan Border's insurance policy	11
3	On captaincy	31
4	Australia A	42
5	Super 8s	52
6	Coaching a state, coaching a nation	59
7	The uphill battle	75
8	A cloud over the game	94
9	Australia in decline	102
10	On batting	110
11	A Centre of Excellence?	126
12	Selector, again	144
13	Pushed out, but still building	163
14	Big Bash battles	172
15	On mental skills	183
16	Selector, part three	198
17	Newlands nadir	208
18	An enduring partnership – by Judy Chappell	222
19	Brothers	233

CONTENTS

20 Recovery, reintegration, retirement 239
21 The Australian system and its discontents 255
22 Loving cricket but not being defined by it 265
23 Last thoughts 272
Acknowledgements 279

PREFACE

M Y LIFE IN cricket has spanned numerous periods of extreme change, from when the game was played by amateurs through to part-time employment and then full-time professionalism. For a significant and well-documented portion of that time, I lived through it as a player and a captain, sampling the English professional game before my Test career began and then experiencing the World Series Cricket revolution and its muddled aftermath, right there in the bubbling crucible.

But I did not finish learning when I walked off the field at the end of my final Test match in 1984. Nor did the game stop changing and evolving, sometimes beautifully and at other times violently. Initially I was not able to go cold turkey in giving up the game entirely – a place on the national selection panel and then the Australian Cricket Board gave me a ringside seat to some of the more far-sighted and ultimately rewarding decisions ever made in the history of Australian cricket. I wonder, now, how many of those calls would be allowed to be made in an era of instant gratification and a much faster news cycle.

After some time away in business, I was first lured back through commentary, only to discover that I really needed to be a participant of some sort to be truly engaged in the game. Coaching Australia A while still doing some broadcasting stints for Channel Nine was close to perfect, but a rare and fleeting privilege, given how cricket and the media who cover it must retain at least some semblance of church and state separation.

With South Australia and then India, I experienced the convulsions being wrought by the professional game. Money had flowed into the game via broadcasters and sponsors ever since World Series Cricket created a much bigger, brassier game – but it also took away some of the spontaneity and breadth of experience many preceding generations had brought to it. In many ways, I felt the jobbing professionals of SA and the international superstars of India's national side shared a common survival instinct: simply trying to make the most of the prevailing system, as distinct from being able to strive freely and collectively for the relatively simple goal of being the best team on the park.

I spent two tumultuous years as national coach of team India, when its leadership was undergoing a transition from the era of Sourav Ganguly, Sachin Tendulkar and Rahul Dravid into the time of MS Dhoni. This also overlapped with the coming of the Indian Premier League, which transformed cricket around the world. These years gave me a rare perspective on the personalities and controversies of the time, and the profound ways in which the IPL, and India's new power, would change cricket. Commercial pressures, and even corruption, became pervasive in unexpected ways.

While my Indian experience ended in disappointment and some disillusionment, it has been gratifying to see the steps followed by the national system in more recent years to find the sort of cohesive, team-oriented approach that I had been first brought in to try to create. At the same time, Australia's hard-won status as the envy of the cricket world was slowly eroded by the pressures of others' professionalism and the ever more complicated priorities of a three-format game, where the 'growth' format of Twenty20 and the revenue-raising imperatives of Cricket Australia butted heads with the more traditional forms of Test cricket – and its Sheffield Shield breeding ground – during every crowded home summer.

Somewhere in this febrile environment, the national team's priorities veered into 'win-at-all-costs' territory, much to the chagrin of all Australians after the Newlands ball-tampering scandal of 2018. To be working in various senior roles at Cricket Australia between 2008 and 2019, including two more stints as a selector, was to have a front-row view of one of the more tumultuous periods of its history. Now we have faced the straitening circumstances of the coronavirus, a challenge that has only helped in sharpening many questions about what the professional era has brought Australian and world cricket, and how we should fashion the game around us to see it endure for many years to come.

Through it all, there are several areas in which my insights and understandings have been altered and, in some cases, totally turned around, even as many fundamentals remain. In looking at areas such as captaincy, batting, and most importantly the mental side of the game, I am sure there will be lessons aplenty for all those who watch, play or coach cricket at any level. I am hopeful, also, that the typically eloquent contribution of my wife, Judy, about how we have maintained an enduring partnership over 50 years will offer something of worth to all.

Some truths take time to reveal themselves; in my case, only now do I fully understand many of these episodes, and I'm ready to address them with fresh candour. This is not my first book about cricket and life, but it is a final reckoning of sorts. It demonstrates how lessons can take a whole lifetime to sink in, how one's actions can keep on evolving new meanings through the years, and how learning never stops.

It is also timely, because although much of what the world has faced thanks to COVID-19 seems unprecedented, history's patterns do repeat, and where else can we look for guidance other than in the lessons of the past?

Greg Chappell, Brisbane, July 2021

1

—

A PARTICIPANT, NOT AN OBSERVER

Australia, 1991–1997

A DELAIDE OVAL, 26 JANUARY, 1993. Just under a decade since my retirement from playing cricket, I was sitting in the Channel Nine commentary box at the top of the Sir Donald Bradman Stand, calling the final moments of one of the great Test matches. Australia, on the long road back from the nadir of the mid-1980s, was a few runs away from beating the West Indies in a series for the first time since 1976, as the last pair of Tim May and Craig McDermott inched their way towards a fourth-innings target of 186. The Adelaide crowd swelled after the tea break, breaking out into choruses of 'Waltzing Matilda', raucously cheering every run from their unlikely tail end heroes.

It fell to me to be holding the microphone and Craig to be on strike for what would be the fateful final ball of the match, as he tried to avoid a Courtney Walsh short ball. The emotion in my voice was perhaps a little more heightened because I'd had a lot to do with Craig through his early years coming through in

Queensland, and then his exceptional efforts to return to international cricket by adopting a fierce fitness regime:

'Oh he's tried to avoid it, it's hit the bat, and he's gone! And the Test match has been won by one run! I can't believe it! The West Indians are delighted, Craig McDermott is so disappointed. It's been a magnificent effort by both sides here today. Courtney Walsh is absolutely delighted, the Australian dressing room will be decimated, but you can bet the West Indian dressing room will be absolutely jumping.'

To be calling such a moment at the end of such a great and exciting day of cricket was absolutely an adrenaline rush and a thrill, as much as I was devastated for Craig and captain Allan Border, who had just seen his last chance to beat the mighty Windies disappear with the raising of Darrell Hair's right index finger. But there were other times when I struggled to be as engaged as that, as a mere observer of international matches and not the participant I had been for my playing days and then for four years as a selector.

As a player, selector or a coach, you have an emotional involvement in the game. You've been part of the build-up, so the result is of interest to you. In the commentary box, it didn't matter who won. You would've preferred Australia to win as a countryman, but if they didn't win it was no big deal. That meant I could struggle to put myself in a similarly demonstrative place purely for broadcasting reasons. Long before I finished playing, during Bill Lawry's earliest days calling World Series Cricket, there was a point when Kerry Packer told him, 'If you don't raise the emotion a little bit, you won't be commentating for much longer.' Bill obviously took the advice on board.

Kerry's aura stayed with us long after he died in 2005. So much so that when the *Howzat!* mini-series about World Series

Cricket was in production a decade later, I briefly thought he'd come back from the grave. Several of us served as consultants on the series (I was more than happy with Damon Gameau's portrayal of me, by the way), and after one production meeting I was heading back to my car when I heard, in that unmistakable voice, a shout of 'Chappell!' I stopped in mid-stride, slowly turned around, and saw Kerry's doppelganger Lachy Hulme, who had tried to inhabit the spirit and size of Kerry as much as possible, to the point of adopting his diet. 'F***, you got me,' I exclaimed. 'I thought he was back!' Lachy was pretty pleased about that.

When you've been there and done that as a player, you're less likely to be excited than someone sitting in the crowd. The danger as a commentator is you don't show enough emotion – and there was never any chance of that with Bill thereafter. We also had the instructive example of Billy Birmingham and the Twelfth Man albums, parodying Bill, Tony Greig and Richie Benaud in particular. He ramped Bill up and then Bill began to follow suit himself. Sitting alongside Bill in the commentary box (he was often standing), I was staggered by how he was always the first one there, he'd get into the No. 1 seat even before the batting order had been put up and be there watching the warm-ups intently. I was impressed that he could get so excited about something he'd seen so often. That wasn't me.

It was Channel Nine's head of sport, Ian Frykberg, who first spoke to me about commentary, and my reluctance to take up a position spoke a lot about how it was never going to be a long-term deal. He wanted to get me into the Nine box full time, something I wasn't prepared to do, because cutting back on travel had been one of the main reasons I had finished up as a selector in 1988 in the first place. In the end I came to an understanding with Nine that I would do Test matches and some one-day matches if I happened to be around. A bit like when I gave up the Australian captaincy at various times, where once I gave it up I didn't expect to get it back again, each time I pushed back on Nine I didn't expect to get another invitation, but they kept coming.

The first time I ever called a game was at Adelaide Oval, and I found myself seated next to Bill. He was commentating and shouted 'and he's got him!' in typical style, when the ball was halfway down the pitch. When the wicket followed milliseconds later I thought 'what a genius you are, Bill'. Or at least, I thought he was, until I realised I was watching the ever-so-slightly-delayed broadcast monitor while Bill was actually watching what was happening on the ground.

My first main commentary gig was on the 1991 tour of the West Indies, which was an attractive first offer of broadcasting work since I had such happy memories of playing there in 1973 and on the WSC tour in 1979. The 1972 England tour has always stood on a pedestal for me, but '73 in the Caribbean had been memorable just because it was so different. You had beaches everywhere, you had music, you had sunshine we never saw in England, how good's that? The day before the first one-day game in '91, we went down to the ground to do a soundcheck, have a look and run through a rehearsal. I gave it the 'and welcome back to Sabina Park' whereupon Geoff Morris, the director, came down the earpiece and said 'Greg, you don't have to welcome people back to Sabina Park, they know which ground they're at'. That was the first and only bit of advice I got. They basically handed you a microphone and told you to get on with it.

Being on the other side of the microphone for interviews was another new experience, in one instance with the former

West Indian captain Clive Lloyd. We were down on the ground in broad sunlight during a break in play, with the monitor in front of us. They were playing a couple of highlights of the session, so I was meant to be referring to what was on screen. But because of the glare I couldn't see a thing and had to wing it, talking to Clive. When I finished, the director blew up: 'Greg, when we throw to the monitor, you've got to refer to what's on the monitor.'

'That's terrific Geoff, but if I can't see it I can't talk about it.'

'What do you mean?'

'The sunlight on the monitor meant I couldn't see the screen, I had no idea what was going on.'

So they then built themselves a glare screen for the monitor.

The cricket itself was certainly interesting enough, as Border's team struggled with their own mental limitations against a fading West Indies side led by Viv Richards. There were terrific players on both sides, and that was always the primary joy of commentating, alongside trying to read the play as I once did in the middle.

Yet I found the amount of downtime excruciating. At least when you're playing or coaching you've got things to do; there's always a meeting on or a training session, or discussion of the team make-up, the conditions at the ground and what a good score might be, or looking at the data from previous games. But in the West Indies there were only so many books you could read or beaches you could sit on. The advantage that my brother Ian and Richie had, to name two, was that they were also writing for newspapers, so they had things to do and I'm sure that helped.

We got to Guyana for the last of the one-day games and the second Test, and by this point I was already bored out of my mind. During the one-day game I was on commentary and somebody hit a six over mid-off and the oval, being below sea level, had a pair of moats around the ground for protection. I'd thought about how to describe this, and I also knew it was about 2 am in Australia, so not many people would be watching – and maybe even Kerry had gone to bed by this stage. So a six was hit and I said 'oh it's gone past the near canal and over the far canal', which just went through to the 'keeper in the commentary box, but I got a couple of messages from mates back home. We used to have a bit of fun with the kinds of things we could try to fit into the commentary without getting banned by Kerry, but it also shows the boredom I was feeling.

Then, between the one-day game and the second Test, I had nothing to do and was desperate for a game of golf. I'd spoken to Tony; he was busy. I'd spoken to Ian; he had to write a story. So I thought 'there's only one left, there's Richie'. Richie was protective of his privacy and his time, and didn't encourage approach. I knew him, but I knew enough to know, be careful, you don't approach him without due cause. But I thought 'f*** it, I'm not going to play on my own, I've got to find a golf partner'. So I rang Richie's room. He answered and I said 'Rich, you interested in a game of golf at all?'

'Erm, Greg I've got to finish an article, but after 12 o'clock, yes.'

I opened up the phone book to look for a Georgetown golf club, found one to my relief and gave it a call. The phone rang, and rang, and rang … before finally someone picked up the phone, huffing and puffing, 'Hello, Georgetown golf club.' So we got a round organised, we didn't need clubs because Richie had his with him, and I called him back to say meet downstairs at one o'clock. It turned out to be about a 40-minute drive out to this course, way out of town, into the sugar plantations. The main road was okay, but then we turned off it and had

20 minutes on this rutted dirt track. Richie's said nothing, but I could sense that he was sitting there unimpressed, looking down his lip, and I was thinking 'this is not going well'.

All of a sudden on the left this golf course came into view, and down in the furthest point of the golf course from the clubhouse I saw a couple of groundsmen working on a green. As the noise of the car coming down the road became obvious, this bloke looked up from the work he was doing on the green, dropped his fork and his bucket and started running. So this must've been the bloke who answered the phone: not only was he head groundsman, but general manager, secretary and caterer too! I was chatting away to Richie as much as you could on the drive, and he was nodding and giving minimal answers. We set off on a nine-hole course but with two sets of tees for each hole, and it was a nice little country golf course.

After about four holes I realised I was doing all the talking. I was either making a statement or asking a question, but it dawned on me that Richie's hardly said a word from the hotel to the golf course. Now we're four holes into the round and I reckon I'm the only one who's spoken. I wondered how long we could go if I didn't say a word, how long it would be before I got anything out of Richie? The answer was not a single word until we got back to the clubhouse. He just wanted to concentrate on his golf; he didn't want light conversation, and so that's what he got. It was a pretty stark lesson about Richie: when he was focused on something, just leave him alone. In the end I broke the silence by asking him if he'd like a beer. Came the reply after some hours, 'Yes, that'd be nice.'

I knew, at least, that this wasn't an issue with me. I recalled being with Ian and Richie at various times and observing how Ian would ask questions of Richie and then answer them himself, because it was the only way he was getting a conversation. It never seemed to bother Ian, and I think Richie enjoyed Ian's company and friendship, so he likely put up with him talking more than he would have put up with most people. But Richie's was such a singular presence that you did enjoy having him around, even if there were times he had very little to say. I'll always wonder how much that reserve was increased by Richie's fame and the degree to which he was (lovingly) parodied.

One year we were down at Bellerive Oval in Hobart for a domestic one-day game, Queensland playing Tasmania. We were in Bellerive's famously swaying gantry with the couple of containers on top, one for the commentary box and the other for Richie's hosting studio, where he would sit alone, either writing or enjoying the peace and quiet when not on commentary. The rest of us when we weren't commentating either had to get off the gantry and go for a walk, or just stand or lean on the wall at the back of the container – if you were about to come on the air, you needed to know what the other guys were talking about lest you directly contradict them. Everyone was by this stage well aware of Billy Birmingham.

I was standing in the back of the commentary box. Bill was in the No. 1 seat, and Richie was in the No. 2 seat. Anyone sitting alongside Bill knew they weren't going to get many opportunities. The old lip ribbon mic, you had to hold it right up to your mouth, because if it was sitting in your lap you could have a regular conversation and not go on air. When you were commentating, the done thing was that when you said what you wanted to say, you put the microphone down so that the other bloke knew he could talk. The worst thing you can have in commentary is two blokes talking over the top of each other.

But Bill never took it down. He'd sit there for the whole stint with the microphone up to his mouth. When you were working with him, you had to sit side by side, watch him, and when his lips stopped moving you had to jump in as quick as you could. Then, when you were talking, Bill would be virtually prodding you to shut up so he could say something. You could sense Bill edging his way into your half of a space little bigger than a telephone booth. I got to a point with Bill where I would sit with my back to him, so that I couldn't get intimidated by him hurrying you along so he could speak again.

Richie was leaning back in the No. 2 seat, knowing that Bill was going to cover it anyway, and if he felt moved to say something, he could always put his hand on Bill's shoulder and he'd know to shut up. The scoreboard got to 2 for 222 and Bill, bless him, actually did what everyone else was thinking: 'And it's chew for chew hundred and chwenty chew.' With that he started rolling himself around in his chair laughing, and we all reeled back with 'oh what's going to happen here'. Richie had his microphone wrapped in his arms and was looking down his lip at Bill. So Richie wouldn't commentate, and Bill couldn't commentate because he was too busy laughing. Each time he got himself together and picked the microphone back up, he looked over at Richie and started laughing again. Two and a half overs they went without any commentary, because Richie wouldn't commentate, and Bill couldn't. We were losing it laughing in the commentary box, and the blokes down in the truck were going 'what's going on up there, why is no-one commentating?'

John Gaylard was a producer on the broadcast, and he kept saying, 'Mate, Richie won't commentate and Bill can't commentate, he's too busy laughing.' Richie's attitude was 'Bill, you got yourself into it, you get yourself out of it'. But not another word was said about it afterwards.

Sitting next to me that dramatic day in Adelaide in 1993 was David Gower, who at that stage hadn't even formally retired from playing for England, and was largely there as a result of his omission from a Test tour to India. At the time, it might have been hard for some to predict which of us would spend the next three decades as a broadcaster, but David's enormous contributions to the likes of the BBC and Sky were still ahead of him.

My mind, though, was drifting even on days as good as that. Because the emotional level wasn't piqued, it didn't get me as enthused as coaching and selection, building teams and putting groups together. Those things challenged my mind more than just turning up and seeing what would happen in the game from what Birmingham liked to call the 'central missionary position'. I knew that if I was going to stay involved in cricket, my involvement would have to be an active one.

2

ALLAN BORDER'S INSURANCE POLICY

Australia, 1984–1989

WHERE WOULD AUSTRALIAN cricket be without Allan Border? It's natural to think that the whole game would have been a lot worse off had he not found a way to slog through the difficult early years of his captaincy to help restore the performances and self-image of the Australian team. Yet as selectors in the mid-1980s, we had to wrestle with the question on what seemed like a daily basis, to the point that we had to bring in the New South Wales captain Dirk Wellham as a ready replacement in the Mike Brearley mould (captain first, batsman second).

At the darkest, lowest point of that era between the World Series Cricket split and the renaissance that started with the 1987 World Cup victory, the panel, comprising chairman Laurie Sawle, Jim Higgs, Dick Guy and myself, had to actively consider what we'd do if Border walked away. He certainly threatened to more than once, publicly doing so in New Zealand in early 1986 and returning to the topic as fervently during the following home summer when the Ashes were lost.

Things came to a head, really, after an innings defeat in three days at the MCG to surrender the series to Mike Gatting's Englishmen. When this was closely followed by the hosts losing all three of their matches in the Perth Challenge held over the new year to coincide with the America's Cup yacht race in Fremantle, we knew we were on the precipice with Allan.

Wellham was captain of New South Wales and a reasonably experienced player. What we didn't know was whether he was good enough with the bat. We had decided to drop the vice-captain David Boon for the last Test in Sydney, and our recommendation through Sawle, who also sat on the Australian Cricket Board, was to install Wellham as Allan's deputy. There was some history here: in 1985, Wellham had been one of the players who decided against touring Apartheid South Africa after being convinced otherwise by PBL Marketing (in other words, Kerry Packer), with the aid of a job offer. This had gone down like the proverbial lead balloon with other members of the England touring party, not least AB himself.

Wellham, then, was an insurance policy and not a particularly popular one. The reason we asked for him to be vice-captain was also to fire a warning shot over Allan's bow to say 'if you don't pull your head in, we'll just move on'. It had got to that stage. When you've started to annoy Laurie Sawle, you've done a good job – he had a high patience threshold and AB went through that threshold.

While the board rejected the vice-captaincy recommendation, meaning that it ultimately fell to Geoff Marsh, Wellham was still included in the side for the SCG Test and the World Series Cup games after it. Border was so angry at the selection decision itself that he threw a tantrum upon hearing about it at a bar in Perth, and flew home early to Brisbane. That left Boon, himself digesting the fact of his omission, to deliver the captain's address at the official function held to conclude the Perth Challenge. A few years later, AB would be similarly ropeable when the decision was made to drop Marsh from the Test side.

Wellham, in the final analysis, was probably not good enough as a player, but he could have been a presentable captain for a short time. We were just trying to get through that period in the hope we could get Border through. He took it all very personally; he took losing personally and didn't enjoy it at all. I don't blame him for that. We'd put some support structures around him and even that wasn't helping him as much as he needed. But if we hadn't done that, he wouldn't have got to 20 Tests as captain, let alone the 93 he finished up with.

Knowing what he went through in the early stages, it's a great credit to him and to Australian cricket that we managed to get him through. Save for this insurance policy, we were really of the view that Allan was the only man who could do the job and we needed to help prop him up until such time as some other blokes stood up and we started getting some results.

Much more renowned is the tale of Peter Taylor. Plucked from supposed obscurity for the final Test of the 1986–87 Ashes series at the SCG, he helped bowl Australia to victory. I'd seen him perform well in the previous season's Sheffield Shield final for NSW. He knew what he was doing, he could handle himself mentally, and we needed a second spin bowler for the conditions, having already settled on Peter Sleep's wrist spin. Of course, when we picked him for the SCG, every man and his dog came out from around the country to say we picked the wrong Taylor, given that Mark was by this time starting to do well as a batsman.

That was a good lesson to underline that, whether as a player or a selector, it is important to have a few people whose opinions you respect and listen to, but to try not to take much notice of the rest. Back then there was no option to watch or stream all the Shield matches around the country, so the selectors in almost all cases had a lot more knowledge of players than the public, the media or even the members of the Nine commentary team.

There was absolutely no truth to the line that we picked the wrong Taylor: we picked the bloke we wanted, and we got a really honest performance on a pitch that suited. Eight wickets and man of the match was better than even we expected, and funnily enough we actually dropped him for Australia's next Test, 10 months later in Brisbane. But 'PT' was a good example of the sort of players and characters we were looking for to bolster Border and the core players we'd identified.

Border's struggles from 1985 to 1987 were just the latest episode in a saga that also swallowed up Kim Hughes and myself as his captaincy predecessors. The story of the underarm has been told to death, but the backstory of the underarm hasn't been told much at all. Ordering my brother Trevor to bowl underarm for that last ball against New Zealand at the MCG was a cry for help from me. We'd gone through World Series Cricket and all the agony that came with it, and come out the other side, but most of the old problems still existed. We now had better pay – we also had a lot more cricket in different formats. In particular, the stress and strain of the captain being the focal point of everything to do with Australian cricket came through.

That was reflected in my closing years, then still more so with Kim Hughes as he took the captaincy in my absences and then full time from the start of the 1983–84 season. The team then faced the loss of Dennis Lillee, Rod Marsh and myself, before back-to-back series against the West Indies that helped play a significant role in the demise of Hughes. There were the unsanctioned tours of Apartheid South Africa that skimmed most of the next rung of players off the Sheffield Shield, and through it all the litany of defeats that Border and his fledgling side then had to suffer, amounting to nearly four full years without a Test series victory against anyone – imagine the reaction to that happening now!

I was new as a selector, but I had the experience of playing and being in teams where I'd seen the right people selected and the wrong people selected. So I had knowledge from the other side of selection to know how important it is to get the right people together, because there are never that many who have the wherewithal to stay on as long-term players. Nevertheless it was a case of trial and error. We used 19 players during the Test matches against the West Indies at home in 1984–85, and then 21 during the World Series Cup and the World Championship of Cricket that ran for a month following it.

At the end of it we sat down and said, 'This is unsustainable, you can't just keep running a revolving door policy. We've got to make a stand at some point and identify who our best players of the next generation are and pick them and play them and stick with them, and let them know we're going to give them time.' As long as we saw the right traits and the right effort going into it, we were going to be patient and give them time to establish themselves, because they weren't going to be ready. Those plans were hurried forward by the South Africa tours.

We'd lost Lillee and Marsh and myself from the previous era, and then all of a sudden we had the loss of the rebels to deal with. The saddest loss out of that group was undoubtedly Hughes. Through the mental pressure and the emotional damage that was done through the captaincy period, we chose not to take him to England in 1985 on the basis that he needed a break. But the conversation around the selection table was that if we gave him a few months off, we'd have a player who at the age of 31 had made more than 4000 Test runs and would be fresh and ready to go for the next home summer. In the meantime, hopefully one or two players would have stood up in England and all of a sudden we'd have the nucleus of our next team.

We definitely had a conversation around making sure the message got through to him that 'we're not picking you to go to England because we think you need the break', but that given a few months away he would come back as that experienced player we needed alongside Border in the middle order. Maddeningly, both at the time and still today, it seems that either the message – which as ever fell to the chairman, Laurie Sawle, to deliver – didn't get through or wasn't received and understood as it should have been. Kim Hughes has no recollection of it. So Hughes remained in such a state of unease that when the offer to go to Apartheid South Africa as captain came he chose to accept it, and he never played for Australia again. That was a tragedy on a number of levels, not least for the huge difference he could have made to our batting over the next three or four years.

The other factor we had was that Border was struggling. He was a reluctant captain in the first place, he wasn't enjoying losing, wasn't enjoying the fact he felt he was out on his own. He was feeling a lot of the same sense of isolation that I had felt prior to giving up the captaincy, and no doubt what Hughes had felt leading up to his resignation.

It quickly became obvious that even if he remained captain, Border wasn't interested in the broader responsibilities, having seen them at close hand. He was happy to do the on the field stuff at most. My experience was useful there to be able to explain the situation, to say to the board and selectors, 'If we don't give the captain more support, we're going to burn through captains faster than we can produce them. We've got someone we know can do the job, let him just worry about what goes on on the field. We need people around him who can deal with the rest of it.'

A major lesson out of my experiences in playing was that there were certain personality traits that worked at the highest level of the game. While you could have a few mercurial characters around a team, you needed a bedrock of stability to support the captain and give young players a clear idea of what was required. The likes of David Hookes, Wayne Phillips and Greg Ritchie were no doubt talented, and on their day produced some terrific performances: Flipper's remarkable hundred in Barbados against the West Indies in 1984, and Greg's unbeaten century against a rampant Abdul Qadir in Faisalabad in 1982 were as good as you can get. Hookesy's best days made him a legend in South Australia. But they all had obstacles to getting the best out of themselves at the highest level.

Some of the hardest conversations I've ever had in cricket were those as a selector when still dealing with players I had been teammates and, in many cases, friends with. Greg and Hookesy were perhaps the two most difficult, as senior players who remained available even during the bans on the players who had gone to South Africa.

I remember a discussion with Ritchie when we dropped him from the national team in 1987. We had been pretty close, because we'd played together, I'd been captain when he first came into the Queensland side, and he was a gifted cricketer. But he wasn't a great fielder, he was overweight and unfit at various times, and in his last series, against England in 1986–87, he had managed to average 40 despite a highest score of 46 over five matches: lots of starts, no scores to really influence the outcome.

During a game at the Gabba, Greg approached me and said, 'How can you leave me out?'

'Mate, you're not doing the job as we want it done.'

'But I'm averaging 35.'

'Greg, there's more to it than the runs you make – you cost us 20 runs in the field so you may as well be averaging 15. We're better off getting somebody who's only averaging 30 but saving us 20 runs in the field. He's bringing more to the team than you've got. We're not going to keep picking you if you can only give us 60 per cent of what you could give us. You should be averaging 45 and be improving your fielding.'

Ritchie was unhappy with that, and he wore the barbs of spectators too. I'm not saying this to denigrate him, and we remain good mates, but someone needed to give him the news he didn't want to hear. For him it had to go from being a matter of us having dropped him, to what he could do to make the improvements the team required. Around the same time, I also had to go through a difficult conversation with Hookesy, this time in Adelaide when he was out of the team.

Hookes would regularly belt domestic bowlers all around the park, particularly when the international players were elsewhere. But he was certainly not as confident a cricketer as he made himself out to be, and that showed in a batting instinct to get runs as quickly as he could, because he didn't back himself to stay out there all day against a strong attack. This is not to say he had to block everything instead, but play the bowling and the situation more thoughtfully.

There had been signs early in Hookesy's career that he could have developed this way. His first tour of England in 1977 was very good for a first-time tourist on a difficult trip given the seaming conditions and also the breaking of the WSC revelations while we were there. The pace-heavy emphasis of WSC, and his status as a pin-up boy of the competition, probably came too early for him to fully round his game.

Once peace was declared and he was in and out of the Australian side, his game was limited by the fact he found that he could score pretty freely in the Sheffield Shield by tugging lots of balls to midwicket and square leg, often from well outside off stump, particularly in Adelaide, with the short square boundaries it then had. He was more or less unchallenged as the best batsman in his state, and was well on the way to becoming a media star. It was during this period that he got a message to me to ask if I could come have a chat in the dressing room. Like Greg Ritchie, he wanted to know what he could do to get back into the national side, given that he was making plenty of runs in first-class cricket.

I replied: 'The trouble is, Hookesy, you've done that before and then played internationally and it hasn't been as successful. I'd suggest one of the things the selection panel are noting is how you're getting your runs and who you're getting them against. You're pulverising the lesser teams and the lesser bowlers, and you get your runs largely through and over midwicket and square leg, especially at Adelaide Oval. I would think we'd be a lot more impressed if we saw you hitting the ball along the ground and scoring runs all around the wicket, because that's where you've struggled in Test cricket. If you can show us you can get runs on the off side as well as the leg side and you're prepared to hit the ball along the ground and not just take the easy runs, because they don't come by as often in Test cricket, then we'll look at picking you again.'

The next thing I heard, sometime later, was that Hookesy has relayed the story that I was the only bloke who ever tried to change the way he batted, and that I'd said 'we want you to show you can get a hundred in five hours, not just in two hours'.

We remained good friends throughout, but those aren't easy conversations to have, and they can be very difficult ones for the players concerned. But they need to be had. To this day we keep hearing about issues of communication between selectors and players, but in the vast majority of cases, the players know exactly what they've got to do. They're informed at every turn, and I know having been involved in three iterations as a selector, that the communication has got more frequent. The message remains fundamentally the same: make runs, take wickets and show the discipline and other required traits of a successful player in a successful team.

The next step as selectors was that we had to put people around Border who were going to support him. We couldn't have the England situation where you had four or five blokes who thought they should've been captain. We needed to be clear he was captain, and was going to be captain for as long as he could stand up. We didn't need someone coveting his job, and we needed people around him who had strong personalities, strong constitutions, who could be his allies and support – his henchmen on the field. The four pillars became David Boon (Test debut in November 1984), Geoff Marsh (December 1985), Steve Waugh (December 1985) and ultimately Ian Healy (September 1988 in Pakistan). These were the guys who we knew would have Border's back, would look after him on the field, pick up any slack that was required, and they were given the strong message that 'you guys are here for as long as you can show us that you're prepared to do what needs to be done to make this a good team'.

Can you imagine giving Steve Waugh 20 Test matches to establish himself today, taking 22 Tests to get his average out of the 20s, and another four Tests to make his first hundred, after four years? Not possible. The world has changed since then, but it took a fair bit of courage from everybody – the selection panel and the board – to persist. There were certainly a few discussions that the board had, and questions Laurie Sawle had to field at times about the direction of his plans. But the panel understood what was needed and the philosophy was carried through.

Even subsequent to that I think we've had a few periods where it has got a bit off track, but, by and large, even in that period in the 90s when we supposedly had two teams you could have interchanged, I reckon there's only ever about 20 players you can pick from. You take someone like Andrew Symonds, no doubting his talent, but he just did not have the appetite for all the peripherals – media appearances, corporate obligations and the like. There's a lot of things to take on with it, other than just playing. I think it's been instructive listening to some of the talk around the Covid hubs in the AFL – they've got to go away for a few months for once in their lives, whereas we did that every year.

There's not many people who can do what an international cricketer has to do. Talent is the first thing you're looking for, but then personality, temperament and all those sorts of things. On performance in first-class cricket you might be able to stretch out to 30-odd names that you can say 'talented enough'. But quite honestly I think I'm being generous in saying 20, it may even be as few as 14. Looking at that team through the 1990s, there was a core of four or five who went through the lot of it, and there might have been another 20 around them. Those who are actually going to make a difference for Australian cricket, there's probably six at any given time.

So you'd better identify who those six are and give them the opportunity and time they need to work it out. Because nobody is ready. I don't care how long you wait, nobody is a ready, fully finished international cricketer when they first make it. It takes about 20 Test matches to truly work out how you see your game fitting in and how you fit into the whole scheme of things.

Sure I made a hundred in my first innings of Test cricket, but that was more good luck than good judgement. It was the easiest innings I ever played, because I think I went under the radar that day. We were 5 for 100, Ian Redpath was the last recognised batsman and I was in at No. 7. England was only worried about getting Redders out. Then reality set in, and the rest of that first series was really hard work – I passed 50 only once more. All of a sudden I had an expectation of myself that I hadn't had before walking out to bat in Perth, and the opposition knew they needed to put a bit of time and effort in as well. It only got harder for that next period, until I got to the point, luckily in the next series against the Rest of the World (in 1971–72) that it all came together.

But it will be anywhere between 10 and 20 innings in Test cricket before you know where you're at, whether you fit and whether you want to fit. That's the other thing – are you prepared to work that hard? If you want to make runs at that level, you've got to work very hard. That was the thing with several of the players during that mid-1980s period that we moved away from. We concluded that they didn't want to work hard enough, and to be fair, maybe they were the smart ones in terms of how they saw their own lives. Certainly, when the time came for me to retire, it was as straightforward as knowing I didn't want to work that hard anymore. You can't afford to be a little bit off your best.

Craig McDermott, for instance, didn't know how fit he had to be to bowl fast in Test cricket until he actually got there. He worked out, during some time on the fringe of the Test team, that he wasn't fit enough. On the Gold Coast he did quite a lot of training with the ironman Trevor Hendy, and he gave Craig a pretty strong idea that he wasn't fit enough or working hard enough. Through training together, Craig realised he wasn't really even scratching the surface, and he got himself seriously fit.

But you had a kid there initially who at 19 years old could bowl 140 kph and had a big, strong body. It's only he and Graham McKenzie who started at that age and didn't have serious back problems or spend extended periods out of the game. But if you talk to Graham about it, he'll say he did have stress fractures at different times, but managed them. There would've been a lot of young bowlers on the verge of serious stress fractures at the end of a season, who then got four or five months off before they had to bowl again, by which time they had healed and never even knew it.

I mentioned that to Jeff Thomson once, saying he didn't have any back problems. He replied, no, not until later on. He had to have an X-ray for something unrelated and they found he had three old stress fractures that had healed and he never knew about them. McKenzie though talked about seasons playing county cricket in England where he had to very carefully manage his workloads, because he knew he was struggling, bowling well within himself and things like that.

Unquestionably, the biggest difference this could have made would have been to the career of Bruce Reid. It's possible you could have got another 20 or more Test matches out of him in spite of his physique if we'd known then what we know now. I met his father once in a hotel in Adelaide when Bruce was playing – I got in the lift and I'd never seen this bloke before, but I saw him and said 'you've got to be Mr Reid', because he was just exactly the same build. Wasn't as tall as Bruce, but he was an older, mini-version of his son. These days there's no way Reid would have bowled in so many games back to back as he did as a young man. Properly managed, we might have got another four or five years out of him at the top level.

We probably should have been more aware then than we were, but if he'd just played Test cricket, he might've played 50 to 70 Test matches and helped get us back to the top of the tree three or four years before Australia finally did so in 1995. But even that trip to the West Indies in 1991, fancy sticking someone with his build – all 202 centimetres of him – down the back of the plane squashed into an economy seat for a journey that long. He was never going to come off that plane in good shape.

Australian cricket's done a lot of good research into back injuries and keeping fast bowlers on the track. The likes of Kevin Sims and Alex Kountouris have collected a lot of data over the years and I think we've got a pretty good handle on it. Nowadays, the medical staff can essentially tell you ahead of time when someone is going to break down. 'He's in the high-risk zone,' they'll say, and as a selector you've got to then make the decision whether you want to roll the dice or not, and almost every time the dice has been rolled, they've broken down.

Peter Siddle was a recent example: the selectors were told 'if he plays this next Test match he's likely to break down' and sure enough he did, against South Africa in Perth in 2016. But that's the decision you've got to make (and those selectors were hard pressed, because of injuries to other bowlers). The fitness guys are not in a position to rule someone out, but they can pretty well tell you when a bowler is on the cusp, and if he goes one more time, he's likely to bust. Generally they're right.

~

The other major pillar of our support around Allan was Bob Simpson as coach, beginning in 1986 and then also becoming a selector in 1987. As a great advocate for doing the simple things well, and drilling his players relentlessly in fielding and running between the wickets, it was always clear what Simmo wanted – a team that played the percentages within their limitations. He and Border built a strong professional relationship, although at times they could be a little too close in terms of personality and out-look. In a coach and a captain you want a breadth of views and a balance of personalities, so one can challenge the other. Border was quite happy for Simpson to come in and run the show, and the proof in the pudding was the 1987 World Cup victory, where a young and unheralded group prevailed largely by being fitter and more disciplined than the rest of the world.

My only reservation at the time was that I felt Simpson should have been titled cricket manager rather than head coach, to help ensure there was no question as to the captain's ultimate authority. People have often said that every other sport gives total selection authority to the coach, so why doesn't cricket? Well, most other sports are football codes, and in those cases the coach has a club team right in front of him, whereas here we are talking about a national representative team, meaning that one person doesn't see the vast majority of the players who may be in his XI. As the years went by the team did stagnate somewhat after that success and others, like the 1989 Ashes tour, meaning that a fresh dynamic was needed to take the team to the very top. Fortunately Mark Taylor was to prove the ideal leader in that regard.

The best players then were, and still are, pretty self-contained and resilient, with personal belief that they can play a part in binding a team together. That's what I saw in Ian Healy. I covered numerous Queensland games as the resident selector in Brisbane, and I'd seen Ian coming through the junior levels. He was more of a batsman than a wicketkeeper to begin with, but what I saw in him stuck with me.

In early 1988 I was down in Tasmania as the selector on duty for a Sheffield Shield game and the first choice gloveman, Peter Anderson, had broken a finger standing up to the stumps to Ian Botham, who was Queensland's big overseas signing that season. As a consequence, Healy got a few games around the time the selection panel was thinking about the composition of the team to go to Pakistan. In later years I discussed what I could see with Anderson: he was a better 'keeper than Ian was ever going to be, a brilliant pair of hands. But his temperament was more highly strung and his glovework could wax and wane with his emotions, specifically those around how well he felt he was keeping wicket.

The Queensland side, which had begun the season as irrepressibly as a road train as often happened due to plenty of early home games at the Gabba, was starting to pop a few rivets. Botham's presence was increasingly a source of distraction to a young team. Border was frustrated by this, and it came to a head in Tasmania. He had stormed back to the team hotel and gone to his room, closely followed by Botham in his efforts to get Border back down to the bar to have another drink – efforts that went as far as kicking down a hotel room door. That evening

I just happened to be in the bar at the same hotel before the shenanigans started, and Healy was with a group of two or three young players in one corner.

At this point it's worth noting that in addition to being an Australian selector, I was on the executive of the Queensland Cricket Association and had been part of discussions about whether to recruit Botham or not in the first place. I'm not hesitant to say I was the sole dissenting voice out of 25-odd members of the executive about signing him. My view was that while Botham would undoubtedly add to the gate receipts at the Gabba, and sponsorships besides, we had a duty to give the young players the best environment possible. I didn't think we would be doing our duty if we put Botham into that dressing room, because it was going to end in tears. I was outvoted there. Then in the matter of how long to sign Botham for, I said make sure it is just a one-year deal because he won't last any longer than that. They signed him for three years.

Back in the hotel bar, I could see Healy's group in a corner, while another, larger group of players was growing around Botham holding court. The best way I could describe it was as bees around a honeypot, preparing to go out, and it did not bode well for the game to come the following day. I could hear as Healy's group began to chat about whether or not to join in the party, and distinctly remember Healy's recommendation that he thought it might be safer if they kept to themselves. Immediately he seemed to be someone capable of reading the play in terms of discipline.

During the match itself in Launceston, Tasmania put up a big score through David Boon, and in reply Queensland were five down, still a fair way behind, and looking towards a declaration sometime after lunch. I needed a drink, so I wandered into the Queensland dressing room to pinch a bottle of water during the break, and sitting in the room were Healy and Glenn Trimble, the two unbeaten batsmen. Trimble had played more games than Healy, but I walked into the middle of the conversation where Trimble was asking 'well, what do we do, what does AB want us to do, are we declaring, what's going on'. As I was walking out, Healy just said, 'Mate, all we can do is our job and keep batting until we get an indication of what's going on – no point getting worried about what the captain might do.' Healy has recalled that I told him 'keep your head down, a hundred is here for the taking' and his thought was 'a selector has said that to see if I'm thinking about the team or myself'. I wasn't testing him to that extent, but certainly a hundred would have raised him up further in wider estimations than the unbeaten 58 he eventually finished on when Allan did declare.

Boon made another hundred and Queensland were bowled out on the last day for Tasmania's first win in 44 first-class matches, and then followed up by winning again in the one-day game the next day. The Botham experiment ended in a police arrest for him in Perth after poor behaviour on the flight there for the Shield final, which WA won with the home-ground advantage that had been Queensland's for the taking for most of the season. Botham did not return.

Those moments with Heals were still in my mind when we sat down as a panel to choose the squad for Pakistan. We had resolved to move on from Greg Dyer, who had held the gloves for most of the previous season. I relayed those stories of Healy to the other selectors, none of whom knew much of him at all, and while we discussed Anderson as the senior 'keeper, I made it clear that I felt Healy's temperament was better suited to the task. Underlining it all was the degree to which Healy reminded me of

Rod Marsh, in that he was going to be able to handle the bad days that would inevitably come in Pakistan and in the early days of what we hoped would be a long career. Pakistan, too, was a tour away from the glare of home publicity and broadcast coverage, meaning he would get a rough but relatively quiet initiation before facing up to the West Indies at home. He also had the advantage of a level of batting skill that we hadn't seen among our best wicketkeepers since Marsh, and we remained conscious that the side, while improving, needed as much depth down the order as we could give it. Unlike the Botham discussion in Queensland, I was able to sway the room.

We were lucky, too, that by this time the panel was chaired by Sawle, a wonderfully shrewd and thoughtful man who brought very relevant real-world experience to the job from his career as an educator in Western Australia. Those insights as to the character and learning ability of young men were as valuable to us as his years in boardrooms, knowing how to reach consensus decisions where all members of the panel felt their views had been given a good airing, even if there had been some disagreements along the way. He had also realised a long time before most that it was critical to start tracking our best cricketing talents from younger ages, and through his assiduous monitoring of junior cricket levels he knew as much about Healy as anyone could without actually spending time with him as I had.

In November 1988 I woke up one morning in Devonport, Tasmania, during another Shield game. Stephen, our eldest son, was 14 at the time, and it struck me that he'd be gone in a couple of years and really I'd been away a lot for most of his life up to that point. If I wanted to have any sort of relationship with him at all, I needed to spend some time at home, rather than working through the week and spending weekends away watching cricket as a selector. So that's when I decided I had to make that my priority. I was confident that in Laurie Sawle we had a selection chairman who would stay the course alongside AB and Simmo, as the likes of Steve Waugh, Geoff Marsh, David Boon and Dean Jones began to repay our earlier faith. And I had gotten out of the Australian Cricket boardroom earlier in the year, frustrating the chief executive David Richards, who had been hopeful I'd be interested in becoming chairman. At the time I'd told him 'I don't need another full-time job, especially an unpaid one', so it was the right time to give up the lot, at least for a while.

3

ON CAPTAINCY

For most of our history, the position of Australian captain has been respected, even if the incumbent isn't necessarily as well regarded. It's a convention that has served Australian cricket well, certainly in comparison to some other nations. But it came off the rails a little due to the critics of Kim Hughes, an unfortunate offshoot of World Series Cricket and the fact that the Australian Cricket Board wanted Hughes to be the next captain, rather than a WSC player in Rod Marsh.

During the latter stages of the saga, I challenged the ACB chairman Phil Ridings about this view. 'Why won't you make Rod captain of Australia?' I asked him. Ridings made various points in response, but the two that have stayed with me were that Marsh had been a part of WSC and that he was also too close to Ian Chappell! All I could say to that was, 'Well I played WSC and I'm Ian's brother, how much closer can you get?' Apparently, though, I was more acceptable to the board than Rod would have been.

I always felt that had they made Marsh captain at some point after I first stepped down in 1981 for the away Ashes series, the ACB would never have needed to reappoint me. Instead, Kim got the job, as he did again when I did not tour Pakistan in 1982. Had Marsh been captain, in time, perhaps after the 1985 Ashes tour, Kim may well have been ready to succeed Rod with a younger team. Each time I did step down, I did so with no expectation at all that I would lead the side again, and there was certainly a part of me that would've been happy not to have it back.

One of the side-effects of the WSC split was that I served as captain but also a selector for the 1979–80 and 1980–81 home Test seasons. The last squad I was involved in selecting was the group to go to England in 1981, which was chosen before I'd decided to withdraw. Trevor Chappell was included in the group and I had to recuse myself from those discussions. Given all that had happened in early 1981 with the underarm and other arguments with the ACB, I would have struggled mentally to lead and needed a break. But when I did drop out of the touring group and Hughes was made captain, he was not made a selector; nor did he get a say in the shape of the team he was to lead. Undoubtedly it would have been wise to reconsider the balance of the squad without me in it.

There are some who have always blamed me for what happened to Kim. But I have to say that he needed to be able to find the strength to do what he ultimately did: resign from the captaincy, or at least decline the opportunity when it was handed to him, on the basis that he knew it didn't yet suit him as a player. Given some more time watching others lead, he may well have found the right balance. But as it was, Kim Hughes' emotions were always worn on his sleeve.

Sometimes you could literally see it: he had a 'tell'. If you watched him in the field you would see him curling his hair. That was his tell that he was searching for ideas. There are times in captaincy when you're absolutely bereft of ideas – but if you let anyone know that's the way you feel, other than maybe your vice-captain or one or two others you confide in, you're gone. If it is apparent to your own players that you have run out of ideas or you think the game is lost, then it's all over – your emotions become contagious through the team. I don't know whether I was born with a natural poker face or not, but I learned very early that a necessary skill was not to drop your guard and let the opposition know what was going on underneath a calm, impassive surface. Let them guess.

Another thing you looked out for on the field was how a player behaved in certain scenarios. You'd take note of the guys who clapped with particular relish any time their fast bowlers used bouncers, because you knew from that behaviour that they didn't like bouncers. Similarly, the ones who yapped the loudest were the ones with the most brittle confidence. Then there were those who wouldn't say a word to the better players in the opposition, but who would start having a go at their lesser teammates. That was another indicator that they were vulnerable – they would only pick on fellow vulnerable people. Like bullies.

Hughes' tells were evident even to a television viewer as far away as I was in Brisbane in 1981, watching the infamous Headingley Test match. I'd been up watching fairly late into the evening as Ian Botham started to take control. Judy had been asleep and got up to take a look, and I can remember saying, 'This could get ugly.' Kim had overbowled Dennis Lillee (39 wickets for the series) and Terry Alderman (42 wickets for the series), overusing his ammunition as it were, leaving the other members of his attack to bowl when Botham was set and swinging fearlessly. It may be argued that Dennis tended to bowl when Dennis wanted to bowl under Kim, but the same could not have been said about Terry.

What Kim's body language and decision-making then did in turn was create a situation where Dennis and Rod, in particular, made it clear from their own body language that they were unhappy. I don't believe either of them are proud of that fact. But Kim would have been frustrating to play under, especially for those who had made up their minds that Rod was the more capable leader. That was true even after Dennis and I retired in January 1984, as Rod hung on through the World Series Cup that followed the Tests and made plans to go to the West Indies before dropping out late in the season.

Something that we are all glad about is that there's no lingering animosity between Kim, Dennis, Rod and myself. Kim and I have always remained in touch, the four of us have socialised since and very much enjoy one another's company. But I'd like to think the many lessons of the era, and of Kim's tenure in the Australian team, will never be forgotten by those who traverse similar ground.

～

At its most basic, captaincy is about giving players the opportunity to succeed. When you've got a new player in the side, you want to see them find out for themselves that they can succeed at a new level. Let's say it's a bowler, bring them on when a new batsman comes in. If someone is starting to get on top of them, get them out of there and wait for a better opportunity to get them back with another new batsman at the crease. But the opportunity to captain itself is not something afforded to everyone.

Of course it would be abnormal human behaviour not to be aware of the benefits of captaincy status at a senior level and to think about the role at times. But if that's your sole reason, or main reason, for wanting the job, then you aren't the right person for it. It needs to be someone with aspirations, sure, but they should be married to a realism about how the opportunity comes as much through chance as through strategy, given how few people ever get it. For your first four or five seasons in a team you're simply there playing and getting established and learning your game. Then you get to a point where you can say 'there's got to be something else to strive for'. That something else can absolutely be captaincy.

That was the only reason I went to Queensland from South Australia: the opportunity to captain a first-class team. I'd never captained at school, because I'd been the youngest bloke in every team I played for and there was always someone older to be captain. Even at Prince Alfred College I had Ashley Woodcock – who went on to play a Test for Australia – a year ahead of me and he was captain. Ian was then captain of South Australia and Australia, so I realised there was more to playing the game. I wanted the responsibility and challenge of captaincy – and if I ever wanted to captain Australia, I felt I would need to have had some experience.

It was only when the incumbent, John Maclean, very generously offered to stand down if I moved up to Brisbane, that I seriously considered it. One would hope that most people come to a captaincy aspiration in a similar way. If it's something that you're coveting, and you want to manipulate your way into the job, then that should be very carefully considered by those who make the decision.

Players who gain captaincy for the right reasons and at the right times in their careers can enjoy a temporary uptick in performance as a result, because it does bring additional focus. The wins and losses go against your name, and that does concentrate your mind. While you're aware of it as a player, you become more acutely aware as a captain of when you're on top and needing to drive an advantage home. If you happen to be batting at the time, you make sure you get to the sort of total you should get, and it is possible to get into a quite serendipitous state of thinking about the team so much that your batting does become almost purely subconscious.

More broadly, the duties of on-field captaincy itself can be very enjoyable – but they come with all the other responsibilities that tend to make the job tougher with each passing year. The number of years you can handle it will vary, depending on your ability to compartmentalise and disassociate from various things going on around you.

When I arrived in 1973, Queensland had been perpetual cellar dwellers. It was the first time I had really taken the opportunity to look closely at a cricket system and figure out what was working and what wasn't. I got my head around the club scene, the way players were being selected and how that was playing out in the Sheffield Shield team. What I quickly surmised was that the players being selected for Queensland were all the same ones who were sitting at the top of the club cricket batting and bowling aggregates: supposedly the time-honoured way of selecting players for the next level.

After a bit of thinking, the conclusion came that Queensland were struggling as a cricket state because they were picking too many players who had adapted their games to playing club cricket. When they got on the faster, bouncier wickets against quicker bowlers in the Shield, their 'prop onto the front foot' games, well suited to slower stuff in clubland, wasn't serving them well at all. And the military medium bowlers who were delivering the bulk of the overs in club cricket, taking wickets by perseverance and getting picked for Queensland, weren't taking wickets in the Shield.

Part of my responsibilities as captain was a place on the selection panel, and so I laid it out pretty clearly that we needed to change tack as a state. We can't keep picking the same guys because they aren't going to help us win games. The longer they stay in club cricket, the less likely it is they'll be able to find ways to adapt to first-class level. We need to identify the good, young players who merit opportunity, and then give them a chance to learn how to play in Shield cricket on first-class pitches. There were naturally some dissenting voices, but ultimately the argument carried the day because everyone in Queensland cricket knew that things weren't working.

Similarly, it was critical to have good, solid discussions with selectors as a captain. When I led Australia, I had many such discussions with the then selection chairman Phil Ridings, whether I formally held the role of selector or not.

A few of the players we identified for Queensland included Phil Carlson, Trevor Hohns, Martin Kent, David Ogilvie, Greg Ritchie, Carl Rackemann and Robbie Kerr. Every single one of that group, having been picked only because we thought they might stand up at first-class level, went on to play for Australia. In the meantime they also helped Queensland become a truly competitive state team. Of course there was a period subsequent to that in the 1980s and into the 1990s when Queensland sought to recruit its way to a first Shield title, and only broke the drought in 1995 after another strong generation came through and, this time, was backed in fully to do the job.

Those lessons are vital to any captain's understanding of what they are there to do in terms of granting opportunities to individuals, and by extension the team, to be successful. Similarly, captaincy is about being able to step back, at vital times, and avail yourself of the bigger picture. Not just within a game, but across series, seasons and careers.

As important as any lesson about captaincy is the one about knowing when it is the right time to step away. I have to admit that I struggled to do it. By 1981 I had personally got to the point that I didn't need or necessarily want to captain Australia again. And it is absolutely vital that the captain feels sure within himself that he has the mental energy required to do the job. The mental energy that captaincy required left me with an ever decreasing supply of mental space that I could apply to my batting. I would've been happier if I'd not been made captain again on a couple of the occasions when I stood down. It was largely through the entreaties of teammates that I kept accepting offers of the captaincy whenever the ACB came calling.

Indeed, I would have been very happy to play the last two or three years of my cricket career as a batsman only. Because I really needed the mental space to apply to my batting if I wanted to play at the level at which I was going to be happy with myself. You don't have to be off by much to be totally off. My 1981–82 run of ducks, after returning to the captaincy, stand as a painful but indelible example of this. I've no doubt that I could have made a lot more runs and brought more value to the team had someone else been able to wholly convince the ACB that they were the right man for the task.

When I was a selector again during the 2010–11 Ashes series, I could recognise in Ricky Ponting what I had seen in myself. He was at the point where batting was a lot harder than it used to be, and he needed every ounce of energy to put into his batting. You finish up having to work a lot harder for your runs than you ever did before, and therefore you get exhausted by the time you're 50-60-70 rather than just getting into your stride.

As coach of India I had the well-publicised episode with Sourav Ganguly, which was exactly the same problem. He didn't appreciate the problem and appreciated the solution even less. He came to me before the 2005 tour of Zimbabwe and said 'how do you think I'm going', and I said, 'Mate, I think you're struggling, just observing from the outside and having experienced it myself. My advice to you would be to give up the captaincy, focus on your batting and I reckon you've got three or four good years in you. But if you hang onto the captaincy you'll be done in less than half that time, you'll finish up losing them both.' He didn't take kindly to the advice, and from that point onwards decided I was enemy No. 1.

The trouble for Sourav was that it was obviously very financially beneficial to be guaranteed a spot in the Indian team, and doubly so to be captain. In his case it also gave him control of the batting order, and where he would be walking out to play. The negatives of him being captain were that we weren't getting the best out of him as a batsman, we were getting disruption and animosity developing in the team as a flow-on from that, and the political implications of any threat to his position were quickly obvious. As it was, Sourav did lose the captaincy and ended up playing for India for another three years – and actually performed marginally better than his overall Test record in that time.

An unfortunate perception did develop in Australia over the years coinciding with the leadership tenures of Allan Border, Mark Taylor and Steve Waugh that it was important to make a clean break once a captain finished. All of a sudden it became forbidden to be a former captain in a team, with the preference that the incumbent carried on until they wanted to give the game away entirely. There were some concerns about this when Ricky gave the leadership up in early 2011. I disagree strongly that it is an issue. On the contrary, I think we lose on both counts if you push a captain too far.

Not only does the captaincy of the individual suffer if they do the job for too long, but their batting is sapped at an escalating rate. Moreover, there have been plenty of former captains still worth their place in the team. We would have been a much stronger side, for instance, in England in 1972 had Bill Lawry been at the top of the order. He, of course, lost his spot when he lost the captaincy the previous year. With Bill's experience I think we could have won the first Test at Old Trafford, on a classic English seamer, and then gone on to take out the series.

I'm also a believer we would have been better off with Border playing his last two years as a batsman and senior lieutenant to Mark Taylor. When Allan did give international cricket away in 1994, he played two highly enjoyable seasons with Queensland as a foot soldier, and was instrumental in the state's first ever Sheffield Shield. Later on, Ricky's final two seasons helped allow Michael Clarke have a honeymoon period as captain. It was important to remember Ricky's quality as a batsman – even at 80 per cent of his best he was still going to be a player more than worth his place in the Australian side. Had he relinquished the captaincy earlier, he may even have had a new lease of life, realising how much energy the role was taking away from his batting.

It's important not to forget that I had Ian still in the side and batting at No. 3 when I first took over the captaincy, which proved a great help against the West Indies. The argument is actually strengthened another way by looking at the two years of World Series Cricket, when Ian was handed back the leadership. The relief of just being able to focus on batting again resulted in what were probably two of the best years of my career, and the 1979 WSC tour of the Caribbean arguably the best single series I played. The fear from Australia seemed to be about too many former captains in the same side. The other side of that coin is having the heir apparent and his allies in the side and getting frustrated. You can have issues either way.

Most captains tend to be batsmen, and of course tend to be among the better players in the team. Recognising that the time is up with the captaincy and then getting another couple of years out of them as a player makes a lot of sense – top-class batsmen don't grow on trees. As ever, this comes back to the critical role played by selectors in ushering in a new leader or encouraging a seasoned one to think about carrying on as a player. That's why selection is so important and why you need a robust selection system to make those hard calls. If we could accept that there's nothing wrong with having a past captain in the team, then I think that would be far more likely to happen, to the benefit of all.

4

AUSTRALIA A

Australia, 1994–1995

My first team coaching job arrived when the ACB chief executive Graham Halbish called me in the spring of 1994. There was to be an Australia A side competing against Australia, England and Zimbabwe in the World Series Cup that summer, and the board thought I would be a good fit to mentor them. I'd been off doing my own thing from a business point of view for a few years and I'd never really considered coaching as a career move, so it came out of the blue when Graham got in touch.

It tickled my fancy, the perverse nature of Australia versus Australia, and there was always still that love of the game in the back of my mind, even though I was doing some commentary for Nine. That was possibly part of Halbish's thinking, that I was going to be on the road anyway, so it probably saved them some money!

We got to Perth for the start of the tournament a few days early and it was my first foray back into cricket since 1989 when

I finished up as a selector. I can remember the distinctly chilly atmosphere between the Australian team and Australia A, and the concept generally. Australia's captain Mark Taylor had fought hard against the idea and would keep doing so through the summer. While I could understand his position as captain of the senior team, I also thought it was short-sighted to be denying an opportunity to not just look at the next generation of players, but give them a taste of that sort of competitive cricket. To have the next tier of Australian players exposed at the top of the one-day game could only be positive for the future, so I thought the members of the first team were looking at it through a narrow lens.

The only bloke who gave our team much time at all in Perth was Shane Warne. They were moving on to Adelaide for the next pair of matches before our first game against Zimbabwe was due to happen when I got a message from Warney wishing the boys all the best, which I think gave us a bit of a lift, because the vibes had been pretty negative not only between the teams but in the media around the concept. Everyone was feeling their way, and the Australia A team were anxious, nervous and keyed up. So to have 'Tubby' Taylor and others giving them short shrift was hard for them. That also meant that when Taylor went public with his distaste for the idea, complaining about the crowd booing the Australian team in Adelaide, to us it felt like a manifestation of the cold shoulders happening behind the scenes.

That being said, as a coach and a mentor, I thought the tension was good, and we were certainly able to use it to give the boys a reminder every now and then that this was an opportunity to show your wares. It was a win/win situation for them really, in that no-one was expecting too much, so it allowed us to really encourage them to just go out and enjoy themselves, something easier said than done in a lot of elite team environments. The message about Australia was that they're obviously feeling the tension, so they won't be quite as relaxed. The more relaxed we are, the more chance we'll play our best cricket and we'll just see what happens.

It really fitted with my idea of what coaching was at that level. Not so much teaching blokes how to play and messing with what they had in a technical sense – just trying to add some value and support to get the group into the right frame of mind on match days. Damien Martyn was captain and that role was new and fresh for him, so I was able to help him a little. Martyn's career was marked by his emotions; at times he struggled to be comfortable with himself and his talent. He had a mercurial nature, was regarded as a bit brash and undisciplined, and I don't know if that always sat well with his captains.

His own experiences, having been dropped very publicly and traumatically from the Test team the previous season, becoming the scapegoat for a Test loss in Sydney, no doubt helped him in being very empathetic and understanding with Australia A. He could understand that not everybody is really comfortable around the dressing room. Leadership is about communication and not everyone receives communication in the same way, so being able to deal with individuals in the group is an important part of it, and I think Damien handled that pretty well. His knowledge and tactical nous was pretty instinctive, he could express himself very well, and when I asked him about his on-field decisions he could always articulate them clearly.

Martyn had been installed as Western Australia captain around that time and that did not go so well. WA's environment has always been a little edgy, in between certain periods where everything was smooth. John Inverarity was the obvious captain when he did it in the'70s, but in periods when Damien Martyn or Kim Hughes led the side, there were others around who thought 'hang on a sec, maybe he's not the obvious choice' and so things weren't as calm.

From what I saw of him with Australia A, he had a lot of the qualities you would want in a leader and he certainly got good returns from the group, with the help of other senior guys in the side. It was also the sort of hectic schedule – Tests, one-day games and domestic games were all meshed together – where most of the time players had to concentrate on doing their job well in the brief periods they had available. That meant there was little thought to rivalries in terms of captaincy or other roles in the team, making it quite a happy dressing room.

Merv Hughes was there, to try to keep the flame of his Test career flickering, and he came in as the big bumbling bear saying 'let's have some fun', which was great for the group, particularly as he went on to bowl very well for us. Paul Reiffel was a solid citizen and a fine bowler, who was also doing his best to get back into the top team and so would set a strong example. Phil Emery was calm, professional behind the stumps, and also a successful state captain with good awareness of the people around him. Players like Darren Lehmann got a chance, having been pushed back a little in the queue for spots after being 12th man for Australia as a teenager in a Test against Pakistan at the SCG in 1990. His omission from subsequent squads was seemingly around issues such as attitude and fitness and declining a chance to go to the Academy. After 'Boof' was dropped for the second batch of games, Greg Blewett came in as a bubbly sort of character who was enjoying his climb to the top of the game. Overall there were enough little aspects to remind players about from time to time to make sure they were focused, and then to just enjoy the fact that the senior Australian team were not enjoying this at all.

A couple of the games were really close, particularly the first encounter in Adelaide and then the first match of the best-of-three finals series in Sydney. They weren't exactly classic games of cricket, but typical of ODI matches of the era: fairly low scoring, a high emphasis on tight bowling, outstanding fielding and plenty of hustle between the wickets to build up to a crescendo in the last 10 overs of each innings. At that stage no-one was really going out to try to blow the opposition away. Some of the pitches we played on would be used wickets from earlier games, which ensured they'd be dry but also quite slow with a bit of up and down bounce. It was another few years before administrators and ground staff got onto the concept of a one-day wicket that was as flat and friendly for scoring as possible.

The final qualifying game at the SCG against England was something of an exception to this, as on a better batting wicket, Blewett and Michael Bevan – a matter of days after being dropped from the Test team – both peeled off centuries. Before the game I spoke to Michael, who wasn't happy to be playing in the 'lesser' team, but I told him 'mate, you've got two choices, you can be as grumpy as you like and go out and play badly and confirm they've done the right thing, or you can go out and do what you do best and show them that next time they're looking they'd better look closely at you'.

As it turned out, Blewey's runs and cheeky medium-pacers would see him elevated into the spot Bevan had previously occupied in the Australian middle order, with back-to-back centuries in Adelaide and Perth making him a part of the victorious touring team to the West Indies a matter of months later. Michael Atherton's team had a litany of injuries to deal with, meaning the likes of Mike Gatting and Graham Gooch were playing and giving us more than a few extra runs with their slowness in the field. It was pretty clear, too, that an Australia versus England finals series was the preferred option for many of those who had dreamed up the concept in the first place, meaning we could really use the message that 'no-one wants us to get there, let's show 'em, we have nothing to lose'. A big crowd really got behind the team in defending the target England had to reach to squeeze past us on net run rate, and that night ended up being one of the more memorable nights of any of those players' careers, whether they went on to play for the top team or not.

The national selectors clearly saw Australia A as subordinate to the national team, and that became still more obvious at finals time, when they took Paul Reiffel away from us to be 12th man in the senior side. We had more or less known that anyway, but that selection decision confirmed it: the worst nightmare for the ACB was Australia A winning the series. If I'd been in the Australian dressing room, yes, I might've felt differently; we certainly felt there would have been a greater chance to win out in the finals if we'd had 'Pistol' playing for us. But we had known what was going on and we had no control over it, so we didn't whinge too much. And the senior side were not going that well in that there were certainly a few players looking over their shoulders. David Boon, though he topped the aggregates for the series, would find himself omitted from the ODI team the following summer and took it as a sign that his international career was coming to a close.

While we lost the finals series 2–0, it was a source of some pride that the most memorable passage of the entire competition took place when Martyn and Blewett batted together with extraordinary confidence and poise early in the second final at the MCG. We knew what a dynamic sort of player Damien could be, but Blewey had some serious talent. I don't know another player who could have used his batting grip and made the runs that he made. His bottom-hand grip was unbelievably strong, and the physics of batting are that if you allow it, once the bat starts moving, the weight of the bat will drop in behind the hands and it'll be on-plane from the top of the downswing all the way through the intended shot, unless you stop it with the bottom hand. Blewey had this grip so underhand and so tight that his bat used to go out to point, it would come via second slip and then go to wide mid-on, and then cross back over the pitch towards cover. That was his bat path. It was on line for the merest fraction of its path, so how he hit so many balls in the middle is a great credit to his ability. It's no mystery as to why he was so good on the pull shot – his bat was going that way anyway! Steve Smith is as close to Blewey as anyone I can think of, but his bottom hand is still nowhere near as strong.

Not that I thought about it at the time, but the enjoyable nature of the Australia A experience contributed later to accepting the offer to coach South Australia. I got a lot of good, solid feedback from the players during that World Series Cup, and that in turn gave me confidence to think I could enjoy it full time. There was, though, an element of difference in that I did the Australia A job while still commentating on the same games. The way that worked was that the commentary roster would not include me at the start or the end of an innings – I'd walk round from the team viewing area to the broadcast area for a couple of stints in between. This might not be great for those who might howl 'conflict of interest', but it was a pretty enjoyable mix, because it meant I was out of the way of the players when the game was up and going, but still there to advise and help before and after play.

I had always looked at coaching as being a little bit like parenting. Your job is to support your charges, develop them, allow them to make some mistakes, and then come back and talk about it later. But the sooner you can make them independent, the better it is for them and the better it is for you. From that point of view, to be out of the dressing room in the middle overs wasn't a bad thing. A few years later with South Australia, we were playing New South Wales at Adelaide Oval, the last day of a Sheffield Shield game a few overs before lunch when we were trying to bowl them out as they stalked our fourth-innings target.

It was Tim Nielsen's first year as assistant coach after retiring as a player the summer before. I was feeling the tension and, as I looked over at Tim, I saw that he was chewing his fingernails, so we were obviously both a bit tense. I said to him, 'We've got to find a way to relax, because if these blokes walk in here and see us chewing our fingernails and wondering whether the sky is going to fall in, it probably won't help them much.' So we spent the last five minutes before lunch telling each other jokes. By the time the boys got there we were laughing. A dressing room can be like an infectious disease ward, in that once a bit of panic or unease breaks out, everyone else has got it pretty quickly. Likewise laughter.

I remember a few times as captain of Queensland I had to send the team manager out of the dressing room by telling them to go for a walk around the ground. On one occasion during a game in Geelong, I sent a very nervous manager into town to get us a newspaper, which I knew would take him an hour and more, just because you don't need that sort of personality in the dressing room. Half your job as a leader is to keep the place as relaxed and calm as possible. So maybe coaching should be a part-time job in that you've got something else to do, away from the group, during the day, certainly in the longer formats.

You can certainly get caught in the bubble if you're not careful. Every coach has a limited life span, certainly with one group, so either the coach needs to be turned over or the playing group does. Those players need to hear different voices and I always believed with my assistant coaches that it was important to give them responsibility, because they're not just helping the players develop, but you're also giving the players a break from your own voice.

Similarly with the captain, you don't need to be best friends with them but you need a strong working relationship that tends towards giving the captain as much responsibility as he can handle. As coach, my role is as the head of the support staff, to support the captain and the team, be heavily involved in preparation and how you want to play and what the balance of your team looks like, but once the game starts, you've got to back off.

The other thing I found with coaching was that while you're in the group and in the room and involved in a lot of the conversations and know the personalities well, once they're out in the middle, I'm no better off than the bloke in row 15. I can't hear the on-field conversations, I can't look into their eyes and see the things you saw when you were playing. Knowing this, I tended to gravitate towards wicketkeepers as readers of a contest – as they are right in the middle of it. I'd always spend some time with the 'keeper once they came off the field before I spoke to the captain or he spoke to me. I wanted to confirm that what I was seeing was what was really happening, and that was as much about your own players as those of the opposition. When I was SA coach, captain Darren Lehmann would always be keen to ask 'what do you think' or 'what are you seeing', and I'd speak to Tim Nielsen as the gloveman in the first season. Tim had a good mind and would be happy to give you the truth rather than telling you what you wanted to hear. With India, MS Dhoni was much the same.

None of these things were specifically in the front of my mind with Australia A, but it definitely shaped my broader view on how the best coaches and captains give players the confidence to believe in their ability to do the job, then give them room to do it. That's not always easy of course, because when you're with them the whole time there are people coming in and out of the team and all of a sudden there are naturally some barriers built up. Players who have been in and out of the team naturally will have doubts about whether you as coach have supported or not supported them in selection.

There's a whole raft of things going on that you cannot always control, and no matter how hard you try, you're not going to get on with everyone. If you try to please everyone you're probably going to end up pleasing nobody, so it's important to be as faithful to yourself and your beliefs as possible, understand what you will accept and won't accept. It's not sustainable to slam the bag down on every little issue, but you have to have something you stand for.

All these thoughts and conversations I found stimulating – certainly more so than going back to the commentary box (as I did for the final couple of Ashes Tests at the end of the World Series Cup). Outside of playing itself, coaching is the most fun I've had.

5

SUPER 8s

Australia, 1995–1997

ONE OF THE business ventures I got involved in after playing was in sports marketing, running events for sponsors like Tooheys and other pursuits like the Sydney leg of the Whitbread round the world yacht race, which included a pro-am sailing event on the harbour. It was in these sorts of surrounds that, over a beer with one of my business partners, Bob Barraket, we started talking about the idea of a shorter format of cricket that could provide instant appeal to spectators and broadcasters.

I'd played some six-a-side cricket, and there was a growing sense that these kinds of formats needed to be better explored. Hong Kong's six-a-side event had been up and going for some time, and the ACB were still in a mood for experimentation after the Australia A edition of the World Series Cup. My former Test and World Series teammate Graeme 'Beatle' Watson had already been talking to the ACB chief executive Graham Halbish about hosting a six-a-side tournament in Australia, and when I spoke to Halbish about our ideas, it appeared he had already made some commitments to Beatle. Halbish tried to direct me towards that project, but they were committed to six-a-side.

Having played sixes cricket I felt it was not enough of a spectacle. There weren't enough of the real elements of cricket – batting and bowling were it. Four fielders other than the bowler and the wicketkeeper essentially made them spectators to a hitting exhibition, and each ball would pass invariably having gone for four, for six or dribbled off an edge for a single. More fielders were needed to ensure there was at least some element of fielding, some running between the wickets. At the same time the old single-wicket format, in which two players square off one to one with a full fielding side around them for a few overs, had more elements of the traditional game but lacked the team element.

I didn't want 11-a-side because I saw greater possibilities in having the game played on a smaller ground and with a softer ball, as in indoor cricket. A turf pitch would not be necessary either. We wanted it to fit into a one- or two-hour format that would be suited to television, because in a day you could play numerous games, which could be packaged more easily for TV. Pay TV had just started to make its mark in Australia with Fox Sports and a competitor in Optus Vision, and we were right in the middle of the explosion of sports rights values generally.

We also had an increasingly professional cricket circuit, which meant you had a growing number of players in year-round contracts with traditional off-seasons, so the cricket talent was available. The last part of the puzzle was the idea that this game would be played away from traditional venues, whether in the top end of Australia during the southern winter, or regionally as in Kuala Lumpur in Malaysia, where we ultimately ended up.

Longer term I saw the format as a way to get more deeply into Asia, China in particular, and also the United States.

That thought about the US has aged better than most, given the vast migration of South Asian lovers of cricket for study and job opportunities. These days, cricket administrators will tell you the US represents one of the largest television audiences for cricket outside of India, and on a coaching visit there in 2004 I could see that flowing through in terms of the number of Indian players in particular who turned out for US teams. Undoubtedly I can see a day when there is a team US at the T20 or 50-over World Cup – certainly much more clearly than I can picture an American Test team.

So instead we put our own proposal to the ACB to run a Super 8s event, with the following conditions:

- eight players per team
- 14 overs per innings
- all players apart from the wicketkeeper bowl one, two or three overs
- a six is now worth eight
- batsmen retire on reaching 50, but are allowed to return if balls are left in the innings
- last batting pair allowed to continue, even after 7 wickets have fallen.

Upon taking that format to Halbish, the ACB ultimately agreed to run a state-based event out of Queensland, while an international event would take place in Asia, announcing in September 1995 that these events would go ahead in July and August the following year. I was sent on a fact-finding mission with the ACB director and treasurer Des Rundle to look for venues and associations that would be robust enough to host. The spectator appeal was largely to the expat population, and given that Hong Kong already had the six-a-side event, we went there for some discussions, but our best hopes were Bangkok in Thailand and Kuala Lumpur. Bangkok had some good facilities but their association was not as strong or large as Malaysia's, which also had a larger expat population at the time.

Rundle was a classic old ACB figure, who I'd known since I was a kid because we both lived in Adelaide and were associated with the Glenelg Cricket Club. Having come up through the traditional administrative pathways and then the SACA, he knew the ropes and the politics of cricket and was supportive of the concept overall. He liked a top-shelf red wine (I would have been happy with the middle shelf), was happy to let me do most of the talking at the meetings and then carried the credit card to dinner.

I also had the good fortune of knowing Prince Tunku Imran, at that stage the president of the Commonwealth Games Federation in Malaysia, at which cricket was scheduled to feature when KL hosted the games in 1998. He played a large role in getting things together, alongside local businessmen Brian Wilmot and Chris Syer. That first event in Kuala Lumpur worked on the basis that the ACB would fund it and arrange for the players from both Australia and overseas. Our company would run the event and look after the venue, at the Kilat Club in downtown KL. Heineken were very keen to sponsor the event to the tune of a substantial fee, but the ACB preferred not to sell commercial rights until after the first tournament had been staged – greatly increasing their own costs, which would become important later.

That first event is still a very happy memory, including the miraculous circumstances of it happening at all. I lived up there for six weeks as we were setting it up and still dealing with the possibility of getting Heineken on board. Meanwhile it rained and rained and rained. I'd lived in Brisbane and seen some heavy rain, but the KL downpours would beat anything from Queensland. You could almost set your clock to the afternoon drenching. So we had a lot of worries about the logistics and whether games were going to be interrupted, because we only had a very brief three-day window for available players, and amid these concerns we chose to stage the games on a matting wicket covering one of the turf pitches on the square.

As the rain kept coming day upon day and the start of the tournament edged closer, we were told by one of the locals that we might have to get ourselves a Bomoh – a Malay Shaman and traditional medicine practitioner – to keep the rain away. So we employed a Bomoh, and he came out to the ground and performed his rituals, and at regular intervals he planted cloves of garlic. We thought no harm done, nothing else is working at this point, but retained our pessimism until the dawn of Friday morning. The rain stopped, we hardly got a drop of it for three days, the flimsy wooden floors in the corporate marquees held together, as did walkways we put down to keep people from treading in the mud beyond the boundary's edge. Then, come the Monday morning when the tournament was safely over and we were packing up, it started raining. Within an hour the ground was three feet deep in water and the floorboards from all these marquees and the marquees themselves were floating across the ground like the most ungainly fleet you've ever seen. We wouldn't have bowled a ball for a month. I don't know what the Bomoh got paid, but it wasn't enough – he saved the tournament.

The players didn't really know what to expect and we had to explain the concept to them. Most probably saw it as the chance for a pre-season holiday with a bit of sunshine, a few beers and some cricket on the side. But it worked better than we could have hoped. The players enjoyed it, the public enjoyed it, and we had some good matches, particularly in KL. It certainly helped Adam Gilchrist's rising star when he launched a young Makhaya Ntini and a left-armer called Gary Gilder into the club pavilion with a series of flat sixes as Australia A beat South Africa in the final.

For the domestic events, we played a couple of night games in Townsville at the rugby league stadium and had a lot of balls launched deep into the stands as a result. Three of the players on one side took the pre-season holiday element a little too far and disappeared for a couple of days on the Whitsundays in between the two events, which created some momentary headaches. But it was a good television product, the spectators at the grounds enjoyed it and it worked well most of all because the players enjoyed it.

There was next to no promotion of these events, as the teams and event staff rolled into town and summoned most of the spectators by word of mouth around the hotel. I've no doubt that the sort of savvy marketing we'd seen in other cricket tournaments to that point, and would see still more of in Twenty20, would likely to have made it a good entertainment proposition – certainly better than six-a-side anyway.

In 1997 we returned to play again, this time at the Royal Selangor Club, on a bigger ground. Funnily enough, those larger dimensions did not seem to work so well, since the fielders were less capable of cutting off the ring. Less workable also was the fact that by now the ACB had taken over the running of the event as a whole, and we also were running opposite that year's Ashes tour of England, meaning most of the top Australian players were elsewhere. Given that Graham Halbish had been sacked as chief executive of the ACB in acrimonious circumstances earlier in the year, it was also readily apparent that much of the board's passion for Super 8s had gone with him. In fact, the unfavourable financial view taken of the start-up events in 1996 was one of many issues that Graham's opponents would offer up when deliberating over his removal.

I could also feel some unease at the idea that the event had, loosely anyway, been drawn up by a 'private promoter', the term that had been used so often to denigrate Kerry Packer and his ideas when World Series Cricket sprouted in 1977. The ACB, as ever, wanted to own and run all cricket. There would also have been inevitable conflict between cricket nations over hosting and commercial rights. A grand plan for the WACA to host the next five editions of the Super 8s was announced in 1998, complete with a then outrageous winners' prize of $400,000. But the tournaments themselves never took place, leaving the format to languish in the memories of those who played them and a few YouTube clips besides. Knowing now what was to come with Twenty20, Super 8s would have had a limited lifespan anyway, but it was fun while it lasted.

6

COACHING A STATE, COACHING A NATION

Australia, 1997–2003 and India, 2004–2005

O N BECOMING COACH of South Australia and in the various roles that followed I was aware that, as a former player and captain of considerable reputation, it was important that I left enough room for others to have their say. If I was forever leading the discussions, they would invariably be short exchanges on the basis that few players, coaches or others would be prepared to challenge me. Experience has taught me that I'm certainly not right all the time, and I need to create the space for other people to have a say. Otherwise I'm not going to learn anything new. Tim Nielsen was my first assistant coach, immediately after retiring as a player, and he will tell you that at times I probably gave him too much latitude!

Working with Darren Lehmann as captain, I made it very clear that I wanted him to have as much responsibility in decision-making as he wanted. It probably isn't a surprise to say that Darren wanted to have a lot of say, and to lead team meetings. That was great, because a captain should want to be in charge, not only in terms of doing the job but being seen to do the job. The space I gave Darren was as much about helping him to learn as it was about not getting in his way.

I know from playing and captaincy that the best way for anyone to learn was to be given responsibility and then to do so for themselves. It was important for me to learn as a coach that it can be next to impossible to give advice when it isn't sought. You may have a lot of knowledge and you will want to pass it on as quickly as possible. But what you learn, hopefully early enough not to do too much damage, is that the 'quickly as possible' approach doesn't work. The only way you can pass that knowledge on is to create the right environment and then recognise good opportunities to share when they come up.

An early example of this arrived when we were training in the old Adelaide Oval nets towards the Clarrie Grimmett Gates. Nathan Adcock, a young batsman who would later captain the state, was struggling with a few things, but this particular problem was footwork. We'd talked about it, but I could see in the training session that he was thinking so much about the particulars of footwork that he wasn't seeing the ball and therefore couldn't play it too well. So I stopped the bowlers and started to walk down the net towards him. I got about three steps away from him and I could see the exasperated look in his eyes that just said 'what has he got to say now'.

I realised I had to get out of there, and I never interrupted another net session. I learned that you had to do your talking beforehand or afterwards, and that it was much easier to do damage than to do good. Coaching, then, should be a bit like the Hippocratic Oath for doctors: first, do no harm. In more recent times I've had conversations with others who have moved into coaching, about the need to understand that as a former elite player, you're like a university professor speaking to high school students. They can't come to your level, so you've got to get to theirs. And if you're going to try to change what they're doing, you need to be able to change their perception and how they think. That process takes a lot more than simply telling a batsman to change his feet position.

Paul 'Blocker' Wilson loved nothing more than to see the ball going through at waist height, miles over the stumps and still rising when it got to the wicketkeeper. It was hard to score from and a lot of players would get out to it, particularly when bowled from his height and with unrelenting line. It seemed, however, that the guarantee of a dot ball mattered a hell of a lot more to Blocker than the chance of a wicket. For my first season I worked with him at South Australia, speaking with him, training with him, cajoling him, swearing at him – everything I could do to get him to pitch the ball up.

Eventually, we got to a Shield game in Adelaide where we were out of the race for the final, and hosting Queensland. They batted first. Blocker was our most economical bowler but he had 10 wickets for the season so far in six games. 'What we need from you,' I'd say to Blocker, 'is 50 wickets, and I don't care if you average 50 to get them.' This day I exclaimed, 'Just make an old man happy, will you f***ing pitch the ball up today, just see what happens?' Matthew Hayden and Jimmy Maher were opening the batting. Hayden facing, Blocker runs in, bowls a big half volley first ball and 'bang' it goes for four. He goes for three driven fours in the first over, and each time Hayden drives him for four. He glares up at the viewing area square of the wicket, as if to say 'I told you so'.

But all of a sudden, a nick, and Maher's gone. A couple of balls later, Blocker hits Martin Love on the pads and gets him lbw.

Next over he nicks off Stuart Law. He finished up with 5-68, the only five-for Blocker got for SA while I was there. And he did it while basically trying to get hit for four! There were other days, too, when Blocker bowled a little fuller because the ball was reversing, and he was incredibly tough to face in those circum- stances. He could have played a lot more Test cricket than those few overs he got in Kolkata in 1998.

The Sheffield Shield was a great level at which to play cricket and it was also a very good level to coach. You had a real mixed bag of personalities and skillsets. Anyone who gets to that level can play, and a lot of what I experienced was about how important it was to watch and listen more than you talk. There is a parenting parallel in that the more you say, the sooner they stop listening to you. With your kids you'll be the font of all information up to a certain point and then all of a sudden you won't know anything. The sooner you realise you haven't got all the answers, the closer you are to being a good coach. And the sooner you can encourage them to realise they can be their best coach, the better it is for all parties.

If they're continually coming back to you, either as a coach or a parent, and not trusting themselves, the less likely it is that they'll become strong individual people. Coaching is so much more about trying to understand players as people and finding ways to impart knowledge in a way that complemented their own. But a lot of the time the very best thing you can do is simply to give them encouragement.

~

For years a contention has floated around that I dodged playing in India. The fact of the matter is that I never got the chance to go.

The only two Test tours of India during my time as a player were in 1969–70, when I had not yet played for Australia and wasn't selected for the trip, and in late 1979, when the peace deal had been reached after World Series Cricket but the WSC players were not yet eligible to be chosen. The next Test tour wasn't until 1986, and so missing the 1979 series is a regret. But having not played in India, there's no doubt the coaching job afforded me the opportunity to immerse myself in the world's biggest cricket nation.

India should have the world's five best teams, let alone the best one. You could, for argument's sake, split the country up along the lines of a few of its most populous religions or regions and make five highly competitive international teams out of them. The best illustration of this came after I finished coaching India, during my time with the Rajasthan Academy. In a state of 80 million people, we compiled a list of the best 20 kids in each of its 17 districts, and over two weeks we culled it down to a group of around 10 players from each zone. At the end of the process we still had 50-odd kids who were really, really good cricketers.

Most of them never played a single game for Rajasthan at Under-19 level, let alone first-class level, and yet I would have loved to have had every last one of them in South Australia, such was the talent on display. If we had been able to transfer that 2008 group to SA, I can guarantee the Redbacks would have won the Sheffield Shield at least a couple of times by now, they were that good. In the same way, India could in time help the UAE become a cricket-playing nation of some repute, or the US or anywhere. Incidentally, it is staggering to me that the contemporary England side doesn't have six South Asian players in their ranks – if we'd had the volume of South Asian kids in Australia over the same length of time as England have, I'd like to think we'd have provided them opportunities far more effectively.

That leads me to one of the things I've ruminated on most often since finishing as India's coach in 2007. The Board of Control for Cricket in India is aware of the power of its position in terms of scale, but I don't think they have a broad enough view of the role they could play in cricket if they wanted to. They're very happy with where they're at, with the market dominance of the IPL, and any bigger picture view of being a force for the greater good of cricket is dismissed as the province of the countries that bossed India around for decades and now experience the shoe on the other foot.

But the inescapable reality is that if international cricket is to survive, even India needs worthwhile opponents to play against, and more than one or two. There are some of course who feel that India shouldn't even do that, retreating completely into an IPL-only attitude that sucks all the best players from around the world into their own domestic system. Such a scenario would mimic nothing so much as the professional baseball and basketball leagues of the United States. That would make cricket enormously poorer than it has ever been, in my view.

Already, some former powers in the game have all but disappeared. The greatest tragedy in the game in my time has been the decline of the West Indies, from the lofty, unbeaten status they held for close to two decades. All countries needed to be thinking in terms of giving up a little bit in terms of money and resources to ensure that the West Indies remained strong.

There are lots of complexities to the issues that have enveloped cricket in the Caribbean, but it certainly hasn't helped that they have had very little money since the turn of the century. Where West Indies had prospered from an old system of tour fees – basically being able to trade off the drawing power of their team when playing away from home – the move to a system of bilateral tours changed the finances of the global game and the West Indies Cricket Board were the clearest losers, because they had precious little domestic broadcast market to sell their home games into. Cricket was seldom seen on television screens in the region, certainly nowhere near as often as basketball, baseball and other offerings from the nearby United States.

That change was exacerbated by the fact that there were few opportunities for the best players to add to their income by playing in the Caribbean, so they instead played in vast numbers in England and also at times in Australia and later South Africa. Over successive generations, the best West Indian players disappeared from domestic ranks almost as soon as they could be identified, and so the quality of the nursery for Caribbean cricket went into decline. Sponsorship dollars became harder to find, grounds fell into disrepair and intellectual property around things like pitch preparation was also lost. Suddenly, the turf on which the great West Indian teams had been fostered was literally turning to dust.

Never during this sad saga – at least not until it was too late – was there a sense from other nations that the West Indian decline was anything other than a relief for their cricket teams and an opportunity for their administrators. Rather than worrying about the loss of a wonderful global force who were happy to tour frequently, there was actually a note of some delight that the immortal teams of Sir Frank Worrell, Clive Lloyd and Viv Richards were to be followed by far less fearsome combinations.

Other nations seem at times to be going the same way, whether it be South Africa or Sri Lanka or Zimbabwe or Bangladesh. It is a credit to South Africa's system that it keeps tossing up quality players through years of administrative strife, but it is impossible to know how long that can keep happening.

In the case of New Zealand, they have punched well above their weight division for a long time through sound management and gutsy cricketers, but it is a constant battle to keep pace. If we want Test cricket to survive, we need these countries not only to survive, but to flourish. India's decision-makers, then, hold much of the future of world cricket in the palms of their hands. The question that has been a source of great angst for many around the world over the past decade or more is about how cricket's powerhouse chooses to wield it.

There was a more broad-minded spirit to the BCCI's decision to appoint me as coach in early 2005, particularly given what I presented to the board as what I wanted to bring to the team. My presentation was entitled 'A Commitment to Excellence', a blueprint based on what I'd seen of Indian cricket and therefore where I felt changes could be made. Pretty much all of these went back to a strong belief that the Indian team was operating as a collection of individuals rather than as a team functioning closely together.

When I arrived in India, they had perhaps the best batting line-up ever produced in cricket to that point. A top six including Virender Sehwag, Rahul Dravid, Sachin Tendulkar, Sourav Ganguly and VVS Laxman, all at or close to the peak of their powers, was a galaxy of riches. What I saw from the outside was an Indian team that had a whole lot more to give than we had seen, even though they had been the only side to genuinely challenge the world's best – Australia – over the years leading up to my arrival.

The fast bowlers they played alongside meant that even a batting line-up as great as that was not always going to dominate opponents, especially overseas. This was an issue that went deeper than who was being picked for India. Conditions in domestic cricket needed significant adjustment in order to provide the requisite encouragement for Ranji Trophy teams to want to develop fast men, who would then be able to compete in far greater numbers for their country.

Nevertheless, that Indian side underperformed relative to their talent, and after being part of the team for a while I could see why. They had a decent record because they were an incredible bunch of individual cricketers, as opposed to the sort of performances that might have been conjured by a totally focused team. There was, to an extent, a divide and conquer element to it. Players did all they could to support other individuals they had relationships with, and otherwise did enough to keep their heads above water so far as their ongoing selection was concerned.

As Sachin put it in an interview in 2004, the reason he felt the team had enjoyed success prior to my arrival was because 'simply, there are plenty of match-winners in this team. There are enough players who can win a match single-handedly'. But there was very little system to what was being done. Not much more than each batsman going out to the middle and aiming to make as many runs as possible, with enough good spin bowlers in the team to take advantage of deteriorating surfaces once those runs had been scored. India knew that if they were in the contest at the end of day four, there was a good chance they could win it on day five. But it wasn't a game plan that was sustainable even in India over the long term. And it certainly would not work too often outside India.

The team's fielding was spotty at best, a quality that would get exposed on bigger grounds outside of India, not least in Australia. Fitness levels were inconsistent, and there was an overall reluctance to do all the things that the best teams do. I'd been lucky enough to play in and against some very fine teams, and so

I knew what they looked and felt like. If you're on the receiving end against one, you pretty much felt surrounded by a united and committed team, rather than a gaggle of talented individuals who wanted to do things on their own terms with few, if any, concessions to the team thing. These were the qualities I thought I had been empowered by the BCCI to bring to the Indian team.

Moreover, when I started in the job I expected that I would have Sourav as a strong ally in achieving these goals. We had dealt very positively with one another prior to the 2003–04 series in Australia, when I aided him in terms of his batting and mind-set on harder pitches against quick bowling.

Our first camp as a team was in Bangalore, and I requested that Sourav come back from a county stint with Glamorgan in England to be part of it. Upon hearing that he didn't want to leave, I got my first sense that things were not going to work as I'd hoped, because it was very important that Sourav and I were on the same page, forging a strong relationship from the start.

Eventually and reluctantly, he came back home and joined the camp for a few days. In that time we sat down on several occasions and discussed a vision for the team, based on what I'd presented to the BCCI. It was a vision to which he seemingly agreed. I then emphasised that as captain, he had to be the one leading the charge and setting the example. We needed him to buy into it and be seen to be endorsing it – something to which he also agreed. 'Greg,' he said, 'you won't have any problems with me.' That conversation gave me some comfort as to where we were going, but it was to be a short-lived sensation.

When we took our first tour together to Zimbabwe, it was immediately clear that Sourav was sticking to his familiar habits: little training beyond a few hits in the nets and very minimal fielding work. In order to make the most of the time we had with the players, my assistant Ian Frazer, a former Victorian batsman with a degree in human movement, and I had decided on high-intensity fielding drills that would also work as fitness routines – very much in the mould of the work that Bob Simpson had done when he first arrived as coach of the Australian side in the 1980s. Fraze was brilliant at devising drills and training sessions that would achieve both ends.

Ahead of the home season, we decided to work the guys pretty hard in Zimbabwe, because we weren't going to get that chance once we got back to India. At one point a few of the players went to Sunil Gavaskar, who was commentating on the series, to say 'Greg's working us too hard, you've got to step in and say something'. To Sunny's credit he said 'no, this is why he's coach and you guys are going to have to put up with it'. There were, in fairness, a few guys like Anil Kumble who had a shoulder issue to manage, and so had reason to be more careful in training. Sourav, though, needed to be leading the approach to improve standards, and I ended up trying to talk it through with him three times. On each occasion he appeared to agree, said he understood and would do the work. But each time thereafter there was no change to what he did.

What I could now see was a contrast between what we had done around the Australia tour, where I had helped Sourav improve his own batting, and wider conversations. In this case, improvement for the team would require numerous senior players to get out of their comfort zones, and also encourage regeneration through the introduction of younger players. Sourav, though, wanted things on his terms. When he came to me in Zimbabwe and asked for feedback on how he was going, he opened the opportunity to have the tough conversation where I told him that I felt he was struggling. Most of all, he wasn't leading the team as he should, and that was a danger sign not only in terms of captaincy but even retaining his place in the side.

I was naive in thinking that an honest conversation was the right thing to do at that point. It was the way I was raised and the way Australian cricket worked. I liked Sourav and I wasn't making these points as a personal attack – it was a professional critique. Sadly, Sourav did take it personally, and essentially from that moment it became a feud, because he felt he had done me a favour in supporting my bid for the coaching job, and now wasn't getting what he wanted in return. In effect this meant that the biggest barrier to achieving what I'd been hired for took the form of the incumbent captain.

While still in Zimbabwe I wrote to the BCCI, outlining the chain of events and my concerns about Sourav's captaincy. I did this not only to get my thoughts down in writing to my employer, but also because I already knew that if I did this, it would leak. Every previous correspondence I had sent to the BCCI had filtered out into the media, and in this case I felt it was imperative that I make my views clear before there were any counter-moves from Sourav's camp. Things were always going to be difficult from there on, even after Rahul replaced Sourav as captain.

Rahul is a very upstanding citizen. A selfless individual and a team player, he bought into our philosophy, and at least initially enjoyed tremendous results. These were helped by the fact that, in the early stages of proceedings, Sachin was right there alongside him. Sachin really enjoyed the way we were training, how energetic and competitive it was. He was a cricket-loving kid at heart, and that was writ large across his contribution to the sessions we had. Sachin was, for a time at least, leading by example.

Another great challenge that I was never able to overcome was to try to get Virender Sehwag to train more effectively and try to expand his game beyond what was an admittedly spectacular comfort zone. His record at the finish was good, but not commensurate with his talent: he's the best ball striker I've ever seen. Sehwag really should have averaged 60 or close to it in Test cricket – he ended up averaging 49 – particularly given he was playing such a substantial proportion of matches in India. But he was uncomfortable against the fast bowlers and we had numerous discussions around trying to get him to understand the value of opening up more areas of the ground in which to score. His preference was to stay leg side of the ball and hit most balls through the off side – be safe from getting hit, and then score from as many balls as he could.

We tried to get him to understand that if he got more into line and tucked straight deliveries around the corner or through the leg side, he'd get many, many more balls outside the off stump he could use his exceptional eye and hands to dispatch. In a way it was the reverse of Steve Smith, trying to force bowlers to hang more balls wider rather than targeting the stumps or the body. A couple of times we did manage to get Sehwag to drill these sorts of things after a run of low scores that may have threatened his place, and on each occasion a century followed soon afterwards.

One of these occasions was in the West Indies where he was battling with the ball sticking in the wicket and so coming slowly off the surface. After opening up some more scoring zones through training, he went back out in the next Test and made a century, but the big score seemed to reassure Sehwag that he was in good fettle, and so the training stopped also, leaving the pattern to be repeated at a later date.

The other occasion was when he was being seriously troubled by Shoaib Akhtar's pace in Pakistan, and so we got him onto cement wickets with some hard plastic balls that Ian Frazer had found in India. They weren't going to seriously hurt anyone but they at least bounced and came onto the bat a little more like a cricket ball. We spent three sessions over three days standing about 15 metres away from Sehwag, trying to pin him to the back of the net. The first session was uncomfortable, but after he realised that it was a helpful process, he warmed to the task. By the third session he had nailed it. He was hooking, whipping balls off his hip and playing all the shots we knew he could play if he chose to.

He came out of the net after the last of these sessions and we said, 'That's fantastic, if you can do that, it'll force them to bowl away from you, they won't keep bowling straight at you.' Sehwag replied: 'Oh, no I couldn't do that in a game.' I asked why not and he said, 'I haven't got time.' Somewhat perplexed, I retorted, 'You don't need any more time than you needed in there, we were throwing at you from 15 yards and you were doing it easily.' But Sehwag wouldn't shift. Over a number of conversations over the course of a year it got to the point where I said, 'You're not really comfortable with fast bowling are you, Viru?' He always talked in the third person, and said, 'Sehwag is frightened of fast bowlers, but fast bowlers are frightened of Sehwag!' He was right, too, because bowlers knew if they missed their mark he'd murder them. But he could have been so much more.

We had a camp in Bangalore early in my tenure and we had the bowlers there first for some skills work before the batsmen were scheduled to turn up. Sehwag arrived a day or two early and asked if he could come out and bat in these sessions. On a fresh practice wicket, with the Indian squad's finest armed with new balls, he just pulverised them. He'd walked out with a brand new bat, and when he walked off the red mark was little bigger than the size of a single ball, because that was how unerringly he hit them. He was freakish.

Another thing I soon noticed about Sehwag was that he was our best fielder. Great reflexes and hands as you might expect, but extremely hesitant to field in the slips cordon where we could make best use of them. He didn't want to stand in there, risk dropping a catch and getting blamed for costing a match.

On the bowling side of things, a challenge we faced was to develop understanding, among batters and bowlers alike, about the best length for taking wickets. It can vary from country to country, pitch to pitch and even over the course of a single Test match, but there is a simple way to illustrate it in a match context. In 2006 I found an article on cricinfo about a series in England, which stated that the strongest correlation between wicket-taking and anything else was in the number of times a bowling team could hit a batting team on the pads. That was the key to finding the right length.

We had been putting down cones to delineate this length, and we'd even had the groundsmen draw white lines to create the 'door mat' we wanted the bowlers to hit. They could hit it in the nets no problem, but as soon as they got into a game they reverted to a default length that was far shorter than would be effective against good players. But once I read the cricinfo article, we went to a team meeting and discussed 'let's start just trying to use the new ball to hit blokes on the pads', because if you don't get early wickets you're in serious trouble and going to spend a lot of time in the field. And if you're in the field for more than 110 overs, your chances of winning go down exponentially. 'If 80 per cent of wickets in Test matches fall to balls of that length, let's try to hit it as often as we can.'

As coach you don't often get to say this, but that approach had an immediate transfer to the middle. Not long at all afterwards Irfan Pathan got his famous hat-trick in the first over of a Test match in Karachi, and the following season in South Africa Sreesanth bowled some of the best sustained outswing it's been my pleasure to see.

7

THE UPHILL BATTLE

India, 2006–2007

IN ACCEPTING THE job, my understanding was that the Board of Control for Cricket in India wanted me to bring to Indian cricket what I knew worked in Australian cricket. So what we tried to bring to the team was a game plan and an attitude that success didn't happen by accident: you don't rely on natural ability and weight of individual run scorers to have a successful team. Instead you have a recognition of periods in a game where hard work needs to be done, by having a balanced team, by having fast bowlers. I often asked the question 'where are your athletes', and just as often got the response 'we don't have any'. But they seemed more often to show up in places like the armed forces, or other sports like volleyball, rather than in cricket. What's more, Indian cricket wasn't looking for them.

An early request to the BCCI was to send for the best 30 fast bowlers in India who weren't already in the Indian squad, so we could look at them. That's where we found Sreesanth, Munaf Patel, RP Singh and VR Singh, to name four. Munaf was a terrific exponent of reverse swing before that skill was widely in use. They all faced the same problem – they didn't have the fitness to keep running in and bowling at high pace all day. They didn't do a whole lot of bowling in domestic cricket and there was very little thought as to how to train and manage fast bowlers to be at their best for prolonged periods.

India also wasn't picking balanced squads. On the trip to Pakistan in early 2006 we took Munaf Patel, Zaheer Khan, Irfan Pathan and RP Singh. The latter three are left-arm bowlers, all the same height, all the same speed. They may as well be one bowler. Very often the reason a change of bowler brings a wicket is because the batsmen have to make a quick adjustment to a different angle, speed or trajectory. But we had three bowlers who all let the ball go at more or less exactly the same point, at the same height, at pretty much the same speed.

The best of them would simply be bowled for every and any available team until they broke down, or until they pulled back a few gears of pace in order to stay on the park and lost the zip that had got them there in the first place. What we tried to do was to get a few of these guys on board and train them for a few months before we played them, so they'd be fit. Another bowler to emerge at this time was a teenaged Ishant Sharma, who I first saw in the nets at Delhi before we toured South Africa. Irfan Pathan broke down on that tour and we needed a replacement: Ishant had made his Ranji debut shortly after the tour began, taking 4-65 against a strong Tamil Nadu.

I rang Dilip Vengsarkar, the chairman of selectors, and asked him to send over Ishant, but got a lukewarm response at best. There was a view that Ishant needed to develop an outswinger, but away swing is overrated. A ball moving away in the air is always going to tell you earlier than any other ball that it isn't hitting the stumps. If you have someone who bowls a straight stock ball and then one that comes back late, they can bowl six balls an over threatening the stumps. The straight ball is then even better than the away swinger because you've already half-committed to playing at it anyway. Ishant is one such bowler. The following season Ishant went to Australia and made as great a batsman as Ricky Ponting look uncomfortable by doing exactly that. A decade or so later, most batsmen, bowlers and their coaches now know this is much the more dangerous combination.

It took a while to figure out the link between India's five zones and five selectors. Historically, selection had been a matter more political than tactical, as the selectors traded off their zones to find a mutually beneficial spread of selections. That had implications not only for the selectors but for the people and associations that had selected them to be selectors, who thought they had a say in selection, and so on up the chain to the top of the BCCI.

One of my early tours was to Sri Lanka for a triangular one-day series, and Ganguly was unavailable because of a suspension for slow over rates. Jagmohan Dalmiya, the most powerful man in the BCCI at the time, said to me, 'Greg, would you like Sourav to go on the tour, we can organise it.' I said, 'Look, it might be an idea if we just let it run its course, I don't think we should interfere in the process, plus it's an opportunity to look at Rahul Dravid and see what options we have.' Dalmiya was happy enough with that response, and so we went to Sri Lanka without Ganguly.

The team was a different place without Ganguly, but he became available again midway through the tour. I sat down with some of the senior players and asked whether they wanted him back, and they said 'no we don't', but the selectors brought him back. We were staying at a resort in Dambulla, and when Ganguly arrived it was conspicuous how cool the reception was.

It was put to the selectors that we needed to be picking the best teams, and if the best players all came from the same zone then so be it.

We took the young fast bowling group to the West Indies in the middle of 2006. Sreesanth had come to a camp in Bangalore and I saw a kid who, while a bit flamboyant and a show-off, bowled fast, late outswing. And he was getting our best players out. The centre wicket we were using at the stadium was not great, and Sreesanth was getting the odd ball to fly off a length and nicking blokes left, right and centre. After asking around I was told Sreesanth was from Kerala, but with some derisive warnings about him not being good because of where he was from and because he didn't take enough wickets for them.

I went up to Sreesanth and asked him to tell me a bit about bowling for Kerala. He said, 'Oh Sir, I have five catches dropped every innings.' They were not a great side, and edges coming from a bowler of his speed were going to be a handful for even the best cordon if they were standing as close as you often had to in India. Understanding that, I convinced the selectors to bring him with us in the squad, and we put him on a strict strength and conditioning regimen once he got there. He made his Test debut against England in Nagpur, and I told him that 'one thing about playing for India is they'll catch them for you'. In his first session he had three catches dropped, just like Kerala!

After that hiccup, Sree went on to take 4-95 on debut, and he performed creditably in the West Indies in the middle of the year. But we had brought him in with the longer-term goal of the 2006–07 South Africa tour in mind. When we got there, we trained for three days at the Wanderers in the lead-up to the Johannesburg Test. By this stage Sree had grooved his 145 kph away swinger and a very sharp bouncer, but his inswinger wasn't as dangerous or controlled. I took him aside before the game and said: 'We know you'll bowl well here, but if you're to succeed it will take a lot of discipline and commitment. Are you prepared to work hard?' He looked me in the eye and said 'yes'.

So for three days I stood at the top of his mark and reminded him, 'What we need here is six of your best outswingers every over. When a new batsman comes in I don't mind seeing a bouncer, but you're going to get wickets here with pitching up your stock ball. If you bowl an inswinger I'll be onto you, because that's going to be a wasted opportunity on this wicket. This will be a low scoring game and you can win it for us, if you stick to your stock ball.' He bowled brilliantly in the nets for three days, and I thought 'if he can do this in the game, we're a chance here'.

I worried that once he got into the game he'd be a bit emotional and there'd be too much variation. But he put together the best Test match of fast outswing bowling I think I've ever seen. He got Graeme Smith, Hashim Amla and Jacques Kallis in each innings, and finished with match figures of 8-99, everything caught in the cordon, bowled or lbw. On top of his amazing display of outswing bowling, he only bowled a couple of roasting bouncers to batsmen trying to get forward to him to cover the swing. Thanks to his bowling – and an aggressive piece of batting in which he hit Andre Nel back over his head for six in the second innings, his only scoring shot – we won the Test match by 123 runs. For a young bowler who hadn't played a lot of first-class cricket, to discipline himself to bowl that well for that long, and get their best three players both innings, was an unbelievable performance.

At that point I would not have minded if that was his only substantial contribution of the series. But in the next Test at Kingsmead in Durban, when I thought he'd be physically, emotionally and mentally shot, Sree backed up with another eight wickets. Unfortunately we batted poorly enough to lose in Durban despite his efforts, and we fell apart in the final match at Newlands after taking a first-innings lead. Even so, we saw with Sreesanth what could happen with just a little more thought and longer-term thinking around a young Indian fast bowler, and a wider plan for the team.

Rahul Dravid was captain by now – an uncommonly intelligent captain who wanted to do the job and do it properly. I had a lot of influence with Rahul. I spent a lot of time with him and we talked a lot about the balance of the team, the style of play that we wanted, how we should go about it and what we needed to get better at. It was a really good working relationship based on mutual respect. I could have the hard conversation with him if I needed to, but he was the boss, the man ultimately accountable out on the field. Rahul was more than willing to take time and effort to see the Indian team make genuine improvements.

Unfortunately, the BCCI did not care enough about doing that. There were some board members who did want improvement, and some within that group who wanted me to push even harder on the existing system. But they were in the minority. As long as India won more games than they lost, and won all their series at home, that was good enough, because everyone was making money. There wasn't a culture of wanting to be genuinely successful or dominant, and there were always handy excuses if they didn't win away. It was the umpires, or the pitches, or the schedule.

For the most part, players were in survival mode, an attitude that went with their continuous treadmill of matches: most Indian players were away from home about 10 months of the year. That's why we were quite happy to get a bit of a squad mentality going, so that we could rest and rotate guys through. We knew we needed to get some bench strength among the fast bowlers in particular. But the survivor mindset took a toll there too. For Munaf, the temptation to stay on tour rather than get himself right for the longer term was overwhelming. He injured an ankle midway through 2006 but didn't tell anyone about it. His pace dropped alarmingly as a result, and we only saw his best for an extremely short time. This was a shame, because he really had a lot of ability.

RP Singh was another example of how difficult it was to take a longer-term view. We introduced him carefully as part of some minor squad rotation: when we won a game or two we would then use the next one to blood one or two players, because it was better to bring them into a winning environment than a losing one. After RP had been with the squad for a while and bowled well when he played, we told him, 'Right, we want you to go home now, play some domestic cricket, dominate there and get used to being a dominant bowler so when we bring you back you'll be better.' He was very quiet, went away, and then returned some time later to ask what he had done wrong. 'Mate you haven't done anything wrong,' I told him. 'We're so pleased with what you've done that we see a long career for you.' His response was to ask, 'Why are you sending me home?' But we'd forgotten about the layers. He'd likely rung home and told them, and the first thing they asked was what have you done wrong. When you've dropped the player, you've dropped the family, you've dropped the association or the zone even.

Player power, or more accurately celebrity power, was also something to contend with. The likes of Sachin Tendulkar and Sourav Ganguly had got themselves into positions in which they were extremely hard to question, even among administrators who genuinely wanted to. In 2004, Ganguly had infamously run afoul of Shashank Manohar in Nagpur, when the local association prepared an evenly grassed pitch for the crucial third Test match against Australia, offering pace, bounce and sideways movement. Despite numerous entreaties to shave the grass, Manohar stood firm, and captain Ganguly didn't play. Australia won easily, winning the four-Test series by going 2–0 up, their only Test series in India in the past 50 years. This was an exception that proved the rule.

Once Ganguly exited the team at the end of our 1–0 series defeat in Pakistan, the rest of 2006 was excellent because that was the closest we got to a united front, with the BCCI happy enough at the time to let us build. Dalmiya's ticket had been unseated from power, Sharad Pawar had come in as the new president, and there was very little paperwork to indicate what the board had committed to or was doing. So in that period, as the new administration caught up, we were left alone and performed well. But once Pawar was re-elected in late 2006 and his wider group had caught up on things, he started to wield more power as a government minister with ambitions to go higher than that.

That led to Ganguly's reinstatement because of his influence in Bengal, the power base of the BCCI at the time, and looking back now, that was probably the time when I should have walked away. From that point onwards it became obvious that not enough people within and without the team were genuinely interested in achieving what we'd set out to do when I took the job. A whole lot of other agendas were at play. I'd spoken to my predecessor John Wright before I went to India and so I understood some of these layers and some of the politics, and I was lucky that for about 12 months things went relatively well. But it came back with a vengeance at the end of 2006 and it was an uphill battle from that point.

When I started with India, their recent ODI record featured just three wins from their past 22 games. It became obvious after a while that they played a high-risk game with the bat and a low-risk game with the ball, and we had to try to switch it on its head. Wickets with the new ball are always valuable, but if you're not taking wickets in the middle overs with spin, you're dead, because of the runs that will flow to set batters in the final 10 overs.

Harbhajan Singh's instructions as to how to bowl in that period were more or less that 0 for 40 from 10 overs was fine. As a consequence, he would value dot balls and bowl wide of the crease into leg stump with a leg side field and make it hard to score. But what was actually happening in those 10 overs was that two players had the chance to get set in a partnership. If they were good players, say Inzamam-ul-Haq and Mohammad Yousuf, or Kumar Sangakkara and Mahela Jayawardene, you're not going to be able to stop them later if you don't even try to stop them early.

We had to work with Harbhajan to convince him to be more aggressive. He was extremely worried about going for runs, and along with several others felt that the negative bowling in the middle overs was almost an article of faith for Tendulkar as a senior player and influence in the team. As a consequence we brought in Ramesh Powar, a fabulous, wicket-taking off spin bowler, and did a power of work on how to manage chasing. These strides, with MS Dhoni right in the thick of it as a middle-order player of tremendous poise and power, meant that the sequence of three wins from 22 was followed by 19 wins out of 22 ODI games, and a world-record 17 successful chases in a row.

By the time of the 2011 World Cup in India, Dhoni led a team that was extremely accomplished at chasing targets. This was epitomised by the way they ran down testing totals against both the defending champions Australia in the quarter-final and then against the repeat finalists Sri Lanka in the final at Mumbai. Most people remember how Dhoni sealed the game with a towering six, but the calm, measured approach to chasing targets was something I looked upon with some quiet pride. That we could not sustain that run into the 2007 World Cup, four years before, had much more to do with disconnection and disunity than it did with talent or planning.

My relationship with Sachin, in particular, was central to how 2007 played out. Earlier on, whether in how he fielded or some of our other conversations, he was very supportive. In late 2005 ahead of the home Test series against Sri Lanka, Sachin was battling to overcome the obstacle of reaching his 35th Test century, surpassing Sunil Gavaskar for the most ever scored to that time. In Chennai before a first match that was ruined by rain, we spoke deeply about his batting. After a morning training session I'd returned to my hotel room when the phone rang: Sachin asked if he could come see me for a chat.

When we met, he asked me 'why does batting get harder as you get older, it surely should get easier?' Hearing this, I replied, 'No, it doesn't work that way. When you're a youngster, you don't know how hard it is, you don't know the pitfalls and the risks – it's just you and a ball. But then as you become more experienced and a more senior member of the team, the opposition take more notice of you and they try to make it harder for you to make runs. But what changes most is your thought process. As a kid it's not complicated, but over time and experience you realise how hard it can be, and you start worrying about ordeals you may have to survive, rather than simply hitting the ball as it comes to you. So if you want to play like you did when you were younger, you need to think like you did when you were younger. If you think like an older player, you'll bat like one, more cautious and safety-first, and the whole thing will become more pedestrian. What you need to work on, rather than hitting more balls, is your mindset. Get the emphasis back on scoring runs and being positive, with defending as a fallback option. If you're looking mainly not to get out, you'll miss scoring opportunities and find your mental resources are sapped. You've got to lighten it up. If you can do that, then I have no doubt you can get back much closer to what you were like in your younger years. You can't see batting as a chore, but as the delight it was when you started out.'

At the end of the conversation Sachin said, 'Greg, that's the best conversation I've ever had around batting. Can we do this more often?' The proof was in the pudding, because after Chennai, Sachin went out and made his 35th Test hundred in Delhi, ending the long wait for the milestone. The majority of the rest of his international career did see a more positive approach, and a return to some of the dominating innings of his younger years. We had two or three of those discussions over my time with the team, and I would have loved it if we'd been able to maintain that line of thinking and conversation throughout.

The breaking point for our relationship was in planning for the 2007 World Cup. We'd been to the Caribbean in 2006 without Sachin and we saw there how many of our players struggled in the one-day games when the ball got older and the pitches slowed up. In particular, the ball would stick in the wicket, a bit like in Sri Lanka, whereas in India it would still come onto the bat. So timing could be a struggle. This meant that we needed a quality player in the middle order to guide the innings in the critical phase between the early overs and the death. After the 2006 West Indies tour I had flown to the United States to see family, and during that time I thought through the issue before concluding that the best thing for India would be to bat Sachin at No. 4 in the order.

When I got back to India a couple of weeks later, Ian Frazer had already returned about a week before I did, and had met with Rahul in Bangalore. By the time I walked into my office at the national academy, Fraze and Rahul had gone through the same process I had, and written on the office whiteboard that they also felt Sachin should be in the middle order. I acknowledge now that the idea, while sound in conception, was also tantamount to trying to move the Taj Mahal from Agra to Delhi: Sachin opening in ODIs was not just a batting position, but a national institution.

We had a series at home to the West Indies prior to the World Cup, and this was something like a pre-season for the cup itself. We sat down with all the guys, and basically told them about our preparation for the global event and the roles they would likely play. In the Pride Hotel in Nagpur, Rahul and I spoke to Sachin and said to him that it was an important discussion because we needed him to buy in to a team plan. 'We think our best chance of winning the World Cup is with you deployed in the middle order.' Immediately, Sachin made his reservations clear, but we reiterated that this was not about him, but about the team. 'You've said you want to play in a World Cup–winning team, if we're to be any chance of doing so in 2007, we think No. 4 is your best spot because the middle overs are the important overs. If anyone can do it, you can, and we have other players capable of going up the top.' Virender Sehwag was better deployed as an opener, and we also had Robin Uthappa coming through, who had the ability to score with tremendous speed.

We finished that meeting with Sachin agreeing, albeit reluctantly, that was the job he would do. The next morning, prior to the game, Rahul came up to me at the ground and said, 'Greg, Sachin's had a word with me and decided he doesn't want to bat in the middle overs.' I asked Rahul if he wanted to rejig plans again, or whether he wanted me to have another chat to Sachin. He preferred the latter. After some of the pre-game warm-ups, I tapped Sachin on the shoulder and asked him up to the dressing room to speak. I said to him that I'd spoken to Rahul and knew he had second thoughts about batting No. 4, to which he said 'yeah, I want to open, I think I'm better as an opener'. I told Sachin I understood and if I was in his shoes I'd feel exactly the same way, but repeated that this was all about forging the right team combination for the World Cup. 'You could be,' I said, 'the difference between us winning and not winning.'

Again, he agreed, and seemed to be buying into the team imperative. Sachin went on to have a good series against the West Indies batting at No. 4, including one punishing century in the final game off just 76 balls. In Sachin's entire ODI career, he only ever made two hundreds at a quicker scoring rate than that. After that innings I went up to him and said 'well played, I hope you enjoyed that'. He just said 'I did what I had to do', and I knew there and then that this would be an ongoing battle. I hoped and expected that Sachin would be capable of doing the job with good grace, but that was the turning point in our relationship and it never recovered. It's fair to say he took that decision as an insult, and it was probably harder to accept coming from me. Undoubtedly I wasn't sensitive enough to his feelings, and I should have tried to get him to more fully express to me where he was coming from in order to find a better solution.

If we were ever to get Sachin to change batting positions and take it on wholeheartedly, hindsight also tells me that the discussions really needed to be between him and Rahul as the captain. Otherwise, it was just another instance of me working as the outsider and change agent who would be less difficult to dispense with once it was all said and done. I got the same impression from some senior members of the BCCI who privately encouraged me to push harder in terms of improving the team, but were nowhere to be seen or heard from when I faced the consequences of doing so.

Another mistake I made in how I approached the role was that I tried to bring the Indian media along with me. I tried to explain what we were trying to achieve as we went, because I thought they would be interested, and I thought the people of India would be interested. The people of India may have been interested, but not enough of the journalists were, because they all had their own agendas and contacts to maintain. Senior players all had mutually beneficial relationships with individual journalists that had existed long before I arrived, and were feeding stories into a hugely competitive marketplace.

A voracious environment for news, in which a story was a story and a headline was a headline – truth tended to be some way down the priority list. The quid pro quo was that the journalist got stories from the player or players, but the player got support from the journalist when he needed it. It was a very challenging environment, and in the end a lot of the information we tried to share was used against us, not least our emphasis on winning processes.

Parallel issues of trust and accuracy could arise in selection. There was one instance in Bangalore where we had a selection meeting after a training session, in which one of the senior guys was coming back and we had to choose between two other players. Upon giving my opinion about the merits of one over the other, I took no more than a couple of minutes' walk from the selection room back to the dressing room, whereupon I was confronted by the player I hadn't preferred asking, 'Why didn't you want me?' After telling the player he shouldn't have been in possession of the information in the first place, I explained that it wasn't a matter of not wanting him, but wanting another player more for various reasons.

He wanted to continue the argument, but I was in no mood to do so. I marched back up to the selection meeting room to give the relevant selector a warning in no uncertain terms that he was never to break the confidentiality of the selection process like that ever again. But the problem was those many layers of Indian cricket. The selector in question had to make sure, certainly before I spoke to the player myself, that he couldn't be blamed for letting down a player from his own part of the country, lest that player go home and blame him for what had happened, putting the selector's position at risk for being ineffectual and not keeping his man in the team.

A major issue I spoke to the senior players about, with an eye to the future, was the way that new players were treated when they came into the team. The atmosphere they walked into was terrible, as senior players disregarded their juniors, either taking no notice of them or actively making their lives difficult. So I sat down with Rahul, Sehwag and Sachin and said, 'Guys, this is unacceptable.' Came the response: 'That was the way we were treated when we came into the team under Mohammad Azharuddin, and Azhar told us that was what happened when he came in under Sunil Gavaskar, and this is the way it's always been.' So I said, 'If we don't break the cycle, this will go on forever, you guys should stand up and be counted.'

But there was no will to change it. One of the things I found in team meetings was that if you talked individually to players about their roles and ideas, most had really good ideas. But in a collective environment like a meeting, nobody would speak. I said to Ganguly early on that he was the captain and while I could prepare things for meetings, he should lead them. 'No, I'm no good at that,' he said, 'you do it.' So the team analyst, S Ramakrishnan, and I would put footage together and whatever else we wanted to present, and one day we spent three hours or so putting a presentation together. I said, 'Ramky, you know all this stuff better than I do, it might be good to have a different voice, why don't you present this.' He said 'Greg, more of them will understand you than will understand me' because he was a Tamil speaker and didn't feel his English was up to scratch.

Then I sat down with a young MS Dhoni, and said, 'Mate, you've got some brilliant ideas, why don't you present them at the team meeting?' He replied, 'Well, if Tendulkar doesn't speak, Dravid won't speak, and if Dravid won't speak, I can't speak.' So there were multiple layers, the senior players, the middle tier players and the junior players. So we had to have meetings in three groups of peers, the young blokes, the middle group and the senior group. That was as close as we got to a semblance of team in the sense I understood it from Australia. The only time you could get unity from top to bottom was if some outside element attacked a player. Then they would fall in behind that individual.

We saw this during the 'Monkeygate' affair during the tour of Australia in 2007–08 when Harbhajan Singh was banned for racially abusing Andrew Symonds, a verdict later overturned on appeal. I was in Rajasthan at the time – no longer coach of India – and became aware of a rumour that the Indian team was preparing to fly home from Australia in the middle of the tour. I found this hard to believe, because I would not have expected a team with Anil Kumble in charge would be thinking like this, but I felt that I should pass the intelligence on to the Australian camp.

I rang Tim Nielsen, who by that time was Australia's coach, and said to him, 'Mate, this is what's rumoured to happen, you've got to back off. Just play the game, don't go looking for a fight.' Next I rang Jack Clarke, the Cricket Australia chairman. 'I've spoken to Tim, this is what is rumoured, you need to talk to your coach and captain and tell these blokes not to get involved in anything to do with the opposition. Just play cricket.'

Some of the team fractures were evident in the West Indies during the World Cup in January and February 2007, where our early elimination sealed the end of my tenure. During a training session, a couple of the senior guys were egging Sreesanth on to bowl bouncers at Ganguly, who was certainly never after a short ball workout in the nets. Sree bowled one and Ganguly gave an irate response, leaving the young bowler to ask 'what do I do now', only to be told 'bowl him another one'. Ganguly just got angrier and angrier, and it summed up what we were dealing with.

We played Sri Lanka in Trinidad in our second game of the Cup, and Sreesanth was 12th man. Zaheer Khan called for a drink on the boundary, so Sree ran around the boundary and took the drink to him. The senior man knocked it out of his hands and delivered a stream of personal invective in Hindi at his squad mate. Sreesanth came back to the dressing room in tears, but refused to tell me what the problem was. Later in the day, I spoke to another teammate, who told me the story. That was pretty standard fare for young players. Sreesanth was an upstart, challenging for the positions of more established players, and that was the general attitude around the group.

Dhoni was really the only one with the self-confidence to move between the age groups a little. He was accepted into conversations with the senior players around the team and would say his piece. Most of the young players would walk past senior teammates with their heads down, only waiting to speak when they were spoken to. In starting to break this cycle, and also in coming from a non-traditional cricket centre in Ranchi, Dhoni was a real force for change and improvement in Indian cricket.

Overall India played 78 completed matches in all formats while I was coach, and won 40 of them, with 31 defeats. We won three of six Test series we played, beating the West Indies away but losing in Pakistan and South Africa. In ODIs we took part in 16 series or tournaments, including the 2006 ICC Champions Trophy and the 2007 World Cup, and won 32 games as against 27 defeats in that time. Of course, the first-round exit from the World Cup was to be the most indelible outcome of the period. Over the next four years, with a less confrontational coach in Gary Kirsten, India took out both the inaugural Twenty20 World Cup in 2007 and also the ODI Cup on home soil in 2011. Much of the groundwork for these triumphs took place between 2005 and 2007.

India could not have achieved what they did in those subsequent years without what had gone before. Things like improved discipline, better fitness, better fielding, a more tactical and less zonal attitude to selection, building bench strength and deepening the well of fast bowlers. Training was done with a purpose in order to improve specifics, particularly things like building on our ability to chase targets in ODIs, or building up our fast bowlers over the year before a tour of South Africa, where we really should have won the series.

But the biggest impact I think I had was that during those two years we were able to demonstrate to the BCCI and the selectors that there was an abundance of talent outside the established cricket centres of Mumbai, Delhi, Bangalore and Chennai. The BCCI had instituted a talent identification program, and Dhoni had come out of that program. That was the first indication of the volume of untapped talent, but we got the selectors to start linking that up to players coming to national team training camps and trials. From there the talent base grew so much wider, as we gained a host of players from places where cricketers had not previously come from. That egalitarian selection opened up the whole of India to the national team, and in more recent times Rahul Dravid has worked tremendously on widening the academy net as far as possible.

Overwhelmingly the saddest thing about my experiences in India was this. For a country that has such a deep and enduring connection with spirituality, the recent domination of material-ism and nationalism have made it unrecognisable in ways that cut to the core of the place. Cliches about cricket being religion in India are just that. The most dominant religion is now money, while the most obvious use of religion is by the national government, to play sectarian groups off against one another.

By contrast, what I am happiest about when it comes to the Indian team is how my time there planted some seeds for wel-come change. Rahul, with whom I remain close, has been pivotal to that process. Fourteen years on from my experiences, there had been enough cultural evolution in that dressing room – and enough coherence in the wider system to make the most of the enormous supply of talent – to mean that the touring side to Australia in 2020–21 could cope with a huge toll of injuries and withdrawals. Not only did they win a hard-fought Test series, but they did so with a young paceman, Mohammed Siraj, right at the forefront of it all. That sort of thing doesn't happen by accident.

8

A CLOUD OVER THE GAME

S REESANTH WAS A very emotional young guy. He came with a lot of histrionics and stuff that wasn't everyone's idea of how to behave, but he was a good man. I liked him because of his emotion and because he wasn't like a lot of his peers, who were much more hesitant to show emotion or speak their minds. Those qualities did not appeal to many people in an established system and hierarchy.

At one point we had a team meeting followed by a team dinner on a boat on the waterways around Kochi, in Sreesanth's home state of Kerala, after he had played a handful of games for us. There was a DJ on board, food and drinks, a dance floor and so on. It was clearly usually meant for a mixed-gender event, but this group was all men. Sree got the music on and had everyone dancing together, and he was at his happiest in the middle of it all. At the end of the trip we docked and got off the boat, and there were blokes arm in arm, a terrific, brotherly vibe.

Apart from the Wanderers, this was my happiest memory of Sree, but every now and then you could see some of the senior guys looking a bit askance at him.

He was young, he was brash, he was extravagant: a very engaging human being who didn't please everyone in the team. He struggled at times in the environment, as the expectations for young players to shut up and speak when spoken to brought him down. Young guys, early in their lives, playing for their country, surrounded by big-name players, they should be thinking 'how good is this'. But all of a sudden the lid was slammed on them. They were also having to adapt their bodies and minds to the rigours of international cricket, backing up day upon day and week upon week. We worked with Sreesanth, through the prisms of fielding, fitness and bowling, to find a balance between his extravagance and the discipline he needed to succeed. To a large degree we succeeded.

What I worried about after I left India was that Sreesanth was still young and operating in a cricket system that had all manner of unhelpful agendas that were very hard to articulate let alone eradicate. Senior players like Anil Kumble and Rahul Dravid, who I respected very much as players who genuinely wanted to see the Indian team be all that it could be, were limited in the degree to which they could push back against things detracting from other players performing with the team in mind to the exclusion of all else. It was a problem that seemed to get more intense the better the team was performing.

I tell you all this because it was the background to Sreesanth becoming the best-known recent Indian cricketer to be caught up in the spot-fixing web. I was devastated but not completely surprised in 2013 when he was banned for life by the BCCI, a penalty later commuted to seven years. It very quickly brought back to mind a conversation we'd had about some of his difficulties with senior figures in the setup, where he told me, 'Greg the trouble with India is that they carry this forever.' I have no doubt that his unpopularity with some players as a new man in the team contributed to the position that he found himself in seven years later, however the specifics played out.

The 2013 IPL spot-fixing scandal was itself instructive, as it established how the network could run far deeper and wider in a team than previous high-profile instances had tended to suggest. That Gurunath Meiyappan, the son-in-law of the BCCI president N Srinivasan, was central to it in his role as team principal at Chennai Super Kings, in a case that led to an IPL ban on the team's owners India Cements, spoke volumes. Prior to that scandal there had been plenty of suspicions about on-field events at previous editions of the tournament.

But as Rahul Dravid said to me at one stage when we were discussing the game's various ills, 'Greg, in India you learn to keep your head below the parapet.' And he was right. Those who have spoken out in the past have found it extremely hard to keep doing what they had been doing, in cricket or any other walk of life. If you want to live and work in the place, you keep your head down. A big reason I've been hammered so often through the media in India over the past 14 years, pretty much whenever I've expressed an opinion on anything, is because it helps to take my voice away so far as Indian cricket is concerned.

When I told the BCCI I wasn't interested in an extension to my coaching tenure, the first thing they did was to send all the heavyweights to ask me what I was going to say, because they were principally concerned I was going to start talking about corruption. From what they said, it was obvious that they had their concerns, but, while I had seen some very strange things, including Marlon Samuels' activities in Nagpur in 2007 that got him banned for two years, I had no hard evidence that I could present to anyone.

One of the areas in which cricket must remain forever vigilant is in trying to eradicate wherever possible the opportunity for questionable figures to form relationships with young players. By questionable figures I mean those with links to the illegal betting and gambling underworld of South Asia, which has had plenty of infamous influence over the international and domestic game over the years.

So long as gambling is technically illegal and thus unregulated in India, there will always be questions and problems. And it is the young players, either yet to be established in domestic ranks or even at the under-age levels, who are vulnerable to getting caught up in a web. That in turn may result, years later, in having to provide inside information or still worse, change the way they are going to play to bring about a spot-fixing outcome for the syndicate whose contacts have trapped them.

As a reminder of how easily this can start, I have vivid memories of an Australia Under-19s tour to Sri Lanka in late 2014. Among the touring party were the likes of Jhye Richardson, Matt Renshaw and Sam Harper, and the majority of the players were under the age of 18 at the time. We'd never had curfews with Under-19s teams or any others for that matter. We'd try to treat them as adults, give them some parameters and trust them to behave accordingly; under a system that was more lenient than those of some other leading nations, there was almost never a problem.

Some time into the tour it came to our attention that a few of the boys had been making visits to the casino in Colombo. Generally on a tour you don't need to be tailing the players everywhere out of playing hours – if you were in the dressing room the next morning you were likely to hear most if not all of the stories of the night before. Usually there's not much to react to beyond a bit of a laugh, but upon hearing the casino tale a few alarm bells went off for us.

So we spoke with our tour security manager, Tony Ross, and decided that rather than putting the foot down right away, it was best that on their next visit he should tag along and see exactly how it was unfolding. What the boys had figured out was that if they got a tuk-tuk to the casino, the venue would provide them with a free dinner and a lift home. So they weren't actually gambling, but availing themselves of the free feed, a few soft drinks and a ride back to our hotel. A cheap evening out on their tour allowance.

More troubling was that during those free meals, there was a guy showing up at the right time to get talking to the players, befriending them, getting to know them and discussing cricket. It was nothing to do with gambling directly, but looked very much like a grooming set-up for more problematic conversations later on in their careers. Some time later, after Tony had shared a photo of the gentleman with the ICC's anti-corruption unit, it turned out that, sure enough, he was already on a list of gambling-related figures – a guy definitely not fit to be mixing with players, especially junior players.

In the meantime, we took the episode as a learning opportunity. The boys were called into the team room at the hotel, and Tony addressed them. He explained the pitfalls of that sort of location and the types of relationships that you might inadvertently build. We also explained that as management on the tour, we weren't just acting on behalf of Cricket Australia but also on behalf of their parents to put them on the right paths.

The players were not banned from returning to the casino, but it won't surprise you to find out that none of them did. As a coach you need a balance between letting players make mistakes and also providing some guidance to help ensure they don't repeat them too often.

The eerie thing about the episode, of course, was that it had been in a Colombo casino 20 years earlier that Mark Waugh and Shane Warne had first crossed paths with another friendly figure. 'John the bookie' offered them gambling money that seemed to be 'no strings attached' and formed a relationship that led to numerous information-sharing conversations over the following Australian season. Those phone calls ended only after the then team manager Ian McDonald investigated the matter during a limited-overs tour of New Zealand in early 1995, resulting in heavy fines for Waugh and Warne right before the Test tour of the West Indies that followed. The ACB sat on this episode for another three years before its exposure, as brand protection took precedence over transparency – not for the first or the last time!

I could sympathise with Mark and Shane, because discussions around gambling with others of like mind had always seemed to be a part of a cricket tour. Without knowing what we know now, I am more than willing to admit I could have fallen for that. You're sitting in a bar somewhere, someone comes up to you and greets you, asks how you're going and by the way what do you reckon you'll do at the coin toss tomorrow? You might instinctively answer 'oh shit mate, I'm going to have a bat' because it all feels so harmless. At some stages of my career I've got little doubt someone did ask me a question that I answered innocently and in doing so provided information that could have been used in the hands of the wrong people.

In 1977 in England, I attended the Sportsman Club in London. We'd been there previously in 1972 and 1975 for a couple of functions, and, as in Colombo years later, our hosts were happy for us to be there as it was good for business, so provided us with free food, free drinks and a few free chips for gambling if we so chose. So by 1977 it was seen as a handy spot for dinner, drinks and a few flutters at the roulette table afterwards.

On that tour I met an extraordinary man by the name of Jack Meyer. A former Somerset cricketer, he was the founding principal of the Millfield School in Somerset, a mathematician by profession, and an early exponent of gambling that was a little more system-based than most. Jack told me he'd invented a 'foolproof gambling system' for roulette, based on certain parameters of odd and even or red and black numbers. While not quite watertight, it was good enough to give us some idea of what we were doing in terms of probability. So long as we didn't start chasing too much we had improved our chances of small wins here and there.

One night at the Sportsman Club, David Hookes and I went and had a go with it, winning two or three times, but most importantly knowing when we had accumulated a level of winnings that would be impossible to get back if we lost. We agreed to a figure at which we'd cash out, and over numerous trips to roulette tables in the various towns of England on the tour we had fun, killed two or three hours, and finished ahead more often than not.

Some players struggled with the gambling impulse more than others, particularly when combined with a few (or more) beers. In those cases, a bit of peer protection was required, such as roommates keeping hold of the wallets of the more impetuous team members at times. Nevertheless, that was the sort of innocent thinking that drew plenty of cricketers into casinos in those days. By the time the grooming for more nefarious behaviour started to happen, I daresay some players were particularly vulnerable to these approaches, simply as a result of the habits preceding generations of cricketers had got into.

I've heard various rationalisations about spot-fixing in particular: that playing out a maiden here or bowling a no-ball there might not influence the result or mean that you're not trying to win the game. That's a slippery slope – and once you slip there's no telling where you're going to end up. I certainly wasn't aware of anyone in my playing era being subjected to that sort of approach, because betting and, most importantly, television broadcasts were not yet widespread enough for the scale required.

Satellite television coverage and a huge proliferation of matches in the professional era has created so many more opportunities than there ever were before. The issues of information sharing and spot-fixing have oscillated over recent decades, but let's not kid ourselves that the problem no longer exists. The simple fact remains: until there is some form of gambling regulation in cricket's largest and most powerful nation, the game's players and governors can never be too careful.

9

AUSTRALIA IN DECLINE

Australia, 2007

B Y LATE 2007 I was working with Rajasthan Cricket Association. Ian Frazer and I had set up their academy and were running the program and had come back home to Australia for holidays. Judy and I came down to Adelaide to see my mum and there just so happened to be a domestic one-day game on between South Australia and Victoria, and we were invited to dinner in the SACA committee room. James Sutherland, who by then had been the Cricket Australia chief executive for six years, was at another table. Once the dinner formalities were complete he sidled over and sat down with us.

At that point, the Australian team was the world's undisputed No. 1 side and had completed a hat-trick of World Cup wins just a few months before. But the Test team had just lost Shane Warne, Glenn McGrath and Justin Langer. We didn't know it yet, but Adam Gilchrist, Matthew Hayden, Brett Lee, Stuart MacGill and Stuart Clark were all destined to finish soon in their wake.

'What do you think?' was one of his questions to me.

'How much money do you spend on your development programs, including first-class cricket?'

'About $20 million a season,' he replied.

'I don't think you're getting your money's worth, because if it was working you'd have six near-Test quality teams running round at domestic level and we're not even close to that.'

We talked a little more about that, but as happens at dinner tables I was distracted by another conversation momentarily, and by the time I turned back towards James he'd vanished. At the time I thought, 'Oh well, there's someone else I've offended!'

I certainly wasn't looking for a job, so I wasn't trying to please anyone, and my honest opinion was that in terms of looking after the future, Australian cricket was falling short. Having had the best part of nine years away from the game apart from some commentary, when I had come back to coach South Australia in 1998 it was noticeable that the game had changed significantly. It seemed now that that process had only gathered speed over the ensuing decade. International players were playing virtually no domestic cricket, which left a back-up pool of domestic teams playing more or less amongst themselves season upon season as full-time professional careers. Those domestic players were dubious, too, about playing club cricket.

That in turn was placing a barrier between the prospective young cricketers at junior and club levels and those precious spots within the six state teams, which of course is where the next national players come from. Essentially if you weren't on a state contract list you were a much greater distance from playing cricket for Australia than you had ever been prior to the onset of professional contracts at first-class level. This was nobody's fault, and all sorts of reasons had been thrown up about what had evolved into the professional system, but, having played under the old system, when I came back into the new one, it was like being hit in the face by a wet fish.

Professionalism might have bred a wider degree of excellence at the top level, particularly in areas of physical fitness and fielding. But it also meant that many players at the level beneath, having staked their lives on maintaining a good income from cricket, were hell-bent on doing whatever they could to survive. This simply created a rehash of the sorts of attitudes prevalent in county cricket in England decades earlier, as I had experienced first-hand with Somerset. They could best be summarised through the conversation topics of the dressing room. In Australia we talked about 'how fast can we score our runs' and 'how quickly can we bowl them out'. In England the discussions centred upon 'how do we avoid getting out' and 'how do we stop them from scoring'. There was another one too: 'How do we get a day off work?'

The emergence of those latter conversations in Australian domestic ranks was an alarm bell for the game in this country. My conversation with James in 2007 was only one of numerous such chats I had with board directors and others over the period, and I had always been vocal in stating that the key thing Australian cricket had to do as it entered professionalism was to avoid the workaday tendencies of county cricket. Now, some nine years after first coaching the Redbacks, I was thinking of ways we could reach a better understanding of what was good about the old system and so make the kinds of tweaks that would get the new system working better.

Above all what I wanted to see was young players being tested and stretched by seasoned opponents at their critical development stages. My first A-grade club game for Glenelg against Port Adelaide had seen me facing up to Neil Hawke and Eric Freeman, who had also shared the new ball for Australia in Test matches. If there was no Sheffield Shield cricket on a given weekend during a summer, lots of other young players were having similar experiences right around the country. And that happened regularly. The next generation of club cricketers were playing against Shield cricketers, and in turn those Shield cricketers were playing often against Test cricketers at the first-class level. Right up to the end of my playing days I was playing three or four Shield games a season in between games for Australia.

Season after season, decade after decade the system also regenerated itself because the rewards for simply being a good domestic player weren't so great that too many players would hang around without stepping up to the top. Generally, by the time a player was in his late 20s, he had to think very seriously about what other career path he was on and then drop out of state ranks. That created space for the next group to come through, and in the half a season when the international players were away, they would often assume the difficult assignments like opening the bowling or batting in the top three.

Of course there are a lot of blokes who go through Shield cricket in any generation who aren't going to play for Australia. But some of the hardest cricket I played outside Test matches and WSC games were for Queensland against Western Australia. They had Dennis Lillee obviously, but throw in Terry Alderman, Mick Malone, Rod Marsh, Kim Hughes and company versus Allan Border, Jeff Thomson, Kepler Wessels and Greg Ritchie, and these were really solid games of cricket. One game, at the WACA in 1981, had nine Queensland players who represented

Australia, opposing a WA side with 10 of their own. The teams were:

WA: Kim Hughes (capt), Graeme Wood, Bruce Laird, Greg Shipperd, Mark O'Neill, Craig Serjeant, Rod Marsh, Bruce Yardley, Dennis Lillee, Mick Malone, Terry Alderman.

Qld: Greg Chappell (capt), Kepler Wessels, Martin Kent, Allan Border, Greg Ritchie, Wayne Broad, Trevor Hohns, Ray Phillips, Geoff Dymock, Jeff Thomson, Carl Rackemann.

Those players brought a healthy share of egos with them, making the battle for bragging rights another consideration. This all made for a very strong grounding. If you made runs against a full-strength WA or New South Wales, to name the two strongest states of the era, you knew there was something there you could work with at the international level. Whereas we have now had a few generations come through who don't get that sort of exposure, which means selectors find it hard to judge how good they really are. The players themselves don't know how good they are either.

Something I discussed once with Darren Lehmann over dinner in Coogee, sitting alongside SA assistant coach Tim Nielsen and players Jamie Siddons and Peter McIntyre, was the fact that playing records went deeper than aggregates. When I played, unless you picked up the previous year's *Wisden*, it was far from easy to know exactly what your statistics looked like. Jump forward a couple of generations, and those same stats were being passed around to everyone in the dressing room every morning. Part of the morning ritual with South Australia was to look at who was doing what and who was sitting where on the standings.

Darren went past Ian Chappell's runs aggregate for the state while I was SA coach, and this night in Coogee after dinner and a few drinks, he made a comment about the record book now saying he was a better player than Ian was. I retorted, 'Right, well, bear in mind you played most of your games against second XIs.' When he asked what I meant, I said, 'Once Ian became a Test cricketer, every Shield game Ian played was against the best team the opposing state had, and you've only ever played against the second best teams, because the top blokes are away with Australia.' Unsurprisingly the conversation got a little bit testy from that point!

The loss of that interaction between the preceding generation and the next generation was vastly underestimated. All the more so as succeeding generations of administrators did not have any knowledge of what things had once been like. So I was seeing the system change, losing some things that worked really well, and then dealing with players, coaches and administrators who did not have any idea of what they were. Something, then, was missing. A vitality, a sense of competition and regeneration. When you've got players who are pretty comfortable at the first-class level and earning a healthy living for doing so, it really does alter the system.

On a similar theme, a move towards playing first-grade matches over full days of six or more hours' duration was another error. While the exact playing hours and formats varied from state to state, the historic convention had been to start around 1 pm. It was not uncommon to have players racing into the ground at 12.50 pm after finishing work at lunchtime: pharmacists, retail workers and the like. Playing until 6 pm with a 20-minute tea break allowed for plenty of overs over two lengthy sessions, with games played over consecutive weekends and leaving Sundays free.

But during the 1980s we gradually saw the start times moved back, on the premise that if we wanted players to be ready for first-class cricket they needed to be playing full days starting at 11 am if not earlier. This stopped players who had to work on a Saturday from having any chance of taking part, while Sunday fixtures doubtless culled another group of players with other things in their lives. I can't think of another single factor that cost the game more mature-aged and capable club players over several generations. While older Shield players who were not advancing further clogged the system, such players at club level had a lot to offer, in terms of guidance, experience and education.

Prior to my discussion with James in 2007, I'd also met with Michael Brown, CA's head of cricket operations, during a triangular one-day tournament involving India, Australia and the West Indies in Malaysia in 2006. He was exploring what my plans were after I finished coaching India and wanted to know Judy and me a little better. Michael was then on the phone to me once I'd gone back to Rajasthan in early 2008 to ask me if I was interested in the role as head coach at the Centre of Excellence in Brisbane.

My interest was undoubtedly piqued by the fact that around that time the political environment in Rajasthan was shifting, and cricket jobs were likely to change hands as a result. Ian Frazer and I were weary, too, of the political intrigues that invariably accompanied any job in Indian cricket. I rang Lalit Modi after Michael contacted me and said, 'Look, I know I've got a contract with you, but this offer has come up. It's a good opportunity to go home, and I don't want to be left here if you're not going to be around as often.'

Lalit was at this stage almost entirely preoccupied with the looming first edition of the Indian Premier League, giving us a free hand in Rajasthan, but at the same time his emotional and intellectual efforts were going pretty much solely towards the new Twenty20 competition. He was happy, then, to say, 'Go for it.' In the end Fraze and I retained an advisory role at Rajasthan, but my course was now very much towards Australian cricket and the issues I had raised with James Sutherland.

10

ON BATTING

Technique is an overused word in cricket, and most of the time wrongly used. Technique is nothing more than your style, your personality being expressed in how you shift yourself from one position to another in order optimally to receive and play a delivery. Unfortunately there has been an insistence, going back to the first-ever coaching book, that in technique lay the secrets to not getting out.

I still consider my father, Martin, to have been my main coach, notwithstanding many lessons Ian and I learned from our family friend Lynn Fuller. While Lynn, a very good country cricketer, was very much of the English, coaching manual mould of mentor, teaching things about a high front elbow and so on, Martin was much more concerned with getting into good positions to score runs. As my own batting evolved, I came to conclude that it was all so much more about your mental processes, routines and skills than about your physical development.

When our youngest son at around nine years old told me he wanted to be taught how to play cricket, I thought, 'Where do I start?' It helped that all he wanted to be taught was how to make a hundred, since he'd picked up that that was a pretty decent achievement in cricket. We had a tennis court at the time, so I took him on the court and threw the ball from the net. He batted on the baseline and I gave him sections of fencing to aim for: square of the wicket on the off side, square on the leg side, and the net behind me. If he could hit those areas that was four runs, and my job was to get it in as close to 25 hits as I could. There was no question of getting out at this early stage. After a while I realised that he was doing it pretty well, and told him 'now you decide which balls go where', and I was amazed in a very short space of time how he was playing square cuts, cover drives, straight drives and pull shots. That session helped me to crystallise the fact that looking to score runs got you into better positions than trying not to get out.

Occasionally over the years I have faced accusations along the lines that I would be against picking someone on the basis that I didn't like them personally. It's true that there are actually very few players I've been involved in selecting who I didn't have time for in a personal sense – but as far as character goes, what I looked for was how their personality might fit into a team in a cricket sense. What I didn't like seeing, though, was a player who would repeatedly make the same mistake – start out as a young player of promise, then, through either their own thinking or the advice of their coaches, try to be safe players who took the risk out of the game. What that meant in practice was invariably a limitation in scoring opportunities. In turn, that gave the best bowlers a pretty large area in which to bowl, when the best means of batting for long periods is to give bowlers as small an area as possible in which to avoid being scored from.

At its simplest, the game of cricket is a battle between bowler and batter for a piece of turf about the size of your front door mat. If the bowler dominates that area, the bowling team is on top. If the batting team can make that thing the size of an envelope, then they're on top in the contest. About 80 per cent of the wickets that fall in Test cricket fall to balls in that area, but only around 50 per cent of total balls bowled actually land there. Even allowing for a few short balls to try to get a batter on the back foot, that's a big gap.

This is the area in which Steve Smith made his quantum leap as a batsman in 2013, and Marnus Labuschagne followed suit six years later. The day that Steve worked out in Test cricket which balls he could attack and which ones he couldn't, was the day he turned himself into a consistent run-maker and innings builder. Once he figured out what the parameters were, and what his best risk profile was in terms of manageable gambles on his feet, eyes and hands, he couldn't stop himself from making runs. The job of a coach is really to help a player to figure out what their parameters are, and how many risks they are good enough to take while keeping the odds in their favour.

Much as Steve has said himself, it was clear that he had learned how to balance attack and defence in a way that would work in Test cricket by early 2013, when he was recalled for a tour of India. He then spent the rest of that year fine-tuning things over the course of an Ashes tour and then the return series in Australia, where he made a trio of breakthrough centuries in Perth, Sydney and then against South Africa on an uneven pitch in Pretoria. Australia won all those Test matches and Steve was on his way, letting dangerous balls go for over after over and scoring from most of the rest.

Steve's mental strength, in terms of wanting to bat for as long as possible, is at an extraordinary level. He is more single-minded about batting than the vast majority of cricketers in any generation. His ability to simply switch everything else off and channel all of his energy into problem-solving the next ball he faces is his greatest strength. Steve lives for batting and for the contest with opposition bowlers and captains in a way that is only truly attained by very few. So much so that sometimes it might even detract from his ability to live the rest of his life – certainly that was the impression I got when I saw how wrung out he had become by the time Australia had won the Ashes in Perth in late 2017 (more of which later). In a way, Steve does not channel his batting talent; his batting talent channels him.

That, I think, is a huge factor in any deliberations around whether Steve should return to the Australian captaincy. He might appear the best candidate on a few levels, but the question needs to be asked about whether it is in his interests and the team's interests, because the need to shift focus to the many demands of captaincy will limit his batting and his longevity in the game. Not least because as captain, Steve will feel – not initially, but definitely over time – that batting becomes a task to be accomplished rather than a fun challenge to be enjoyed. We saw instances of that during his first stint in leadership, when the joy he experiences while batting seemed to leave him at times. And that is another essential quality for the best of batsmen all through history: somewhere within them they always retain the sense of fun and joy in batting that they had as teenagers. As long as Steve maintains that, he can keep playing for as long as he wants. But the day he loses that is the beginning of the end.

My several vacations away from the game in the latter part of my playing days were all about being able to prolong that sense of fun, enjoyment and engagement with the contest when I did go out to bat. Had I continued to tour from 1981 to 1983, my retirement would have come around quite a bit sooner. But being able to have that space, get winter time away from the game, go and do other things, spend time with my family, regenerate and come back, I was able to push things out a few seasons further. By 1983–84, however, I knew that I was losing that instinct even having had those breaks, and so I knew it was time to get out. It was an easier decision for me than it is for contemporary players, too, because at that stage I was going to be making a better living off the field than I could by being on the field.

When I'm looking at batsmen, I'm looking at their set-up and their initial movement before or at the point of the bowler's release, because that predicates what will follow and how much chance they have of dominating that door mat. It was really through working with Ian Frazer towards the back end of my time coaching South Australia that this view, although I had it for years before, was finally clarified and classified with the collation of video evidence. In SA I was seeing things that I intuitively could see weren't working, and I could see others that did work, and I knew from watching good players what had worked. But I didn't have the footage that could isolate the human movement elements of it.

Fraze played 17 games for Victoria and was part of the first ever intake of the cricket academy: a doughty, determined opening batsman. His mind was nimbler than that, however, university-qualified in human movement and possessing an endless fascination for such things. In the days before the internet and information sharing becoming so much easier, Fraze had a cricket video collection far beyond the norm. In the early 2000s, having been connected by the legendary Swan Richards – the bat-maker and co-founder of the Crusaders travelling cricket academy team – we met up for several days in Melbourne at what is now the Pullman Hotel above the MCG. Locked in my hotel room, we watched hours of footage of all the top players. Into the third day of this process, we almost simultaneously exclaimed 'That's it!' What was it? The fact that all these players shared a virtually identical position at the point of the bowler's release, despite finding all manner of different ways in which to get there.

We described it as the 'active neutral' position. Basically it meant that at the point of release, their weight was mainly on the back foot but with their front foot lightly touching or just off the ground, ready to move forward if required by the early release of the full ball, or back if a delayed release meant the shorter ball. It was a similar position to the one I'd taken at the same point, and applied almost universally to players who managed to average better than 50 in Tests. Gary Sobers and Brian Lara were there despite their big backlifts, Adam Gilchrist was there with his long handle batting grip. Even Shivnarine Chanderpaul found a way, somehow, to get into this position. He started out looking at square leg, but by the time the bowler got into his load-up, he was around with 80 per cent of his weight on the ball of his back foot, ready to attack the full ball, but knowing that if the ball is still in the hand at a certain point it can't be full, so the front foot goes down and you push back.

Steve Waugh, we found, was the only player up to that point who managed to average over 50 in Test cricket without adopting this position across his whole career. He did it only for the second part of his career. But if you have a look at his record he averaged a little over 36 in his first 46 Tests, and then nearly 57 over his last 122. The difference is he went from looking for short balls to getting ready for full balls.

When I spoke to Sir Donald Bradman late in his life and asked him a few questions, once I realised he was up for a chat and not rushing off elsewhere like he usually was, I tried to get as many in as I could. So I asked him about his mental routine, to which he replied, 'Oh I didn't have one.' When pressed, he said, 'No really, I just saw it and hit it.' When I asked him whether there was any one bowler he feared, he said none, before clarifying that on their day and in the right conditions any number of bowlers could get him out. So then I followed up by asking 'was there any one thing that you were concerned about' and he said, quick as a flash, 'Yes, the full ball, because it could get me out every way: lbw, bowled, caught.' That answered the question for me, because when we looked at Bradman, he was the benchmark. And yes, he was in a very similar position at release. On further inspection, it was possible to conclude that around 75 per cent of his dismissals were to full balls: bowled, lbw, caught by the wicketkeeper or behind square on the off side.

What Fraze, then, was able to give me was an academic framework and confirmation of something I knew by instinct but not necessarily in a way I could easily show to others. The best batsmen, regardless of era, get there in part because they are consciously or unconsciously setting up to deal with the full ball. A lot of players I spoke to didn't realise they were doing it; it wasn't intentional. But on further questioning they inevitably came back to, 'Yeah I was getting ready for the full ball because that's the first one that leaves the hand.' In Steve Waugh's case he couldn't remember why he changed. It was after a tour of India, and I thought maybe he had looked at Sachin Tendulkar or someone similar, but he was sure there was no conscious decision on his part.

Either way, the ability to risk-manage this fundamental of batting – being prepared for full balls that you get the vast majority of the time, but being in position to cope with short balls – is clearly vital to being among the best. What might work at lower levels, or perhaps even in limited-overs cricket, is to have a more rigid, upright stance with feet planted and the bat raised. Some players double down on this by then having a pre-delivery movement that moves their back foot across and their front foot forward *before* release, essentially trading one stuck position for another that leaves an awful lot to the hands to catch up.

My counter to those sorts of approaches is to say that even if they make runs it is going to take a lot of time and enormous mental effort to get there. If it is a low-scoring game, not only do you lessen your chances of scoring runs, but increase your chance of getting out. Because if you can't make that 'door mat' area smaller, by punishing balls that stray either to the fuller end or the shorter end of it, the ball that will get you out is that much closer to arriving. The message has to get to the bowler that if they don't hit exactly the spot they're aiming for, you're going to score runs.

Footwork, in essence, is about being able to move from one position to another more optimal position for that particular delivery. Flat feet and an upright stance both detract from this goal by meaning less of your weight will be on the balls of your feet. Partly, both approaches have come from the era of helmets and the extra weight they place on a batter. Wearing the early versions of helmets during World Series Cricket, I found they affected my balance, and by going more upright in my stance to try to counter that, I'd lose the ability to stay light on my feet.

That then brought me back to the conclusion that the bat-tapping stance is the best one, because it gives you the best chance of being on the balls of your feet, the better to react positively to each delivery.

Much of this simply gets back to human movement of the kind Fraze knew so well. If we want to go from a standing start to walking we've got to get our weight onto the balls of our feet to access the ground reaction forces to work against gravity. It doesn't matter whether you're playing cricket, football or any sport, the same things apply. If you put an implement in your hands like a bat, that's going to have an impact as well, so that has to come into account. And if you hold the bat upright, it forces you even further onto your heels, it creates tension in your arms, which creates tension in your chest, which creates tension in your legs – a whole raft of muscles that you need to release and re-engage to get moving. All of that takes time.

You can try any stance and you can make it work, as a lot of players have done. For example, you wouldn't teach anyone to bat like Simon Katich, with his bat raised high and pronounced sideways movement before delivery. His absolute willpower, determination and skill made it work. Nevertheless, it was often the case that players looking for improvement on their level of performance could find it here. On one occasion I spoke to Ed Cowan after an Australia A series in 2010. Ed had built his technique to survive the moving ball in Tasmania, his bat raised high in preparation for pull and cut shots, but he couldn't hurt bowlers who went fuller. We had an exit interview in which he asked me what I thought.

'Mate, you've tried to make yourself too safe and you can't move. So you've got a limited number of balls that you can attack. To make runs, you've got to bat for a long time. At some point you'll get tired, you'll make a mistake and you'll get out. So you'll do the hard work and then not be able to capitalise. I really think you need to free yourself up – you had a really relaxed stance as a kid, very natural and the sort you'd expect if you just told a kid to pick a bat up and hit with it. But at the moment you're full of tension and you can't move.'

That conversation ended badly, as Ed was expecting some positive feedback after making a hundred. Many years later, ironically after Ed had been chosen and then dropped by Australia as a defensive foil to David Warner at the top of the Test batting order, he went back to his old, natural stance and started blitzing it, because he had shots available that he didn't have before. In a piece for cricinfo in 2015, Ed summed it all up rather well:

'Finding your way as a young professional brings you up against the ultimate paradox. You may try to find consistency to ensure a lengthy career in a tough but financially rewarding environment by minimising risk and simply "surviving", but this will no doubt diminish your ability to put pressure on the bowlers. The more pressure the bowler feels, the more likely they are going to serve up more run-scoring balls and fewer wicket-taking ones.'

Movement patterns follow the mind.

If you're in a positive frame of mind and looking for scoring opportunities, that improves your ability to move, because you're lighter of mind and lighter of body. When you're thinking about not getting out, there's a lot of tension, fear and anxiety. That goes through the body and affects your ability to move. Whenever I've had the opportunity to talk to young cricketers about it, I try to say 'this will help you, but you work out how to get there'.

Shane Watson was a perfect example. In early 2009 I was head coach at the Centre of Excellence and he rang me up to ask if he could come up and do some sessions, having been dropped from the Test side and then struggling with injury. We did three or four sessions, as I explained to him about the active neutral position, looking for the full ball and being set up to attack it. Watto is seldom one for half measures and he took it to a bit of an extreme, almost finishing up standing on one leg for a while. It certainly looked funny, but he was in a great position, and over the next two years he averaged 49.88 as an opener in Test cricket. The full ball was pretty much fruit for the sightscreen then. One innings I recall, against the West Indies in Adelaide, was almost like watching a batting machine calibrated to drive balls anywhere from forward point to forward square leg.

What Shane was able to do, at least over that period, was get himself into a position where he could go wherever the ball was. If the ball was outside the off stump the front foot goes that way; if it is in line with middle stump it goes there. That in turn serves to ensure that he could keep the ball on the off side of the front leg when it was full, and then keep the ball on the leg side of his body if it was short. That way you've got perfect access to the ball and you're taking your head to the line of the ball. That's done most easily when the ball is on the off side. What's harder is if the front pad goes to the line of the ball, the head and most of the body weight is to the off side of the ball and you've got a terrible view of it. Hence 'falling over' and succumbing lbw as Shane would do so often later. If you can keep the ball on the off side of the front leg, only the very best ball, moving late, is going to get through.

That's why you don't want batsmen who have committed weight to their front foot before they've picked up the line and length. I would say that up to 90 per cent of batsmen that I watch have a first movement that gets weight onto the front foot before the ball leaves the bowler's hand – leaving them rooted to the spot. All they can do is gain a little bit of height if the ball bounces, but absolutely nothing about making the door mat smaller.

If you're stuck in that way, it also becomes even harder to make the mental and physical adjustments that are required to cater for the vast array of subtle or pronounced differences between bowlers. If I had Richard Hadlee bowling to me, I knew he would largely bowl a fullish length and take it away from me. His error ball is going to slide onto my pads, because he's either going to be trying to move it too much from leg to off or it just won't swing. So I knew that straight down the ground, through the covers and just in front or behind square leg were the most likely areas I'd get my boundaries.

That's not premeditation, but it is awareness of the angles and areas for scoring ahead of an instinctive reaction to what comes. A left-arm over-the-wicket bowler creates different angles and scoring zones. Someone like Colin Croft, a right-hander sliding everything into you from wide of the crease, another set of boundary areas. Understanding the angles of each bowler is important – knowing where you can score your runs but then parking your ego and reacting to what comes. When you let the ego take over, as I did once to Lance Cairns and assumed he would give me a loosener to hit – only to miscue it straight to mid-on – that's the difference between preparation and premeditation.

The biggest statement you can make as a batter is to hit a fast bowler straight back down the wicket. Then you've put them on notice. Only the top one or two per cent of bowlers are resilient enough to come back to that area right away. As for the rest, if you punish a ball that is at your end of the door mat, you can almost guarantee they'll over correct and the next ball will be short of the door mat. One day I was with Greg Ritchie and he asked me, 'Do you get the script every morning? You obviously get a script about where they're going to bowl the next ball, the rest of us don't get that script.' Obviously there was no script, but I was applying the idea that if you punished the balls you should punish with the bat, it pretty much dictates what will come next.

That is one reason why I've never been a believer in the idea that the first hour is for the bowler and the rest is for the batter. When I'm in the middle I want the bowler to know that if you bowl me a half volley from the first ball I get, I want to score from it. If you bowl me a half-tracker or a wide ball, I want to score from it.

What I'm looking for, and tried to be, is a batsman who can hurt the bowlers. I, like so many others, used to love watching Ricky Ponting bat, and there were not many players for whom I would turn on the TV just to watch them bat. When Ponting was in his best rhythm, he could put the bowler's best ball – full, targeting the stumps, the pads or the edge – back down the pitch and into the gap between the umpire and the non-striker. If he hit one of those straight drives early on, I'd almost slap my hands together as if to say 'this is going to be fun', and sit back and enjoy it.

Part of what was enjoyable about watching Ponting or others of similar quality is seeing how often a batter putting bowlers under pressure makes judging the location of the next ball easier. I know if I get a full ball and I punish it, the next one is not going to be full. I can't go to the bank with that assumption, but I know he's more likely to go shorter. Then the pull shot becomes something you can be thinking a little more about. If you then get short and wide, the cut shot. All of a sudden you can have three boundaries in the space of a minute or two, and guess who's under the pump? Unless that bowler is Andy Roberts, John Snow, Jimmy Anderson or Glenn McGrath, you know they're not coming back there again.

Conversely, if it is a bowler of that quality and they are coming back again, you need to be aware enough to know that's what's coming, because they will try to make it that little bit harder each time. Their ability to do so won't just be dictated by them either, but by the field settings and the attitude of their captain. If the captain sets defensive fields, with a sweeper on the off side and the leg side, they'll encourage shorter length bowling and fewer risks for the batting side. Some bowlers, good as they were, would have been nightmares if they'd pitched a metre or so fuller. Joel Garner might have taken 1000 wickets if he'd done this, but I certainly wasn't going to be the one to tell him!

~

Combinations are very important in batting. All of the best teams I have seen over 60 years of watching and playing cricket had someone at the top of the batting order who could take the opposition down. If you've got two stodgy players together it doesn't work, because they will bat the opposition bowlers into form by not punishing their wayward deliveries often enough. In turn, the batsmen further down the order are invariably going to be under pressure because they're already behind in terms of run rate if not wickets.

But if you inject someone into the contest like David Warner or Virender Sehwag, who can get you a hundred in a session, that sets up a Test match and changes the mentality of both sides.

Of course you're not going to see that happen every game, but often it is enough to know that the threat is there.

Batting with Warner is a lot different to batting with Simon Katich. Opening with Katich alongside Ed Cowan would be unlikely to work in a Test match, but both would have done well with Warner, as Chris Rogers subsequently did from 2013 to 2015. The best thing that ever happened to Justin Langer was getting to open the batting opposite Matthew Hayden. Had he batted with Katich, his record would not look anywhere near as rosy. Equally, Katich benefited enormously from his partnership with Shane Watson between 2009 and 2011.

Years before, Bill Lawry and Keith Stackpole were an ideal combination; Lawry and Ian Redpath not so much because both were intent more on survival than on scoring. During my time playing for Australia, Ian Chappell's positive run-making at No. 3 served a similar purpose even though we did not have much in the way of successful opening stands at the time. Those circumstances suited Ian's personality, because the sooner he could get at the opposition, the better. Stacky, though, was something else. Like Watson, Stackpole didn't start out as an opener, but found that his temperament was just right for it; not to mention that he was a seriously good, fearless player of fast bowling. Stacky was the only player I ever knew who would say 'bring me as many fast bowlers as you like, as quick as you like, I don't care' and actually mean it. A few others might have said similar but with a veneer of bravado rather than genuine relish.

When we heard that Uton Dowe, Jamaica's hyped young fast bowler, wasn't playing in the tour game immediately before the first Test in 1973, I'd never seen someone as angry as Stacky. The rest of us were quite relieved we weren't going to see him for another week, but he was seriously filthy they hadn't picked

Dowe. More famously, when they did go head-to-head in the first Test, Stacky's hundred was so murderous that it led to the immortal barracking from the crowd to the West Indian captain Rohan Kanhai: 'Hey Kanhai, you not heard the eleventh commandment? Dowe shalt not bowl.'

Similarly, Watson was ideally suited to opening and in those two years after our technical work, he seemed to have a very wide bat. You rarely see a fuller face of the bat than the one he was offering – even Ricky Ponting's bat was slightly closed towards the leg side. The rarity of this comes from the fact that most of the time, facing a right-arm over-the-wicket bowler, you're basically hitting into the angle towards leg stump. I enjoyed watching Shane do this for the underlying reason that at the top level, you really need to have as many scoring options as possible. You can't afford to close any down in terms of deliberate technical decisions, because runs are too hard to get as it is.

11

A CENTRE OF EXCELLENCE?

Australia, 2008–2010

MY INVOLVEMENT WITH Lalit Modi meant that one of the first things I was able to do, having joined Cricket Australia, was to help broker full use of the Rajasthan Academy facilities for the touring Australian team. A training camp at the outset of the Test tour of India in late 2008, offering the full range of pitches and training spaces that Ian Frazer and I had set up, was undoubtedly a better acclimatisation base for Ricky Ponting's team than some of the BCCI members might have had in mind.

This proved to be very true on the next major Test tour in 2013, when the pitches on offer for warm-ups bore absolutely no resemblance to those prepared for the series, as a young Australian team was trounced 4–0. By 2017, Pat Howard had the Australian team preparing on practice pitches made-to-order at the ICC global academy in Dubai instead. But that 2008 camp was a pleasant experience for all concerned, the Australians and Rajasthan both, and, while the Test series resulted in a 2–0 defeat, it was certainly a more competitive showing than some of those that followed in Asia in subsequent years.

Coming back to Brisbane and the Centre of Excellence, I set about making numerous changes to the way things had been done for some years. The centre itself had been a marked departure from the much-admired Cricket Academy based for many years in Adelaide and run by Rod Marsh with help from his cadre of cricketing friends including Ian Chappell and myself, Dennis Lillee, John Inverarity and Terry Jenner. In moving up to Brisbane, where outdoor training was possible through the southern winter, the focus had shifted more to fitness, strength and conditioning. I felt more game awareness training was required for the young players coming in.

One concept Ian Frazer had developed at Rajasthan was built out of the fact there was some vacant space at the academy next to where they had built accommodation. Basically a sandy waste. Due to the heat, we had run sessions from 6 am to 9 am, then move indoors and only return from 3 pm to 6 pm. The sandy spot was in the shade of the building, making it exceptionally useful on hot afternoons. Ian set up a netted area roughly the size of the inner fielding circle in a limited-overs game, and during sessions the ball had to be kept inside the net while remaining live the whole time. The concept was dubbed 'cricket in a ring'.

This added a dimension of intensity to the game. The pitch was challenging because it was dusty and barren, meaning spin for the spinners and up and down bounce for the fast men, and the Rajasthan academy intakes loved it because of how much it resembled backyard cricket. Coming back to Australia, we refined it a little more and called it the battle zone. Matches were played with scores kept, even if it was just one-on-one between bowler and batsman.

This idea was met with mixed reviews from the players. They were used to going to the nets for the usual sessions, and they couldn't quite understand what we were getting at. Players were of course reporting these ideas back to their state or personal coaches, meaning we would get questions back about 'where are they getting their training volume from'. The expectation was that CoE scholars would come to Brisbane and hit 1000 balls a day outdoors rather than the 1000 balls a day they'd have been hitting indoors at home.

But I totally disagreed with that form of development. If the centre was to be one of excellence as it said on the front door, we had to be a point of difference. If all we were doing was replicating what was done in the states, then there was not much point in players coming up to work with us in the first place. I hated even the use of the word 'volume'. The way good players differentiate themselves from the rest is by being better competitors, better decision-makers, picking up more of the cues and adapting to a situation more quickly than most. That's where our focus was.

So the battle zone was a big part of the first six weeks of any intake, and I had lots of discussions with the likes of Glenn Maxwell and Steve Smith to talk them through its value. This was a chance to develop your game, develop new skills and have a competitive edge to everything you do. During Glenn's first couple of sessions in 2010, he persistently hammered balls as far out of the net as he could, as if to make the point with his bat that he had been trying to get across verbally. We said to him, 'Maxy, we know you can do that, but your team won't get any points for those big hits. What we're trying to do here is develop your all-round skills and ability to manoeuvre the ball into different spots.'

Guess what? Once Glenn bought into the concept, he was the best player by so far it didn't matter. He did the things that good players do: manipulate the field, work the ball into gaps, drop it at his feet and run. All of a sudden his decision-making was being exercised in a real-time way that a typical net session could never achieve, like a childhood game of backyard Test cricket once did. A lot of the best lessons I learned about the game were in those backyard contests, and what we were trying to recreate in the battle zone was the same attitude. Six-ball overs, scenarios for the batsman to overcome, limitations within which they had to work.

Ricky Ponting once said that he never got much out of net sessions because everything about it felt false relative to what he would encounter on match day. Similarly, when I was playing, going into the nets day after day would have done my head in. I wanted a contest to keep me interested. I wanted to pit myself against the best the opposition had, and I wanted to challenge myself with finding answers to the questions they posed. Cricket is a problem-solving game, and the best players are the best problem-solvers. You don't solve many problems in the nets. What we were looking for was a bridge between the nets and the game.

Game-sense training is not simply a matter of putting a game on. It's about trying to create an environment to focus on the specific outcomes that you want. As an example, what I saw with Steve Smith was that he was a brilliant leg-side player who could play almost any ball to that side of the wicket with precision. I could relate to that, because up until early in my Test career I only made runs on the leg side, in part because in the backyard the house was on the off side of the pitch and I was less likely to break a window playing to leg. I also had a leg-side-heavy batting grip.

I didn't want Steve to change his grip, but I wanted him to understand the limitations it brought, because when you get to the highest level, the standard of bowling is going to go up, the standard of captaincy is going to go up, and the opposition will have more intel about where you can and can't score. You want to play on the leg side as much as you can – but if you don't have an off side then there's no danger for them to bowl there, making it harder and harder for you to score runs. They might not get you out, but they can slow you down. At least if you can get off strike and manipulate the ball through the off side, guess what, you'll get more balls bowled straighter and then you're in heaven, you're playing to your strength.

What we did then was to try to change the environment for him to help him to hit there. Essentially we told him, 'You can hit any number of balls through the leg side but we won't award you scoring points unless you hit them through the off side.' To say Steve was reluctant to try this would be an understatement; he was grumpy about having to do something outside his comfort zone. We gave him the explanation that once he got to the top level, opposition captains, bowlers and fielders would be good enough to plug half the field, so he needed at the very least to be able to turn the strike over by deflecting balls to the off side. That would then draw opponents into feeding his strength and the runs would follow. The battle zone was there to expand his range.

Eventually, Steve saw the fun in it and started to work at it, both in 2009 when he was a full-time scholar for 18 weeks, and again in 2010 when he was there for six weeks in the same intake as Glenn. On balance, he probably only bought in to about 50 per cent of what he was capable of, but he played the game and showed he was more than good enough to score runs all round the wicket. I was conscious, too, that you can push players only so far away from what they want to do; beating them over the head won't work either. Once I could see that he was making some attempt to do it, for the sake of his team's score as much as anything else, I was happy to move on to focus on other things. Even when we had the battle zone going, we did have other nets and other opportunities for guys to train more normally if they chose to.

It was later in that 2010 intake that we had a training session up on the Ray Lindwall field above the main oval, and bowling into the northern nets. Steve was batting and Joel Paris, then still a teenager, was bowling. We'd gotten towards the end of a session and Steve wanted more of a hit. I was working with Joel on his run-up and a couple of other things he was trying to get right.

Chris Simpson, then the captain of Queensland, came up to join us ahead of a state training session and asked if he could have a bowl; at the end of a net session we were more than happy to have the extra help. I didn't take much notice for his first few balls as I was preoccupied with Joel, but Chris came back to his mark and said, 'Wow, hasn't this bloke changed. I've just bowled him three balls, last season he would've hit every one of them through the leg side, and now he's hit them all through the off side.' So maybe the message did get through – certainly the impression was that a lot of guys got more out of the experience in hindsight than they thought they had at the time.

I had my frustrations with these debates, either with the players themselves or their state coaches, over the first couple of years. But by 2010 when I was travelling around to different states, I saw battle zone–style training was starting to become a part of the language and other states and coaches were taking it up. Moreover, players were expecting to take part in it and enjoying it when they did, so it became part of the way Australian cricket evolved its training. It was always important to know the context, trying to augment game sense and awareness skills in a heightened environment without actually having to put games on.

That challenged coaches too, because the easiest thing to do with a squad of 15 or 20 players and three or four nets is just to rotate them through and run the session. That might work as a tune-up between matches in an ongoing series, but it isn't the sort of exercise that will develop players.

Often there was pushback from the states about the fact they no longer wanted these development intakes or squads getting together and going to Brisbane, arguing there was nothing they could learn there that wasn't happening in their home towns. In addition to some of the different things we were doing, this viewpoint missed the fact that if you put a young group of talented players together from around the country they will feed off each other and learn. The energy that comes from the group will help individuals, and the energy from the better individuals will help the group. They would also get more chances to be placed in vital scenarios over the course of a match, rather than being the junior batsman at No. 6 or the young bowler coming on third or fourth change.

In 2010 there was that very debate around Mitchell Marsh and Josh Hazlewood being included in the squad for the Under-19 World Cup in New Zealand. Both were already playing first-class cricket, and when we said we wanted them for the Cup, Western Australia and New South Wales made their opposition very plain. We won the argument on the basis that it was an opportunity for Mitch to captain Australia and be the premier batsman, and that Josh would open the bowling for Australia. They would also be exposed to the pressures of playing in a global tournament televised around the world. All of these elements were not things their states could give them, and the cost would be missing a couple of Shield games.

But that pushback in turn I think influenced the attitudes of Mitch and Josh, who struggled to get into the right frame of mind for the tournament and did not perform well as a consequence until the Cup's closing stages. In the end, with the aid of some encouragement from the coaching staff, Mitch and Josh warmed to their tasks and ended up playing vital roles in the most recent instance of Australia winning the tournament.

Young players will learn more from each other than from a coach who isn't of their generation. Aside from my early exchange with Sir Donald Bradman that compelled me to adjust my batting grip, all the best and most enduring lessons of my playing days came from experiences in the middle and conversations with other players.

It was in the dressing room at Adelaide Oval in December 1967, prior to South Australia's tour match against India, that I had my first exchange with Sir Donald Bradman, who compelled me to adjust my batting grip. We had said good morning to one another before the Don commented 'I'd change that grip if I were you'. My grip, front hand turned around the front of the bat, was very much in the English style. Sir Donald proceeded to show me his neutral grip, with both hands in vees down the back of the bat. 'You'll find it's uncomfortable because you haven't used it before, but it'll help with your off-side play … And by the way, I gave this advice to one other player. He didn't take it and he's no longer in the side.' That other player, I soon found out, was the former SA batsman and then journalist Alan Shiell!

Perhaps the best lesson of them all was from spending time with an opposing team after play in an early Sheffield Shield game. We were playing Victoria in Melbourne, and though the

Test team was away in South Africa that summer, they had the likes of Ken Eastwood, Paul Sheahan and Alan Connolly, all of whom would represent Australia, in the side. I looked at them as much better players than me, and assumed they were pretty confident and that the game came fairly easily to them: in the course of an innings victory over SA it had certainly looked that way. But in discussions I realised that they were just as nervous and apprehensive as I was. It led me to conclude I wasn't as far away from coping as I thought, because I realised everyone had doubts and worries they wrestled with daily.

At the same time, if you put one young, talented player amongst a group of experienced players with less upside, they can get lost. First of all, the experienced players are seldom trying to help them as much as they think, or claim to. It is, quite frankly, bullshit to overplay the idea that you need experienced players around any dressing room. Because experience doesn't work that simply: there will be 10-year players in any dressing room who only really have one year's meaningful experience in them that they've repeated 10 times. Young players can be bullied, and for many generations were expected to be seen and not heard. That had been the case in Australia and England, and I also saw it in India. Unless you have a very good and giving dressing room, older players will feel threatened by youth as much as they feel a duty to show them the ropes.

A part of the philosophy of the Centre of Excellence was that in conjunction with its move from the Cricket Academy in Adelaide to the Brisbane-based model in 2004, the program became a much shorter one that only covered an off-season. In Adelaide, scholars had trained together through the winter and then played together for an Academy team through at least the first half of the summer, famously beating an England touring side in a couple of one-day matches played over consecutive days at North Sydney Oval in December 1994. That in itself was an evolution from the initial system, which had somewhat inequitably allowed South Australia to pick scholars for the state team, suddenly bolstering the SACAs with the likes of Michael Bevan, Darren Berry and Joe Scuderi.

That aside, the Adelaide model worked well, and Rod Marsh was rightly lauded for helming its most successful era. He was the perfect personality: a hard but fair task master, more or less treating the players like an older brother would, and calling on an unrivalled network of former players to come in for specialist coaching. That those former players also got to spend an evening or two with Rodney and some bottles of South Australian red didn't dampen their enthusiasm either! Something else the scholars did was work jobs for some minimal payment, whether that was Ricky Ponting replacing screws in the bench seats of the members stands, or Shane Warne working in the SACA admin office with the then chief executive Barry Gibbs.

I, however, didn't like the idea of a 12-month program that took players out of their states during the summer. Our schedule was designed to give them back to the states in time for the season, and moderated the intensity of the cricket training environment with a designated day for study or other work each Wednesday. That idea had come in partly as a response to the behavioural issues that had seen David Warner, Aaron Finch and Mark Cosgrove sent home from the CoE in 2005, but what we found was that by the late 2000s, players coming up to Brisbane did not like the idea of doing anything other than either training for and playing cricket, or playing golf or relaxing.

That in itself was a fundamental shift from the earlier years in Adelaide, as successive generations threw themselves into professional cricket. My strong sense was that the game's custodians had a duty of care to set up these young men for their lives, not just for their cricket. They were coming to Brisbane for months on end, often over multiple years, quite a few straight out of high school if they had even completed secondary studies. The Australian Cricketers' Association has tried to provide those opportunities and support in terms of tertiary study and career options, but history has shown that some will engage with that and some won't.

I've often been criticised for an over-emphasis on youth. A misconception of my initial years at the Centre of Excellence was that I was the sole voice agitating for the removal of a generation of senior players from the system and the Sheffield Shield second XI and club cricket fringes. Nothing could be further from the truth. The fact of the matter was that when CA high-performance staff and management sat down to actually look at the way the professional game was evolving, we found a problem even more advanced than we had suspected, and which required immediate remedial action.

When we did the review of the pathway from junior cricket to the top, there was a total of just five players under the age of 25 with full contracts on state lists. That is an extraordinarily low number. It set alarm bells ringing, because we had already been talking to the states about the importance of providing chances for the best of the young players to show their wares, because that was the future of Australian cricket.

History, bolstered by our research, told us that if you hadn't debuted in first-class cricket by the time you were 21 or 22, and if you hadn't debuted in Test cricket by the time you were 23 or 24, the likelihood of you making much of an impact on Australian cricket was minimal. Sure there was Adam Gilchrist and Mike Hussey, who did not debut for Australia until late into their 20s, but they were outliers – and even then they were still recognised with selection for their state at young ages.

When Simon Katich was first picked for Australia in 1999, Ian rang me to ask what I thought of him. I said, 'He's a good player but they missed a better one. I would've picked Mike Hussey.' So someone like Mike could easily have played plenty of international cricket at a younger age. It was a further six years before he made his debut, in late 2005. Matthew Hayden is another who could easily have played a lot more for Australia at a younger age, having missed out narrowly to Michael Slater for the spot opposite Mark Taylor at the start of the 1993 Ashes tour. Australian cricket had traditionally been good at giving youth a chance. Our success across many eras had been based largely on the fact that we'd identified and picked a lot of good players at young ages and seen them have long, fruitful and often brilliant careers.

But we could see that on current lists, there were very few players in that age profile. The primary reason for this was that states were contracting players towards the bottom ends of their lists as senior players for their second XI sides and then back-ups for the Shield side. New South Wales was the one state that gave more chances to younger players than most, but this was largely a product of two things: they generally had more Australian representatives unavailable, and many of their second-tier players were poached by smaller states.

Even then, we were pleading with NSW to pick David Warner in the Shield team and give him opportunities at the top of the order. But for the bulk of the three seasons between his Twenty20 debut for Australia in January 2009 and his Test debut in November 2011, Warner was dismissed by the NSW brains trust as a one-day player, and it didn't matter how often we asked after him. In our discussions with the states, if there was a choice between youth and experience, even if that experience had let them down repeatedly, they would still choose the experienced player.

In a way it was the sort of thinking that dominated football lists of 40 or so among the top six clubs, with plenty of 'top-up' players just outside the first 22. Where this thinking fell down of course was in the number of available places in any given cricket team or squad: about half that. Even those football clubs expecting to play finals the following year were still drafting four or five teenagers every season! In Australian cricket circa 2008, those sorts of developmental talents weren't even getting a look-in, when the Shield and second XI competitions were research and development for the national team.

These words from Mark Sorell, at that stage the coach of a South Australian side that had underperformed and so was topping up with players culled by other states, were typical: 'It is no coincidence that the average age of players currently on the Cricket Australia contract list is 29 and that successful state sides such as Victoria dominate the domestic competition with squads with similar age profiles. With the retirement of Greg Blewett, Darren Lehmann, Matthew Elliott and Jason Gillespie last season the average age of the Redbacks squad lowered to 24. I have been looking for players in 27 to 30-plus age group.'

As a consequence, any of the conversations we had with the states about this issue saw them nod their heads and then go away and do the opposite. The number of state contracts was not going to be cut unless the Australian Cricketers' Association agreed, an unlikely proposition given that it would, at a stroke, reduce the size of their membership base. So the states were free to keep topping up their squads by whatever means necessary, the better to meet the needs of domestic coaches who were still employed to win the Sheffield Shield. That performance imperative forced them into short-term thinking and a preference for experience over youth.

I had empathy for the coaches after many of the conversations I'd gone through at the SACA myself. A balanced philosophy, taking in the fact that it wasn't just about the number of games won but the quality of players developed to go to the top level, was in short supply. Our arguments with the high-performance managers of each state were that they should be choosing coaches to produce and develop players for Australia. If they are doing that properly for you then the Shield wins will doubtless follow. But if the focus was only on winning the Shield, the selection thinking would be geared far too much at the here and now and nowhere near enough at the future.

For years we had discussions with the states about the incentives for coaches: don't employ them just to win the Sheffield Shield. That might be one criterion, but the other criterion that was more important was producing players to play long-term for Australia. That sort of change had a positive impact on someone like Greg Shipperd, who in his later years as coach of Victoria became much more helpful in looking for international players within his state, with some noted successes. I like Greg, have admiration for what he's done and his passion for the game, but we had plenty of discussions where we'd bump heads around how to produce players for Australia and giving opportunities to young players. His attitude changed a little too, I think, because we made an effort to involve him with Under-19s, Australia A and other pathway programs so he could see beyond Victoria.

The other thing often at odds between state and national levels was that many of the coaches in the system liked making players dependent: guys who would, upon reaching the top of the game, be happy to say of them 'that's my coach'. The best players at international level are adaptable to a wide range of scenarios, conditions, parts of the world and time zones, and can think on their feet without recourse to their personal guru. They are able to size up the risk-management element of a particular contest with an opponent more quickly than most, and they can do it for themselves. No-one can fire off a WhatsApp message for advice in the middle of an innings or a bowling spell anyway.

The structure was such that it created little knots and glitches because you have people employed to have their focus on the domestic here and now, when we needed everyone's focus on the national team and the future. Virtually every element of Australian cricket was, and still is, predicated on the success of the Australian men's team. That is what paid *everyone's* salary. We needed as many people as possible focused on producing the best players for Australia.

So having failed to impart any positive change through conversation, our next best option was in regulation. We agreed to impose age restrictions on the second XI competition, allowing only three players over the age of 23 in each team, starting in the 2009–10 season. I'm not sure where the name 'Futures League' came from, but the optics gave fuel to the naysayers to take potshots; there were plenty to fire over the next two years, especially after the 2010–11 Ashes went the way they did (a 1–3 loss, with each of the losses by an innings, if you need reminding). The states made their unhappiness known, as did the ACA.

A lot of the blowback that came my way was a product of the fact that I was left to sell the concept once the changes had been put in place. I didn't mind being the target because I felt very strongly that what we were trying to do was in the best interests of Australian cricket. There were certain players who were extremely agitated by the whole thing, generally those who were experiencing life on the fringe, either of Australian representation or that of their state. I can only conclude that they felt if too many young players got opportunities that had previously been almost impossible to come by, they might be on the way out the door.

Unpopular as it may have been, we had to try to find a way to provide a circuit-breaker, and my job was expressly to develop talent to play for Australia. The restrictions were only ever devised as a temporary correction, and as such worked with great efficiency. Within two years, the numbers of young players on state lists went up exponentially. There had also been some tweaking done around rookie contracts, limiting the number of years for which a player could be listed in that category without either being promoted to a full contract or returning to grade ranks.

While the second XI age restrictions were gradually pared back, starting in 2011, the important thing was to ensure that the states recognised the need to be moving fresh talent through the system all the time. They have followed this to varying degrees over the intervening decade, but it is telling that all the established members of today's Test side – even the captain Tim Paine – made their debuts at a young age, seldom any older than 25. Let's go through them.

David Warner – first-class debut at 22, Test debut at 25
Marnus Labuschagne – 20, 24
Steve Smith – 18, 21
Tim Paine – 21, 25

Mitchell Starc – 19, 21

Pat Cummins – 17, 18

Nathan Lyon – 24, 24

Josh Hazlewood – 17, 23

Even so, the debate continues. A similar move to the Futures League was made when we included a Cricket Australia XI for young players in the domestic one-day tournament for three seasons. That was a consequence of further discussions with the states when we said 'if you blokes aren't going to play these guys in first-class cricket, we have to find some form of a higher level of the game to expose them to'. That created a battleground where states did not want to release fringe players to play in the CA XI on the grounds that they were back-ups for the state team, meaning the XI itself was often composed of players at the rookie and under-age levels.

One discussion I had with Justin Langer after he became Australia's coach went along the lines of, 'Justin, you're on the board at the West Coast Eagles, and you don't leave blokes in the WAFL for five years to get them ready for AFL level; you play them at 18 and 19 years of age, because you have to.' The AFL clubs accept that that is what has to be done; Chris Scott, the coach of Geelong, spoke at a cricket conference on the Gold Coast after his first year with the Cats. He talked about playing players before they were ready, playing them before you need them. He said it was important that you don't play them in the back pocket against the bottom team, you play them at centre-half back against Buddy Franklin, because they had to find out what good players do.

There's no hiding a player. You've got to expose them to how tough it is, throwing them in at the deep end of the pool. Some will swim right away and some won't. If your selection and ID processes are good enough, you won't drown too many. Every now and then you'll have to throw them a life belt and get them out of the deep end if they need to, and put them back when they've learned those lessons and grown a bit more.

12

SELECTOR, AGAIN

Australia, 2010–2011

IN EARLY 2011, a group of coaches and mentors from Cricket Australia ventured to the United States for a couple of visits with two of the world's most renowned sporting organisations: baseball's Boston Red Sox and college football's Texas Longhorns.

One big similarity struck me more than the differences.

We spent some quality time with Mack Brown, who was at that stage coming towards the end of a 15-year run as head coach of the Longhorns that ended with a win/loss record of 158–48, earning about US$3 million a year. He was essentially the Wayne Bennett of American college football. It was around the time that high-profile recruit Brendan Fevola had been sacked by the AFL's Brisbane Lions after one chaotic season.

I asked Brown, 'How do you deal with the really talented but disruptive player?' His reply was succinct. 'Each team,' he said, 'can afford to have one asshole, and that's gotta be me! I would rather be beat by them twice a year than deal with them 24/7, because they'll take 80 per cent of your energy and give you less than 20 per cent of what you need from them.'

One of the most celebrated examples of a strong-willed character was Shane Warne, of course. He worked in the Australian team, both as a young player in the era of Allan Border, David Boon, Mark Taylor, the Waugh brothers and Ian Healy, and then in later years as a senior one, because the vast majority of the characters around him were all strong and mature individuals. If Shane had come into the team in the mid-1980s with that unsteady young team around Allan, it might not have worked quite as well. Border would have struggled to manage it on his own, and the other players would not have been sure enough of their own ground to step in. Even with the experience and the talent of the team in the 1990s, and then the later group under Steve Waugh and then Ricky Ponting, he was still a disruption. But at least when he was on the field, he gave you what you needed.

So in evaluating where your team is at, you can take more risks when you've got a mature group in that sense, with those mercurial sorts of players.

In assessing a player, you generally want to be getting a feel for them as a person as well as a cricketer, and that's where spending time around them early on at under-age, academy or Australia A levels is a real advantage. If they were selected to go to the academy for instance, you knew they had ability. Then it was a case of getting to understand who they were. I found plenty of valuable insights as national talent manager when being around them in the off-season at what is now the National Cricket Centre in Brisbane, and then taking them on tours and really getting to understand how they operated.

From that you'd get a pretty good idea of who were the ones you felt had a good chance of surviving long enough to make a success of their careers.

Every player who should have played a lot for Australia has done so. In 50 years of being aware of what's going on around me and even before that, watching cricket in the 1960s, there has never been someone who was good enough who has failed to find a way to make it there. Those who don't, despite showing potential at an early age, will invariably fall short because they are unable to expand their games beyond those promising beginnings. Often this can happen as a consequence of moulding, either deliberately or simply out of habit, a game that is safe and reliable for the level below the top.

But as a game of risk management, cricket requires a constant weighing up of how much is achievable at a given moment. To make runs, you have to risk getting out; to take wickets, you have to risk going for runs. The evolution and expansion of a player's methods of dancing with those risks is critical to long-term success as an international player. Domestic players who make the same mistakes time and time again can still have careers in the second tier, but after a certain point they will be stunted in terms of what they can achieve at the top.

~

My move onto the selection panel in August 2010 had come in conjunction with the creation of not just my new position, national talent manager, but the formation of a network of state talent managers. We felt that we needed somebody in each state who could put the national team cap on in their thinking, and not be sitting there as the Victorian talent manager or the

Queensland talent manager and be thinking about the team in the same way the coach was. There were already enough people in the room in each state worrying about the team in a conventional manner; what we needed was someone who would think about Australia.

When the role was mooted, I felt that my time as a coach was winding down but that as a talent manager and selector I could work for another 10 years. Plus it was a hugely challenging role, it was a role Australian cricket needed, and when I saw the direction they were going in I decided that was a role I was qualified for and that I should at least apply. My suspicion was that Michael Brown and James Sutherland would've been quite happy for me to stay as head coach of the Centre of Excellence, so in the interview process I had to sell myself moving into the new roles in part as an advocate for how vital they were.

It was a long interview. I got the distinct impression that at the start, James and Michael were going through the motions because I wasn't their preferred candidate. So I had to convince them that this was another and more important challenge for me that would also create room for another coach to come in at the Centre of Excellence, perhaps someone with greater coaching ambition than I had. Midway through the discussion I got the impression that the tide turned and all of a sudden James and Michael were looking at each other and getting excited about the potential of the role.

Most importantly, the establishment of a link between the head of the youth pathway and the national selection panel was absolutely imperative. It was a perfect amalgamation of my skills and the role, because getting the insights that came from being involved in the youth side of the system offered a whole range of knowledge to the selectors of the senior team. Between the end of Laurie Sawle's tenure in 1995 and the creation of the national talent management role, the selection panel had been a satellite in somewhat loose orbit around Australian cricket. Its appointments were tied, by tradition, to the Cricket Australia Board, but in what had become the professional era there was no link to the wider system.

Sutherland and Brown were also coming at it from the perspective that they wanted a greater level of professionalism on the selection panel. That ideal was blocked in part by the fact that selectors were still chosen from the small pool of nominees raised by the state associations through the CA board. Brown's recommendation to the board had in fact been that the chairman of the selection panel become a full-time position, but this had been blocked. As a compromise, one position was freed up on the panel to appoint the national talent manager. I'd enjoyed my time as a selector in the 1980s, and could see that maybe in time that would be my sole role again. But initially it was ideal to take on both. Another area in which the two felt I had a role to play was as a lateral-thinking challenger to the selection status quo.

As part of the commission, I was going to all the national under-age carnivals, I was touring overseas with the Under-19s team and also Australia A, and so I was able to relay what I learned to the national panel. It meant I got to see young players operating under all conditions, in foreign environments and outside the comfort zones of their home towns and states. Soon, you could get a pretty good idea of what each young guy was capable of.

One of the more contentious elements of the compromises that led to the role was that I was depicted as becoming a spokesman for the selection panel, when the chairman Andrew Hilditch really needed to be. He had not enjoyed that element of the job, not least when he was hunted down by News Corp cameras while walking his dog on the beach in Adelaide when not the selector on duty for Matthew Hayden's last Test match at the SCG in January 2009. But it then got messy as to who was talking to the press on behalf of the panel. The description was of a 'two-headed monster' and it did neither of us any favours.

I took the job entering into the 2010–11 season, one where Ricky Ponting's team were broadly expected to regain the Ashes lost in England in 2009. I did not share this optimism, because looking down the team I felt that if Ponting and Michael Clarke did not make runs we would be incapable of cobbling together enough scores to win matches.

My concerns around Ponting's workload and the toll of captaining a young and uncertain team were manifest in his response when I met him in Sydney before the summer began and asked him if he really thought he should still be at No. 3 in the batting order. 'What do you mean,' he replied, taken aback.

'Your recent record suggests that you've probably not been at your peak, maybe if we give you a little bit of breathing space batting at No. 4, you might actually do a better job for yourself and your team.'

'No! I'm going to bat No. 3, that's where I bat.'

At the Gabba, the day before the series, Australia had an optional training session. Ponting would have had to do his mandatory media appearances on match eve, but apart from that I didn't see how the extra training was going to help him. I told him he would've been better off hitting golf balls and freeing his mind of cricket. As it was he went to the nets and had one of the worst sessions I'd seen a quality player have, and it only got worse the harder he tried. He averaged 16 for the series, bettered by Peter Siddle and Mitchell Johnson, besting only a few bowlers.

Once Michael Clarke became captain, Ponting's centuries thereafter came at No. 4.

A couple of years earlier in Chandigarh before the second Test against India, I watched the intensity of Australia's training in hot conditions and felt that the energy being expended was not sustainable. You can't keep going that hard for that long; in a never-ending season you've got to manage your resources well. I watched Matthew Hayden train, pounding countless balls against bowlers and bowling machines, a high physical and mental energy session. Then I saw Michael Clarke come in and do exactly the same thing and thought 'he can't survive'. Hayden is a man mountain, a bull of a man, who might be able to get away with it.

After watching Michael do it, I took the opportunity to walk back with him from the nets to the dressing room to ask him about his approach. He said, 'Oh mate I'm going really well, I'm working so hard, there's runs just around the corner.' I said, 'Mate, be careful. I've watched your training on this tour and you're doing exactly the same thing as Matthew Hayden. I'm not sure Haydos is doing the right thing and I'm not sure most people understand what he's also doing is spending time in the middle of the ground, on his haunches, just imagining himself making runs. I wouldn't be sure which one of the two is more important. You're only doing the physical stuff, and to be fair, you're not half his size. You're a batting artist, finely built, fast twitch muscles, a touch player. In art terms, Haydos is the equivalent of a house painter and you're Rembrandt. You're going to break yourself if you're not careful.' He nodded, kept walking and the subject was never mentioned again.

I'm not convinced that the legacy Ponting left around training as intensely as that was necessarily a great thing for Australian cricket, because it wouldn't have worked for everybody and it focuses training primarily on the physical aspects of the game. There are going to be different personalities – treating them all the same can be dangerous. While Ponting's theory was that if golfers hit 1000 balls a day, why don't cricketers, I'm not sure that worked too well for all golfers.

But apart from any individual selection for the Ashes series, the most confronting thing we had to contend with was Cricket Australia's desire to build a big event and marketing hype around the announcement of the Test squad – on a pre-determined date and at a setpiece event near Circular Quay, Sydney. It was annoying for Hilditch because he had to front it, and it was scheduled to take place before the final round of Sheffield Shield games and an Australia A tour game against England in Hobart. Where CA argued that this was the same timing as in 2006, our counter-argument was that the team was far less settled this time around, having come off a drawn series with Pakistan in England and then a 2–0 defeat in India in a series that was shoehorned into the schedule by the BCCI.

If we'd known exactly what the XI was that we wanted for the Gabba, it wouldn't have been a problem, but there were still some issues we needed to sort out, one of which included a recurrence of back problems for the vice-captain, Clarke. To have an extra couple of games and a few days' time was going to help us, but CA was insistent that we give them something. The result was that we responded, here you go, have 17. We didn't want to see it as a broadcast event or reality TV, that wasn't our job, and we found it intrusive to have to do it two weeks before we needed to. It almost made the Australia A game redundant.

Something I saw quite quickly around this time too was how much Ponting was leading selection discussions. This is not to say that a captain shouldn't do so, but his word was certainly carrying tremendous weight. We saw that in how the selectors switched from Nathan Hauritz, who had been the No. 1 spin bowler since early 2009, to the Tasmanian Xavier Doherty, on the basis that Kevin Pietersen had an indifferent record against left-arm orthodox tweakers. Both Haury and Xavier were lovely guys, but neither were the sort of spin bowlers likely to impose themselves on a game, either in terms of how they bowled or the personalities they possessed. Steve O'Keefe was chosen for Australia A at that time, but Xavier was ultimately preferred, having just played for Australia in a limited-overs series at home to Sri Lanka.

Ponting was tough on spin bowlers. His expectations, no doubt built up by playing alongside Shane Warne for the first 12 years of his international career, were extremely high. That was a tough environment for Hauritz, who in technical terms had most if not all of the gifts of Nathan Lyon but struggled to make the mental graduation to feeling like he genuinely belonged. I saw how high those expectations were after Xavier debuted in Melbourne, and took 4-46 in a game where Australia lost thanks to a Houdini act from Angelo Mathews. Despite the fact the next game was at the SCG, Xavier was dropped: we lost again.

Nevertheless, Xavier was included in the team for the first two Ashes Tests. He reminded me a little bit of Brad Hogg in the sense that neither of them offered a huge amount of side spin, but bowled with plenty of over spin that would cause the ball to drop tantalisingly onto a good length when they were in rhythm. So Xavier was someone who could do a job and had shown that for Tasmania, but he was never the sort of bowler who was likely to bowl a side out in the fashion of Warne. Given that we had issues with the rest of the attack, not least Mitchell Johnson,

Xavier was left exposed as the new kid on the block, something England didn't fail to notice.

Johnson's case was one where we tried to perform some mid-series remedial work and got a short-term result from doing so. At the Gabba, Mitch's control was almost entirely absent, and his pace was down too. In consultation with coach Tim Nielsen, captain Ricky Ponting and bowling coach Troy Cooley, we chose to take Johnson out of the side for the Adelaide Test and send him to Perth ahead of schedule so he could spend some time with Dennis Lillee, who had mentored him with some success previously. As much as those sorts of sessions could create a brief upsurge, as we saw during his first-innings burst at the WACA that helped square up the series at 1–1 with two to play, Johnson's biggest issues were of the longer-term kind, both in terms of keeping his mind focused but also keeping his lower body strong enough to support the upper body exertions of his violent bowling action. When he produced a couple of series to remember in 2013–14, his body and mind were equally strong.

After it was decided to move on from Doherty after the first two Tests, we plucked another left-arm spin bowler, Michael Beer, from what appeared to be considerable obscurity. We liked his height and accuracy, the word from Western Australia was that he was a pretty durable character, and a little like Peter Taylor in that he had played plenty of premier grade cricket to hone his game before starting out in the Sheffield Shield. Beer played one Test in Sydney that series, another in Trinidad a couple of years later, and went on to considerable success in the Big Bash League. He was, undoubtedly, a stopgap until such time as we found a longer-term option.

The flip side of my pre-series conversation with Ricky about the batting order was that I also felt we needed to have Steve

Smith in the top six. Though unpolished at that point, he was our next superstar, and while we had Ponting and Clarke in the middle order, there was an opportunity to have Smith come in at No. 6 and learn from them, having not long made his debut against Pakistan as a spinning all-rounder. I felt he was as capable of making runs against England's attack as Marcus North, who had held the spot since 2009 without ever making it his own. I could see, too, that Smith was ultimately going to run past North. The compromise was to give North the first opportunity in Brisbane and Adelaide, leaving Steve to come in from the third Test onwards.

As a selector, if it is 50/50 between two players and the captain wants one of them, you should always go with the captain unless there's a very good reason to do otherwise. There's no point having a grumpy captain out on the field because he didn't get his way at the selection table. Nevertheless, there are occasional times when it is important to say 'no, we think this guy has got to play', and choosing a young Steve Smith was one such example. By the end of the series, though it was a nightmarish one for Australia overall, Steve had shown a few things, and came back much better for that initial experience a couple of years later.

Another point of conjecture had been around Mike Hussey, who after a tremendous start to his international career had started to struggle – not long after promotion to the No. 4 spot in between Ricky and Michael. Entering the Ashes series he'd averaged a little over 30 over the preceding couple of years and only made two hundreds in that time. His start to the season was interrupted by needing to juggle his place in Chennai Super Kings' team in the T20 Champions League with Test and Sheffield Shield commitments, and during a game for Western Australia against Victoria at the MCG he looked a long way from his best.

Watching his first innings in that game wasn't pretty. With the approval of the WA coach Mickey Arthur, I had a conversation with Mike between innings in which I essentially told him, 'We back you and you're going to get picked for Brisbane, but can you please score some bloody runs.' He duly made a hundred, and went on to have, alongside Shane Watson and Brad Haddin, a solid personal series in an awful one for the team.

When Simon Katich tore his Achilles tendon in Adelaide and limped out of the series, we also recalled Phil Hughes. It was a decision that met with some criticism on the basis that he was not scoring runs in Shield cricket at the time. While it is true that we could have opted for an older player in Katich's stead, there were actually remarkably few making top-order runs in a season where plenty of pitches were bowler friendly. In that context, we felt it was best to look forward rather than back. A cricket team is never the finished article; there's no such thing as standing still – you're either going forward or going backwards. So you need to be looking ahead, and I would certainly rather invest games in someone who you believe has the potential to play a lot of them.

In doing so, we ignored the claims of players like Chris Rogers, who had made his debut in January 2008 and would later prove to be a more than capable Test batsman. I have since spent quite a bit of time with Chris and found him to be a good person with a sound cricket brain. He was steeped in cricket of course through his father, John, who played for New South Wales and was later general manager of the WACA. But around 2010 he was – rightly or wrongly – not a popular cricketer among his peers, something that was undoubtedly an undercurrent whenever we discussed him. It was a shame because there was, and is, a lot to like about him.

Something I admired subsequently about what Chris did as a Test batsman was that he played a lot of the most expansive and positive innings of his entire career at the highest level. Very few players are able to expand their range, particularly guys who have come into Test cricket later on, at international level. In those circumstances, most players go into their shell and then wonder years later why they couldn't bring their best stuff on those days. When I spoke to Chris about this once he'd retired, he wished he'd been able to play more like that earlier on in his career. I think that had he done so, he may well have played a lot more Test cricket.

Andrew Hilditch is a remarkable bloke who did an exceptional job as a selector, not least because he juggled it with partnership in a law firm. A solid citizen of the game, he was incredibly passionate about the role, to the extent that he put in a superhuman amount of time and effort – in my experience only Pat Howard has come close. Often he would bring his legal papers to the cricket, and on occasions on tour he could be seen pounding away on the treadmill while simultaneously reading through what seemed an endless supply of documents.

Conscientious to a fault, he was unfairly maligned for decisions around the top team when the system beneath it was the most significant thing that had come unstuck. The way his selection tenure, begun in 1996, ended in the aftermath of the 2010–11 Ashes series was terrible, and I pleaded CA chairman Jack Clarke to avoid making him the scapegoat, because the system had problems far deeper than the selection of the Test team.

The frustrations all were feeling at how the summer unfolded were manifest in how, in the new year, the selectors were barred – temporarily – from going into the Australian dressing room.

The underlying problem here was that Cricket Australia did not provide any specific place at a venue for the selector on duty to sit and watch the game. We had to make the best of the available spots. Of these, I wasn't going to sit in the general public or members areas, just on the basis that it would be hard to concentrate without getting engaged in conversation. Similarly, the CA corporate function areas may have been comfortable and well catered, but you'd quickly find yourself the centre of attention if you spent any length of time in there. In that sort of environment it was hard just to say 'mate, leave me alone, I'm trying to watch the cricket'. Some of the team viewing areas were roomier and better for us to find a spot somewhere, but the SCG in particular was very cramped. Often, even if you found the least obtrusive corner available, you were still in the way. What that meant in practice was that some of us found ourselves in the curious position of being at the ground but watching the game on television, simply because there was nowhere else that would work.

We were coming to the end of an era and we were short of options among the next generation, but with some young players starting to come into the side – Smith, Hughes and Usman Khawaja, who debuted at the SCG – I felt there were better times to come. First, though, we had to face some of the issues relating to the end of that former era.

The squad for the 2011 World Cup faced some criticism, largely around the fact that it was very heavy on pace bowling for a series to be played in India, Sri Lanka and Bangladesh. That was forced, in part, by injuries that ruled out both Xavier Doherty and Nathan Hauritz from consideration. But there was also still a sense that speed was our strength regardless of the conditions. Ponting was definitely more comfortable captaining a pace bowling attack than a spin bowling attack, which was a factor, but the paucity of spin options was more so.

It fell to Jason Krejza, he of the 12 wickets on Test debut in Nagpur in 2008, to be the spin bowler, and he was cast into a very negative, holding role. After Australia lost their quarter-final to India in Ahmedabad, I expressed my frustration to Jason about the role he had played, feeling it had been a missed opportunity for him to exert more of an influence on proceedings. Based on my previous experience in India I knew that if you're not trying for wickets at all stages of the game in those conditions, you're going to struggle, because once partnerships are established, batting sides have the chance to more or less tee off with wickets in hand.

Krejza was almost freakish with the way he could bounce and spin the ball, and he could undoubtedly have been a match-winner in those conditions had he been handled differently. As selectors we felt he was a bowler who could get us wickets through the middle overs with that bounce and turn. But Ponting was besotted with the approach of Harbhajan Singh, because the Indian spinner had caused him so many problems personally. What he wanted from a spinner was Harbhajan, who fired balls in from wide of the crease with a leg side field, and that made life tough for Krejza relative to what he could have produced. It was almost an impossible commission.

While Ponting's batting powers were on the wane and there needed to be some consideration as to the future direction of the team, we did still feel that he should remain captain as long as he continued to play. Various theories have been floated about whether he received a tap on the shoulder to resign the captaincy in 2011, but we had absolutely no desire to push him out ahead of his chosen time.

So his resignation upon returning home from the vanquished World Cup campaign was cause for some quite animated CA board debate about whether or not Michael Clarke should succeed him. Andrew Hilditch was firm in thinking that Michael was the best candidate, and even before I came onto the panel there was always an air of expectation that it was close to inevitable. We weren't always privy to the angst within the dressing room, and while there were certainly two cliques around Ponting and Clarke, we never discussed it as selectors.

What became clear either side of the captaincy appointment was a significant body of criticism that, regardless of how good a tactician he might be, Clarke's ambition for the job had left quite a few players wary of playing under him. It is very hard to be a good leader if you haven't been a good follower, and it is fair to say now that this served to undermine Clarke's captaincy at various points over the next five years. It was a personality flaw and perhaps should have been taken into greater consideration than it was.

Once he had been appointed, the next major task was the central contracts list for the following year. This was the first time I'd been involved in a process that had evolved from a relatively simple process in the late 1980s to a multifaceted exercise that was also heavily influenced by the shape of the Memorandum of Understanding between CA and the Australian Cricketers' Association. Players were ranked according to their value in each format, with Test cricket weighted most heavily, and from an accumulation of those ranking points we came up with a list of 25 contracted players. There was one major casualty: Simon Katich.

As we have seen with the most recent CA contracts list in 2021, the system tends to favour all-format players over specialists, particularly if you are not one of the first three or four players picked for the Test team. Undoubtedly, Katich's Test-only status hurt his ranking, and so when he was missing from the final list it was the cause of considerable hubbub. At this point it is important to point out that whether someone is on or off the contract list doesn't create a cast-iron case that they will or won't play. Looking back on the list for 2011–12, no fewer than 12 of the 25 names didn't go on to play a single Test match over the next year.

But I had learned over the years that there's no such thing as a finished article. You don't have a team where you say 'right, that's it, we've got the team settled and let it run for the next period'. Sporting teams and certainly cricket teams are never standing still. As I said, unless you're moving forward you are going backwards, because the opposition is going to be doing all it can to get ahead of you. Having seen the results of a group of top Australian players retiring together in the 1960s, then having that happen again in the 1980s and for a third time in the late 2000s, there was always an awareness that we had to plan ahead.

We could see the likes of Katich, Hussey and Ponting all coming to the end around the same time. As it was, Ponting retired first in late 2012, before Hussey followed in early 2013. Katich kept playing first-class cricket via Lancashire until about six months later. I had no problem with players going on for as long as they wanted to and were able to, but that's also why you needed a robust selection process so that tough decisions are not left to the players to make themselves. In that sort of environment, plenty of players will give every indication that they can't see the finish line, despite knowing in themselves that their own departure date is within the next six months.

So somebody has to have the responsibility of keeping an eye on the clock and the other eye on the future, assessing who we have in the pipeline to come in next. It's no good waiting until the clock runs out to make those decisions; you've got to be planning ahead and looking to give the next generation some opportunities while members of the previous generation are still there. We had already done some of that work by including Smith, Hughes and Khawaja in the Ashes series (made somewhat easier by Katich's absence through injury).

I was also a believer in giving the very best players too many opportunities rather than too few. There may be players at the next level or even the level below who might end up getting the odd game too few rather than too many. But the Pontings, Clarkes, Smiths, Gilchrists and Haydens, I'd much rather see them go on one tour too many than the opposite. In a professional era, too, it is only human nature to try to eke out every last year of your maximum earning capacity; I can hardly blame the players for that. But somebody has to have the responsibility to keep an eye on what's in the short-, medium- and long-term interests of Australian cricket: the selectors.

Katich's repudiation of the contract decision, and the selection panel in general, cut deeply. But we all knew that in taking on that role it inevitably came with some days as a punching bag. You don't get to throw punches back, and that's a good thing. I don't think it's in anybody's interests for the panel to be publicly slagging off current or past players. Privately we certainly talked about the fact he was telling only his side of the story, but ultimately we acknowledged that it goes with the territory. We also knew how emotional a time it is for a player, dealing with the end of the line. So you need to give them a little bit of room. If you've got a thin skin, don't become a selector.

What stuck in the craw most of all were the supposed issues of communication. Apart from the formal contract meetings every year, there were also discussions with individual players, either with the chairman of selectors or other selectors on duty, about where they stood at any given time. We were constantly chatting to people and giving them the opportunity to ask questions. If someone sits down with you and asks, 'where do I stand', I took it upon myself to answer as truthfully as possible, which sometimes meant you weren't telling them what they wanted to hear. That came, at times, to be construed as a lack of communication, when it was actually a lack of sugar-coating.

13

PUSHED OUT, BUT STILL BUILDING

Australia, 2011–2016

A DECADE ON, I still don't think Australian cricket needed the Argus review, put together to examine cricket's structure after Australia's third loss by an innings in the 2001–11 Ashes series. Much of the work to free up the system to move new, long-term talent into it had already been done, but it seemed to me that James Sutherland, Jack Clarke and the Cricket Australia board fell into the corporate thinking that if ever things aren't going well, you have a review.

I disagreed entirely with the Argus review's decision to pull apart the link between the national talent management network and the national selection panel. I don't blame Don Argus for that. Nicknamed 'Don't Argue' in corporate circles for his straight-ahead manner, Argus was a former chief executive of National Australia Bank and former chairman of BHP Billiton and, at 72 years of age, had assumed elder statesman status in Australian life. However great a captain of industry he might have been, he did not know enough about the game to know what he was doing.

Others on the Argus panel did know more about the game, but knowledge of cricket from playing it is not the same as wider knowledge of the system. As an example, a current international player, no matter how knowledgeable, is hard pressed to know what's going on at a first-class level they only seldom take part in, let alone anything below or beyond that. Someone who played the game 10 to 15 to 20 years ago and hasn't been intimately involved in the game during the intervening years has no idea of how it's changed. I still don't think the people who made the decision were well-enough informed to do so. As it turned out, it took just five years before the national talent manager position was returned to the selection panel.

Whether that role is held by me or whoever doesn't matter. What was important was the connection. It's very hard if you're thinking only about selecting senior teams for Australia to keep track of other issues rising and falling that are going to hurt you in the next five years, but not necessarily the next five Test matches. Laurie Sawle said as much when interviewed by Mark Ray in his final year as chairman of selectors in 1995. At the time, a member of the selection panel also served as chair of the panel to select Under-19 teams: 'I was most involved in the Under-19s from the mid-80s for six or seven years. I thought it was important for us to know what talent was coming through so that we could fast-track them. Players like the Waugh twins, Ian Healy and Mark Taylor all came through the system.'

The last couple of squads I was involved in selecting actually provided some idea of the advantages of knowing what was coming through. Pat Cummins, Mitchell Starc, Nathan Lyon, James Pattinson and David Warner all got early chances to be around Test cricket during the spring tours to Sri Lanka and South Africa in 2011, and all had worn the baggy green cap by the end of that year. Selection comes with a lot of brickbats – but there is also the deep satisfaction when you see guys achieving what you thought they were capable of, and the team coming together.

Those players were more or less the embodiment of what I thought the job was really all about: finding long-term players for Australia who are going to be match-winners. It's not so much our job to be looking for bit-part players or short-term options at the end of an era. Our job as selectors is to find the players who will *be* an era, a group who will learn, play and succeed together to form the core of a three-, four- or five-year period. You've got to be constantly looking for those players.

Cummins, Starc, Pattinson and Josh Hazlewood, who made his international debut for Australia the year before, were pace bowlers of the class that had traditionally defined the best teams in the world. If, as a country, you're not producing fast bowlers, your chances of being the best over a substantial period are extremely slim: to do so you need to rely on luck that no other country boasts such an attack. Bowlers of high pace and high quality bring with them a fear factor that unsettles opponents and wreaks havoc on their confidence. They also benefit spin bowlers, who can capitalise on the mental frailty – and hence failing footwork – that the best fast bowlers can draw out of their quarry over the course of a series. Mitchell Johnson, with help from Ryan Harris and Peter Siddle, got things right for about a year; the younger New South Wales trio and their Victorian off-sider were capable of doing similar things over a decade together.

But perhaps the most extraordinary story was that of Nathan Lyon, who had emerged, via country New South Wales and then

Canberra, as a spin bowler, then also serving on the Adelaide Oval ground staff. During the 2010–11 Big Bash, his talents for flight and dip had deceived plenty of opponents, and he ended the season as a member of the South Australian Sheffield Shield side. We picked him for an Australia A tour of Zimbabwe in mid-year, and on that trip he was the best bowler in both short and long formats of the game. He changed the game every time he came on to bowl; you could see the difference in quality relative to both opponents and teammates. My first thought was that we'd found another Ashley Mallett.

At the tour's end, I reported back to the rest of the panel that Lyon was our best spinner by so far it didn't matter: technically, tactically and mentally. Underlining it all was a clear intent to take wickets. At that stage he was, if anything, slightly more dangerous in limited-overs games than first-class encounters, something worth noting any time you hear that he is better suited to red-ball cricket. Numerous influential voices around the Australian team have at times shown a reluctance to play him in ODIs and T20Is out of fear that it might mess with his Test bowling, but I feel that has done him a disservice relative both to his abilities and the team's options.

He also showed himself to be a good contributor to the team on tour, always having ideas in team meetings and being happy to help out with whatever needed doing. He wasn't the best fielder in the group but always fielded well off his own bowling, indicating that he had plenty of upside there as well. His competitiveness and heart were evident in other areas like his batting, where he never looked – as many bowlers do – like someone in a hurry to get on with bowling.

A couple of months later I was again on duty and had the honour of presenting Nathan with his baggy green cap on the first morning of the Galle Test. This in itself was a bit of a change under Michael Clarke, as his predecessor Ricky Ponting had presented the caps to debutants himself for a time. Nathan went on to take 5-34 on debut and contributed well to what was one of only three victories by Australian teams in Tests in Asia since 2004, and the only series win in the region since then.

While Nathan didn't always have the highest regard for his own ability, leading to a few moments in which it looked doubtful whether or not he was going to become a fixture in the Test team, he had enough determination if pushed in the right directions. I wondered if some of his early advice, particularly about being a stock bowler while the pacemen attacked at the other end, meant that the process took a little longer than it should have. As recently as the summer of 2016–17 there were discussions about his future in the team, particularly relating to the level of self-belief we wanted to see in the No. 1 spin bowler in the country.

Subsequent to those conversations, he was able to broaden his repertoire and thinking enough to make himself a highly effective spin bowler in all conditions – exactly what the team had needed ever since Shane Warne's retirement. There was real delight in seeing Nathan put together series like the one he had at home to India in 2014–15, away in India and Bangladesh in 2017 and in each of the past couple of Ashes series. He is a genuine person, and it was a good call by Mike Hussey to entrust him with the team song in 2013.

Once I got back from Sri Lanka I was still heavily involved in the youth pathways and development programs, but without the selector status I wasn't speaking a whole lot to the new panel of John Inverarity, Rod Marsh, Andy Bichel and the new coach Mickey Arthur. It was quite a strange adjustment, because only a year before the talent management network and the position of national talent manager had been brought in to connect the selection panel to the wider system.

The Argus review tore that apart and took the selectors back to their previous position as a satellite in their own orbit. While I didn't agree with the decision, I accepted it as the immutable verdict of the umpire and wasn't about to throw my bat. I also didn't blame Invers, Rod, Andy or Mickey for not seeking out my counsel either, because I knew that one thing a selector doesn't need is extra advice: plenty of the unsolicited variety will be coming their way without adding to it. I also knew that we were, at least to some degree, operating with different philosophies.

Of those selectors, Rod and I had the longest relationship, and we have agreed to disagree over many things for much of our lives. This was particularly the case around selection. We've had some great discussions over the years about different players and differing views on them. I can remember one heated discussion about Marcus North, where we debated his all-round skills. The other big one we disagreed on was Tim Paine, who I rated a lot more highly as a wicketkeeper and a cricketer in his younger years. As two strong-willed friends tend to do, we have had many more such arguments, but they never stopped us maintaining a relationship forged in playing Test cricket together.

It was at this time that we also saw the high-energy Pat Howard, a former rugby union international player with the Wallabies and then a coach and administrator in the sport, welcomed into CA as the new head of team performance. I enjoyed working with Pat. We didn't agree on everything, but Pat was very much a doer, and he was very helpful to the talent management network in order to get changes and improvements made to the pathway system. He also never shied away from a robust discussion – you could agree to disagree and then start afresh the next day. He didn't hold grudges, but he was willing to fight his corner and he expected you to do the same. If you wanted to sell a new concept, you had to make sure you had figures to back it up – Pat felt strongly that cricket had always been heavy on theories and light on evidential proof.

Pat's appointment didn't please everybody, but his ability to pick up and retain information was quite incredible, because he was coming from a long way back as an executive new to cricket. He got some concepts through in all areas – changes to the Sheffield Shield points system and the use of the Dukes ball, to name two – that others wouldn't have dared to try. Like head of high performance Sonya Thompson before him, who I felt should have gone a lot further in Australian cricket, Pat was very clever and also hard working. The hours he put in were extraordinary, and got ever more so as his role grew broader over the years: he was catching 6 am flights from Brisbane to Melbourne a couple of times a week and going on bike rides before heading to the airport! One of those mornings he came off his bike quite badly and still made the plane.

Regardless of Pat's contribution, the inconsistent link between the talent management network and the selection panel remains a huge issue that is not well understood. That was made plain once again when I finished as a selector for the final time in 2019, with no replacement in my role. Once more, this opens up the danger of outstanding talents getting missed. The recurring issue tends to be that if a strong prospect comes through, there need to be authoritative voices to communicate that to the coaches, particularly at state level. Otherwise you see players of great promise being asked to spend numerous years in club cricket before they are recognised, by which time they are starting to develop habits that won't help them at the top.

State coaches, and in some cases national coaches and selectors, have not seen it as their responsibility to worry about players who won't be relevant to them in the short term but are highly likely to be in the long term. They can be similarly unknowing about opponents in the same system. Before Justin Langer's first selection meeting as Australia's coach, at the National Cricket Centre in Brisbane, he said to me 'mate I'm going to need your help here – I don't know half the players we're talking about'. When I asked 'what do you mean, you've been coaching against them for the past five years?', he countered with 'oh no, I don't watch them, I only watch my players'. Coaches are seldom looking out a broad window, but through a single looking glass.

Another example came when Ashton Turner emerged in Western Australia, just as Justin had commenced as coach of the Warriors. I told Justin that Ashton, a middle-order batsman and off-spinner, had match-winning qualities in him, particularly in white-ball cricket, and given the right sort of development there was the chance he could do it in the red-ball forms as well. Justin was slow to be convinced, on the basis that Turner wasn't dominating club cricket, which can be an extremely tough school but not always a definitive one.

If you are overstating your requirement for the hard currency of runs or wickets with which to select someone, you are doing a job that is closer to accounting than selection. Players who take the opportunity to perform at a high level three or four times – against good quality opposition it must be added – have demonstrated they have it in them to do so at the next one, provided they are nurtured in the right way. Leaving them to languish for years at a level where they don't have to stretch themselves all the time is likely to have them operating at less than their best when the chance belatedly does come.

Similarly, the body of work of a young player should not be strictly defined as how much club or first-class cricket they have played: things they show playing at under-age or Australia A level need consideration also.

Eventually Ashton started to get opportunities via the BBL, and proved himself as a middle-order batsman in a role that can be fiendishly difficult. JL rang me after his first breakthrough innings for the Scorchers to say, 'Oh I expected a phone call from you last night about Ashton to say I told you so.' To that I replied, 'Well I don't do I told you sos, but I told you so!' Fast forward to early 2019 in India, and Ashton played what should be remembered as one of the most vital innings in the rejuvenation of the Australian team after Newlands, a rip-snorting 84 from 43 balls to conjure the biggest ODI chase in our history. Turner's knock meant that Australia won the series – and just as importantly, had started to play some good cricket in the absence of Steve Smith and David Warner. I'm not sure the importance of that has been fully appreciated.

Apart from Laurie Sawle and myself, it has been hard to figure out which selectors have taken a particular interest in that sort of emerging talent. Rod Marsh, with his cricket academy background, took some interest, but it is vital that someone on the panel takes greater ownership of it. If you disconnect the top level from the grassroots, players are going to fall through the cracks, and Australian cricket will suffer.

14

BIG BASH BATTLES

Australia, 2011–2019

I SAW THE FIRST edition of the Indian Premier League up close as a commentator in 2008. From the moment that tournament took off as a mighty commercial juggernaut it was only a matter of time before Cricket Australia followed suit with its own Twenty20 tournament, but it was always going to be harder to replicate the IPL down under.

For a start, the window effectively created for the IPL meant that the top-quality overseas players elevated the standard of the event beyond comparable T20 events and even some international matches. The Big Bash League, as it would be known when it launched in 2011, was always going to have to share calendar space, not just with Australia's international fixtures but those of the majority of major international countries all sharing a southern season.

That crammed calendar space was a challenge in itself, as there were mixed reactions to the BBL and mixed views about where exactly T20 should sit in the programming. Some of us who had had experience of some earlier changes to the game, for instance when India fell head over heels for 50-over cricket after the 1983 World Cup, knew that there would inevitably be some cost to the interest in and quality of Test cricket. The logic went that if we, as administrators, denigrated Test cricket with our programming or commercial decisions, we couldn't expect the general public to retain the love of the long game that we were trying to sell to them. There was duly a level of fear about exactly what the BBL would take away, relative to what it added.

Even so, CA had concluded, not unwisely, that too few cricket followers were actively supporting their traditional state teams during the domestic Big Bash that had started in 2005. While the contests between the states are still avidly followed by many, it is a long time since a significant number of those followers had been anything more than passive – listening to radio, getting online updates and reading reports on a day's play. New identities, shared across six capital cities with two teams apiece in the biggest centres of Sydney and Melbourne, would offer a fresh start.

Over the first 10 years of the competition, the record would suggest that this was the right move. Particularly in the smaller markets of Perth, Brisbane, Adelaide and Hobart, populations have latched onto their local team in a much more active way. The dual-club models in Melbourne and Sydney have not been without their problems, but they can also point to a good degree of success on the field and also moments like the biggest single crowd for a domestic game in Australian history, when 80,883 spectators descended on the MCG to watch the Melbourne Stars host the crosstown Renegades on a warm January evening in 2016.

What else has T20 added over the past 15 years or so? Undoubtedly it has challenged bowlers and batsmen to come up with different ways to operate. When I was young, limited-overs matches had expanded my game, helping me to realise it was possible to hit the ball in the air and not necessarily increase the risk. Two other players who I saw greatly expand their games due to the constraints of limited-overs matches were Geoff Boycott and New Zealand's Glenn Turner. Both were openers, very good defensive players, extremely hard to get out in long-form cricket, but in one-day cricket they were dragged out of their shell and became excellent takers of calculated risks, like chip shots directly over the heads of the in-fielders. Taken away from a 'don't get out' mindset, they were almost revelatory.

Bill Lawry was another who, given a limited-overs scenario as an older player, found himself able to shed the 'corpse with pads' reputation and unfurl shots seldom seen since his earliest years in Test cricket. In the final of the 1971–72 one-day knockout competition, the season after Bill had been harshly dumped from the Australian captaincy, he led Victoria to a thumping eight-wicket win over South Australia at Adelaide Oval after we'd set them 191 to win. Opening with Keith Stackpole, Bill dominated a stand of 116 and then raced to an unbeaten century as Victoria won the match with more than six of their 40 overs to spare. I just remember standing in the field and thinking, 'Where have you been hiding these shots, Phantom?'

Similarly in the T20 era, players and coaches alike have really had to think about the very limits of their games, particularly in terms of bowlers becoming ever more inventive to try to combat the hyper aggression of opponents with a widening repertoire of shots and a growing fearlessness about how often to play them. Switch-hits and ramp shots existed before T20, but the short form has seen them develop far more fully than they would have otherwise.

Concerns were raised that this aggression and invention were going to destroy batting techniques. My view wasn't quite as extreme as that, because I'd learned that technique wasn't as critical to success as most in the game seem to think it is – it is an outcome of sound mental application rather than a driver of it. So my initial thoughts about what T20 could do for batting were that it was a great training ground, an environment where there was less fear about getting out. The fact that the format now existed in tournaments meant that we could help players to expand their thinking as much as their stroke play.

I was enthused, then, by the idea that T20 created more opportunities for players to experience and figure out match scenarios rather than spending more time in the nets, where conversations and improvements were invariably technical. Most players are better when they're not thinking too much about what they're doing – the subconscious being so much faster than the conscious – so the more you can get them away from think-ing about what's happening at their end, the better they react. If you're preoccupied by your own set-up and 'technique', you won't be watching the ball anywhere near as closely as you need to. The fearlessness is seen at the lower levels, where six-hitting is so much more prevalent now than it ever was. I can barely recall hitting a single six in under-age cricket, and yes the bats are much springier these days, but the kids are generally freer of mind – encouraged, not discouraged, to take risks.

Something else T20 and the BBL did was help to create more opportunities for fringe first-class cricketers to play not only at a higher level but also under the glare of floodlights and televi-sion coverage. Where there were many areas in which the gap between first-class and international cricket was perceived to be growing, this was at least one area in which it could be bridged. It also, here and there, encouraged some older players to make calls on the ends of their international and first-class careers in order to play in T20 leagues, which helped create room for younger talent at the other end of the cycle.

In 2013 at the Bradman Oration delivered by Mike Brearley, Rod Marsh floated the novel idea that T20 cricket should be exclusively for players over the age of 30. He saw it as a good way to reward players who had already given a lot of time and effort to mastering the longer forms of the game, while also meaning that younger cricketers had years of mastering the fundamentals behind them before they played it. That would also mean there was less chance for younger and less powerful players to get lost somewhere in between the two extremes. I don't think Rod or I could ever see this actually happening, but I got where he was coming from.

My worries about what T20 would take away were elsewhere. At least in the start-up stage, before Cricket Australia raised significant broadcast rights fees for the BBL, it took resources away from the longer game, so there were fewer funds for other things. And after a decade or more there would be consequences of the emphasis shift: fewer incentives for batting for long periods of time or bowling to take wickets as much as to keep the runs down. We also saw very quickly in the lower levels of the pathway that there were lots of voices calling for T20 to be played more frequently at under-age levels, in particular at the national championships.

The offshoot of this desire was that for several years, the youth championships model became a hodgepodge of formats: a couple of T20 matches on the first day, a few one-day games and then a few two-day games. It was trying to be all things to all people and not achieving what we wanted, which was to expose promising under-age talent to higher competition that would help them to grow but also help us to better identify who was coming through. The states do a fine job of identifying the talent in their respective patches, and most of the good kids do get picked up. But at the national championships level you wanted to be able to see that talent on display for a decent amount of time, and in T20 games you'd often see very few members of the teams able to gain that exposure.

Not only was the shortness of the format a problem, but the difficulties it created tended to favour players who had developed early, to the disadvantage of others who were less obviously gifted or powerful at the same age. Plenty of great batsmen, in particular, are late physical developers, Ricky Ponting and Mike Hussey to name two. So T20 wasn't going to tell us much about their ability to rotate strike, find gaps in the field or demonstrate mental skills. At the same time, shunting the longer-form games to the end of the program meant that players were tired by that stage, injuries had taken a few out of the picture, and most games anyway would be winding down by halfway through the second day. 'Junk-time' is a term used for what happens after a footy match (or basketball game) has been decided; it applies just as well to the latter stages of most two-day games.

These issues resulted in a decision to revert to 50-over games for the duration of all under-age national championships. That was done on the basis that these games were long enough for batters to make hundreds, for bowlers to deliver two or three spells, and elements of both T20 and longer-form games were required at various points of the day. Overall, it meant that talent spotters got to see more of the better players over the course of a championship. But the presence of T20 and the incentives created by the BBL meant that calls for more short-form games were always lingering somewhere.

At the top level, the influence of T20 can also be seen in the decrease in the size of boundaries and also the increasingly generic nature of pitches. One-day cricket had an impact in both these areas, but T20 has doubled down. The economic need for as much cricket to be played as possible outside of rain delays has contributed too, as drainage at venues has vastly improved – while also serving to denude pitches of some of their former moisture. Years ago you could get to July in an English season and pitches would still be damp, green-tinged and offering side-ways movement off the seam. Nowadays surfaces are much more likely to be drier and harder earlier in the year.

Something that should always be made clear is that the advent of the BBL was for reasons both directly and indirectly financial, as opposed to cricket reasons. In direct terms it created the opportunity for more revenue through broadcast rights fees, and indirectly it afforded the chance to grow the game's audience beyond its traditional base and thus expand the number of 'customers' that cricket served in Australia. The cycle that CA was attempting to break in terms of revenue was the fact that when India tours Australia, the governing body makes a lot more money than any other season, including the Ashes, because of the value of selling the rights to that tour back into India. While CA is a bigger and healthier board than many around the world, it was still in the same boat as all those other nations equally dependent on the extra money flowing from an India tour.

But by creating the BBL and lavishing resources upon it in its early years – a significant proportion of which came from a joint stake in the short-lived T20 Champions League – CA was able to sell a purely domestic product to broadcasters for a significant sum of money separate to international rights. That had never been possible before, as even a figure as keen on cricket as Kerry Packer never showed much interest in non-international matches. In one move, the BBL increased the value of domestic broadcast rights and reduced CA's reliance on rights from an India tour. That reliance had been at the front of many minds on the CA board in 2008 after the 'Monkeygate' saga, where for several days a touring India team might have upped sticks and flown home in the middle of a tour, with the financial ramifications that would have had.

The decision to invest so much in the BBL, over the grumbles of the states who had wanted the investment to be balanced by the sale of at least some of the clubs to private owners, has paid off, and it is to CA's credit that it went down that path. But 'paid' is the operative term; the BBL is a tournament that exists for commercial reasons and so has never been considered in the cricketing terms that might otherwise have influenced much of its shape. These sorts of considerations include where it should sit relative to other formats, and how much it detracts from the focus of players, coaches and selectors upon the home Test series that were, until 2011, always the undisputed centrepiece of a summer.

If you were thinking only from a cricket point of view, then you would schedule the BBL in the slot proposed by the Australian Cricketers' Association in 2014: in October/ November, before building into longer formats later in the sum-mer at both domestic and international levels. But the reason the BBL is played when it is played is because December/ January is the peak viewing season, people are on holidays, and broadcasters can now segue from a day's Test cricket into BBL matches in prime time. Those slots then spin off a whole range of other advantages in terms of spectators, sponsors and partnerships that would not be anywhere near as healthy if the BBL were played at another time. 'How best to schedule the BBL' is thus subservient to 'how best to showcase it'.

The notion of growing the game, finding a younger and more diverse audience for cricket in Australia, dovetailed with the finances. There were some scary demographics developing in the mid-2000s even though the national team was the world's best at the time. 'Pale, stale and male' was the catchphrase, with white males over the age of 40 comprising the vast majority of Test cricket's audience, while anyone under the age of 40 couldn't give a hoot about it, even more so if those people were female. Consequently there was a need for new ways to attract spectators and players, in the same way 50-over cricket brought a younger and wider crowd to the game in the 1970s and '80s. Had we only played Test cricket over the past 40 years, cricket would be a niche game played by so few countries it wouldn't matter: in India it would probably sit a distant third behind football and hockey.

On the flip side, South Asian immigration to Australia has only made the BBL more vibrant, as it attracts lovers of the game who are not automatically drawn to the traditional image of the baggy green cap. India, by its sheer size, is not only a giant on its own terms but it has the capacity to create other cricket nations around the world simply through large-scale migration. The subsequent expansion of the BBL into a full home-and-away competition, occupying more than two months of prime summer real estate, has been about chasing ever more of this and other audiences for broadcasters.

Ultimately, this is the biggest worry I have about T20 cricket in general and the BBL in particular. Ever more expansion of an entertainment product like this runs the growing risk of killing the golden goose through over-saturation. The pressure is there from broadcasters for ever more content during the summer holidays, causing offshoot conversations about growing the number of games or even the number of clubs from the current eight. That in turn creates a danger of over-exposing the flaws in T20 cricket, particularly the fact that by fielding eight teams, it is already stretching the talent resources available in Australia.

Given that no Indian cricketer has yet been permitted to take part in the BBL, and that the vast majority of other nations share the same southern season as we do, there is far from an endless supply of quality reinforcements. The most recent expansion of the BBL to a 14-game season also saw numerous overseas players, previously solid contributors to the tournament, decide to ply their trades elsewhere, earning more money for a shorter time commitment.

A gap has now emerged in the broadcast rights value of the tournament and the percentage of that value being paid to the players on BBL contracts. While CA has sound reasons for the gap, wanting to prioritise international cricket as the ultimate for any cricketer in this country and therefore the most handsomely paid, it can only be pushed so far. At the same time, making more money available to overseas players now choosing to play in Bangladesh or Pakistan leagues instead will only place further pressure on the boards of less wealthy nations like the West Indies. The conflict between CA's responsibilities as a global citizen and a domestic commercial entity is never clearer than here.

Challenges, then, are many. But it is important to remember too that shortened formats of the game have now brought fresh audiences to the game a couple of times. There is plenty of evidence from the way that 50-over followers graduated to Test cricket that in the coming years we should see a similar graduation from T20 fans as well. The generous diet of one-day games, especially of the day/night variant, that came out of World Series Cricket and then the decade or so after it, created a bigger and younger supporter base to turn out to watch Test matches once the ACB started to market them properly in the mid-1990s.

15

ON MENTAL SKILLS

GOLF AND CRICKET are the two games that I think are both over-coached and under-coached. They're two sports that train in one environment – the driving range and the nets – and then play in another. What is over-coached is technique, volume and repetition, trying to groove a physical activity until it becomes second nature. What is under-coached is that nothing becomes second nature without going beyond conscious thoughts and actions to subconscious ones.

My golf got better when I stopped hitting balls on the range and went and played on the course. If I had time to practise, I'd practise playing golf. What I had to do was to groove my swing under a game scenario. I can hit 1000 balls perfectly on the driving range, then walk over to the first tee and hit my first drive into the water. It's more about what I'm thinking about and my mental state than my physical state.

If I'm standing on the first tee and worrying about the out of bounds on the left, the ball is most likely going to go left because of the tension in my body. It doesn't matter how many balls I've hit if I haven't got the mental game right. Similarly in cricket, what I had to get good at was making good decisions. What I had to do was to respond appropriately to every ball that was bowled to me. If I could do that, then my technique was going to be ok. Training for me was to face a few balls, not many, and be satisfied when I walked out of the net that I had responded in the right way to every ball bowled, because that's what I had to do in a game.

To get the mental side right, you need to stop thinking about the past. Whether you're Ricky Ponting, Sir Donald Bradman, Steve Smith, Steve Waugh or even those in the next rank like Mark Taylor or David Boon, anyone with a Test batting average of better than 40 has the ability to divorce themselves from the previous delivery and play the next one as though its predecessor never took place. You don't make runs regularly at that level unless you have that ability. Just as importantly, you also have to stop worrying about the future.

If you want to be healthy in life, let alone cricket, staying in the present moment and thinking about what's happening now rather than worrying about what's happened or might happen is vital. There's no such thing as an empty mind; we're always thinking, even when we're asleep. But what there can be is an ability to let thoughts go whenever they're not helpful. A good, healthy mental state is being aware of what's going on at this moment, and not allowing yourself to get stuck in the past or projecting forward. One thing I can say from more than 72 years of experience is that most of the things you worry about happening in the future never take place.

The author W Timothy Gallwey, who wrote *The Inner Game of Tennis* and *The Inner Game of Golf*, recognised the real game that exists for more or less anything we do as humans. You could cross out tennis and golf in either of those two books and write 'cricket', and his lessons would be just as applicable. Gallwey spent considerable time with pro tennis players and golfers when he was writing those books, and they are classic accounts of what is really happening when you play a game. Prior to reading those, I had been fascinated by the lessons of Maxwell Maltz in *Psycho-Cybernetics*, published in 1960.

What Maltz found was that he could take accident or burn victims, having come to him seriously depressed by the experience and their wounds, and rebuild their bodies and faces. He noticed that even when he restored their good looks or their ability to move freely, a lot remained depressed, because they still had the image of themselves being disfigured or incapacitated. The ones who could now see themselves in a new light were the ones who prospered. What they thought of themselves was more important than what they saw in the mirror. That had a powerful impact on me.

Then, as now, these type of ideas were largely untapped by cricket. All the best players use their mental skills better than the average players, but I don't know how many of them are consciously aware of the fact that they're doing it. Either they're inherently positive people, or they have trained themselves to do it by a combination of good luck, circumstances and their natural cricket skills. I don't think I was inherently positive, it was more something I learned along the way.

It was a joy to watch Shane Warne use his mastery of the game's mental side, both between the ears and between the wickets. Shane was perennially trying to get the batsman to play the shot he wanted them to, and in the same breath get the umpire to make the decision he wanted them to. He talked a good game in the media about new deliveries when there were none or close to it, and he was able to master the subtle touches of the inner game. He exuded confidence, so anyone who was doubting themselves was doubly doing so when they looked down the wicket and saw this bloke who appeared to be supremely confident.

There's little wonder that Shane developed an interest in playing poker, because he has got the ability to project an image of confidence that went as far as making opponents think he always knew something they didn't. That was, to some extent, a mask, because Shane could also be very much in need of reassurance off the field. He used the inner sanctum of dressing rooms, hotel rooms, bars and the like to express those doubts. But he would clear his mind of them the moment he stepped onto the field. Interestingly, Shane's career coincided with the gradual disappearance of frequent dressing room conversations with opponents after play, meaning it was harder for batsmen to see that side of him.

A less ubiquitous name who I rated similarly highly as a master of the mental side of spin bowling was the Sri Lanka-born Malcolm Francke, who plucked 146 wickets at 29.61 in 46 matches for Queensland. While not a big spinner of the ball, Malcolm was pretty cocky, reckoned he could bowl a bit, and didn't mind letting blokes know this. But it worked for him because he repeatedly backed it up. As captain of Queensland I brought him on to bowl many times against the likes of Doug Walters and Ian Chappell, who tried to go after him every time they saw him. Not once did Malcolm shirk the issue or get defensive, and he often won the day. A courageous bowler, who could easily have played international cricket and made a success of it.

The antithesis of Warne and Francke was Abdul Qadir. Though a fine bowler, I knew from experience that if I could take Qadir on early, particularly by hitting him down the ground, he would go defensive and bowl far fewer of the sorts of deliveries that were going to enhance my chances of dismissal. But if you let him get on top of you, he would get more and more aggressive, mixing up variations and paces and flights. I'd also notice that Qadir was a very different bowler with Imran Khan at mid-off, as counsel. There were plenty of other opponents who you could influence by your body language and actions, particularly early.

These sorts of conversations are common to dressing rooms down the decades. But what I know now from plenty of research and discussion is that the more profound elements of the mental skills area are little more understood by cricket today than they were in the early 1970s. In an age of full professionalism and vast financial expenditure, that in itself is extraordinary. There are enormous numbers of talented players who are not achieving their potential because they're still thinking it's a physical game, and the more balls they hit or bowl, the better they'll be. On the contrary, history tells us that is often the worst thing you can be doing.

Being an observer of your own thoughts and words is really important. I've been listening to conversations in and around dressing rooms for the majority of my life, and I can't believe some of the things that people say to themselves. One of the most amazing characters I played with in this sense was Allan Border. In the dressing room, Allan couldn't have been more negative if he tried. I had to speak to him on one occasion to say, 'Mate, I wouldn't even let myself think what you're saying out loud. If you want to sit and think it, that's fine, but please don't infect the rest of us.' The great thing about Allan was that the moment he walked through the gate onto the field, he couldn't have thought like that, because he couldn't have been the player he was if he genuinely did. AB was a contrary individual. He saw himself as the underdog and perhaps that was how he motivated himself. He needed to see himself with his back to the wall to produce his best. But it doesn't work for most of us.

Playing the occasional innings in retirement helped to clarify this even further for me. About 18 months after my final Test match I played in a charity game for Terry Jenner at Adelaide Oval, as part of a group of ex-cricketers against a team of businessmen paying for the privilege. So it wasn't particularly challenging opposition but I hadn't held a bat in a long time. I came out to bat and Ian was at the other end. As I walked out I thought 'I haven't done this for a while, I'd best be careful and play myself in' – and I couldn't have batted worse. After a few overs, Ian walked down the wicket and said 'what are you doing', and I replied 'oh I'm just trying to play myself in'. Ian's response was typical but telling: 'Well whatever it is, it looks awful.' Having started in that state of mind, it was really hard to change it, and I struggled for the rest of the innings.

Some years later I played in Derek Randall's testimonial game at Trent Bridge, featuring a couple of teams of former players. We got over there, it was wet, had been raining for a few days, and there was some doubt about whether we were going to get a game. Some of the guys went to the indoor nets on the Saturday, match eve, for some training, but I knocked that back, reasoning I'd rather be stiff and sore once than twice. On game day they had marquees on the ground and we were having lunch, hoping for the weather to clear. A waiter came round and offered a glass of red wine, which I accepted, and then came around a couple more times, topping it up.

Judy was sitting alongside me and she said, 'What are you doing, you're going to have a bat soon.' And I said, 'Yes, but the last game I played, I worried about it so much I batted like I'd never played before. Today I'm going to pretend I'm in the best form of my life and see what happens.' John Lever bowled the first ball to me once we played; it was a half volley and I creamed it to the cover boundary. I ended up getting 73 and I couldn't have hit them better. It was just a great example of the difference that can be made by thought processes: against better bowlers, several wines in and on an English wicket, I was much the better player than against a bunch of businessmen on an Adelaide Oval track.

There is research in music, for instance, where novices are given piano lessons. One third are given instructions to practise the keys only, another third to practise the keys for half the time and then imagine themselves playing, and then the other group go away and simply imagine themselves playing the piece without any practice. The group that has just done it in their imagination perform as well as the groups who have been practising. But in sporting studies too, the overwhelming evidence is that those who see themselves doing things well do as well as – if not better than – those just doing the physical training.

I don't believe we need to do as much physical training as we do, particularly not long sessions at low intensity. The beauty of imagined training sessions is it is the only place where you can do things perfectly, having success. We have all heard of the law of attraction, but I don't know how many people fully understand that you do basically attract to yourself what you think about. If you're expecting good things to happen, invariably they do. If you're expecting all the traffic lights to be red, guess what you're going to get?

I've spoken to as many people as I can at Cricket Australia for the past decade that this is the last frontier. If we want to get a fresh advantage over other countries, then we've got to utilise this knowledge. When I first started down this path, you had to go to libraries, find books, audio and videotapes of people talking about this sort of stuff. Whereas now you can find enormous amounts of material online, such as YouTube clips about visualisation and mental skills. It's readily available, but cricket is hesitant to go there.

We live 95 per cent of our lives in our subconscious. The first seven years of our life are in a near hypnotic state, learning by observation rather than instruction. We learn to walk through trial and error. Most of our belief systems are learned in those first seven years, again through observation of family members in particular. You're just absorbing information over those years, and much of that information sets in for the rest of your life. Many people don't go beyond that, and believe what they've been told about themselves. So unless you actually go in there and rewrite the software, that's what you've got to work with.

This is never more clearly the case than in dealing with fast bowling. When you have problems coping with the ball delivered to you at faster than 135 kph, it's not actually possible for those issues to be solved in your conscious mind. When you've got Pat Cummins bowling to you, you've got less than half a second from the time the ball leaves his hand to when you play it. So you are making decisions on very raw data, but that data says 'this is a short ball'. Your brain then adjusts and your eyes go straight to the pitch length where you expect to see the ball next time. You cascade ahead of the ball, you don't watch it all the way; that's physically impossible. You might be able to do so against a spin bowler, but against a quicker bowler, the brain picks up the early data, says 'this is short', then moves to the short section of the pitch, picks it up again and adjusts with the feet and hands.

If you're then dealing with something deep inside you that makes you uneasy about facing up to and reacting to fast bowling, all the self-exhortations of 'concentrate, watch the ball' in the world aren't going to help you. When a fast bowler is running up in a limited-overs game for instance, you're saying to yourself 'just work it around, work it around, two runs a ball, that's all we need'. By the time the bowler is halfway through his run-up, your subconscious is going haywire saying 'get the hell out of here, you're going to get hurt', so you're not seeing the ball, and all of sudden you're out of line and relying on your hands and eye to make a late intervention.

Ben Johnson is a name most commonly associated with the 1988 Seoul Olympics and anabolic steroids, but the namesake of the Canadian sprinter opened the batting for South Australia in the late 1990s. A left-handed batsman but a right-arm medium pace bowler, he had a brief run of success bowling to Allan Border in Sheffield Shield games. Ben was also just about the only golfer I've ever seen who could have played off a single-figure handicap as either a right-hander or a left-hander. So he was a gifted athlete.

He never quite reached his potential because whenever the bowling inched up above 135 kph he struggled to find ways to deal with it. When I took over as South Australia's coach, I could see Ben had a lot of ability, but he wasn't playing to the level that he could. Other players saw the same things, and offered up critiques of Ben's footwork and therefore his mettle against pace. All the fast bowlers of the era, such as Brad Williams, Michael Kasprowicz and Andy Bichel, used to give Ben a helluva time. I felt that it was a bigger problem than just telling Ben to keep his back foot in line. Unless I can unlock that, I don't think I'm going to change much.

Around that time a friend of mine wanted to start an early online coaching program. I noticed in the group there was an American fellow by the name of Dr Charles Krebs. He was a kinesiologist, working with kids with learning difficulties – issues of the subconscious. After learning a bit more about Charles, I emailed him and explained the issue with Ben, and asked whether what he did could help with batting. He said 'of course it could' and sent me a copy of his book, *A Revolutionary Way of Thinking*, while he travelled overseas.

As a younger man, Krebs had suffered from a very serious case of the bends, affecting his spine, after going diving with a group of friends off the Victorian south-east coast. Fortunately, a nearby doctor was an expert in handling the bends, and directed him to an oil rig in Bass Strait – the only available decompression chamber that was big enough to accommodate both Krebs and his doctor. He survived, but was going to be a quadriplegic, before a revolutionary course of treatment, injecting pig's blood into Krebs' spine, helped to some degree. What helped more, however, was a background in martial arts, eastern medicine and biology. He imagined himself bypassing the break in his spine, getting messages to the rest of his body. Eventually, he taught himself to walk again, against all the odds, and moved into kinesiology.

In 2001, South Australia were in Melbourne for a one-day game against Victoria. I met with Charles to see what sort of guy he was and it was a fascinating conversation – probably the smartest bloke I've ever met. I explained more about what I was seeing with Ben, and he said, 'The problem is when you consciously recognise that you're at the edge of your capabilities, all of your resources go to the part of the brain that deals in survival and so the subconscious is telling you to get out of the way, you're going to get hurt. So to all intents and purposes, he's got no resources left to deal with fast bowling, because all his resources are being used for survival. You can overcome it to a degree with willpower, but at great cost, because it drains energy very quickly.'

We were staying in Fitzroy, and Charles' office was not far away, near Carlton Gardens. Ben said he was open to meeting with Charles, and I asked if I could sit in, because I wanted to see what he did. Charles works with muscle groups, so he'll get you to hold your arm out and he'll press down on the arm and you resist the pressure. Then he'll hit a pressure point, and no matter how hard you resist him, you can't avoid him pulling down on your arms. What that's telling him is the brain is working correctly, because he's just switched that muscle group off by hitting the pressure point. So by checking all the muscle groups he can tell which part of the brain is working properly and which part isn't. Charles said that it wasn't necessarily the first fast bowler Ben faced, or that he'd been hit by a fast bowler or anything like that, that was causing his problem. He said he might have had a difficult birth, he might have fallen out of bed when he was younger – some sort of traumatic incident could have set this off. Unless you go in and switch the mechanisms back on again, you can't solve the problem in the conscious mind.

Ben, who had been out of the Shield side, was recalled for our next game at home to Western Australia, who had Brad Williams in the side. Despite the presence of his former nemesis, Ben went out and not only made a hundred at the top of the order, but accomplished the rare feat of carrying his bat. You could see that Ben was still consciously aware he should have been worried, but he was in there getting behind the ball and he got a hundred. Next game, back in Melbourne for the Shield game against Victoria, Ben made another hundred, this time staring down Mick Lewis and Mathew Inness, another two of the fast bowlers to give him a rough time. A third terrific hundred arrived in the last game of the season against Tasmania, who had David Saker and Damien Wright. Having missed the first three games, Ben finished with 653 runs at 59.36, behind only Darren Lehmann on our averages.

At the start of the following season, I got Charles to come to Adelaide and spend a week with the SA players who wanted to work with him. Johnno had a couple more sessions with Charles, and then peeled off another big hundred, this time 165 against Victoria to help us start the season with a win. Ben's scoring trailed off after that and it turned out to be his final season of Shield cricket. But in the course of a calendar year, he'd notched four of the nine hundreds he made in his entire first-class career, and he'd done it against all the blokes who'd given him so much trouble before. It's impossible to know anything to 100 per cent certainty, but I'm 99.9 per cent convinced Johnno couldn't have done any of that without the help of Charles. It was remarkable to see.

I got in touch with Ben while writing this book to ask him about his memories of it. He couldn't recall feeling overly different, which goes to the point that this was about dealing with the subconscious. The difference was something others could see in how he was batting against specific bowlers, even if he did not register it in his conscious mind.

I subsequently took Charles to India for a couple of weeks when I was with the BCCI, and he did more work on a voluntary basis with a few of the players. The pair who got the most out of it were MS Dhoni and Ajit Agarkar. Ajit was a very talented bowler and not a great batsman, but he had more ability than he was showing. After a 45-minute session with Charles, Ajit remarked, 'I don't know what he's done to me, but I'm a different person.' So there are skills available and ways to access them that can bypass the conscious mind, but the vast majority of the cricket system won't have it. I've seen it work, I've experienced it personally, and I really think it needs more consideration.

No coaches talk about it. Sports psychologists don't know the game well enough to talk about it in specifics, sticking only to general things like being 'in the moment' and having processes, which is all good stuff, but there are times when that's not enough, and it's a very slow, laborious way to get to where you want to get to. That's because, under pressure, the emotions kick in before you have a conscious thought: if something frightens or worries you, you've leapt backwards before you even know you have. You've reacted emotionally before the realisation reaches your conscious mind. And it's not just against fast bowling. Shane Warne ruined South African Daryll Cullinan's career due to undue concern about Warney's flipper.

Some players have been able to recognise that they have been working with mental routines to get them as far as the elite level, and so they're open to further discussions. Matthew Hayden, for one, looked after his mental game as much as his physical one through spending time visualising and 'grounding' himself in the middle before a game. What's funny though is that the vast majority of those who use Hayden as an example will reference the thousands of balls he hit and not the mental work. It shouldn't just be about a hard grind, but there are a lot of coaches who have ingrained the importance of quantity over quality. Sound judges in other sports have spoken about the tendency to want to create robots rather than living, breathing, thinking human beings who happen to play sport at the highest level.

The trouble here is that the more professional a sport gets, the more robotic the training becomes. It evolves into a situation where the type of training is very much dictated by the amount of time there is to fill a working week, rather than by the best fit for the development of the individuals concerned. Using the AFL as an example, a couple of decades of full professionalism have brought the game to something of a defensive standstill, where coaches have totally dominated thinking over the individual expression of the players for several generations. It took some clever rule changes to open the game back up momentarily, before the coaches worked out how to combat the changes.

Looking at the current scene, one of my wishes would be for someone like Charles to work with Glenn Maxwell. Given some time together with someone capable of working on the subconscious, it's downright scary to think about what we might be able to see from Glenn. Emerging Victorian batsman Will Pucovski is another who may benefit. At the same time, the best way for these ideas to be more widely accepted is through being picked up by top players. Steve Smith and Virat Kohli, to name two, are both miles ahead in mental terms and absolutely use things like visualisation. Yet whenever they talk about it, the wider cricket populace takes next to no notice. This is what we should be coaching, this is what we should be teaching in school. We need a few more of the current generation to speak about it.

In terms of competitive advantage, Australia should be looking more closely at this than anywhere else because of the size of our system. We simply don't have that many high-quality players to pick from that we can afford to lose them through not exploring all ways to extract their best. In recent years, I have

sand in the oyster who can set off the chain reaction that might one day lead to a pearl.

The other thing that was a longstanding factor in my thinking was the knowledge that from the advent of professional cricket, players tended to go on a little bit longer. And more or less every former player I've spoken to has admitted, however great their career was, that they more than likely played on too long: Allan Border, Steve Waugh, Ricky Ponting to name three. They played a season or two longer than they would have in previous eras. It's much harder to make that final call, in particular because of the financial implications.

One November morning in 2016 I arrived at the National Cricket Centre for a day's work. It wasn't just any November morning: Australia had lost their fifth Test match in a row, by an innings and plenty to South Africa in Hobart, and Rod Marsh had resigned as chairman of selectors the previous afternoon. I walked past the office of the head coach Troy Cooley, who had his door closed and was on a video call. He motioned by putting his hand to his mouth to see if I'd had a call yet. I indicated by throwing my hands up: 'what call'. He then pointed down towards Pat Howard's office, whereupon I shook my head and sat at my desk. When he finished, Troy popped his head in and said, 'Have you got the call about selection yet?' And I said, 'No, they're not coming back here', laughing.

Maybe half an hour went by and Pat popped his head out of his office and said 'Greg, have you got a sec?' I walked down to his office and at no point on that walk did I expect that it was going to be a conversation about becoming a selector again. Just a few months earlier I'd negotiated to reduce my workload to three days a week, with a commensurate reduction in remuneration. I could see my time was winding down: I'd been offered the opportunity to grow my role when Belinda Clark had moved down to Melbourne to take a different management role with Cricket Australia, and I'd knocked it back. If anything I wanted to focus more on the cricket and less on the administrative work, to allow Pat to work on a succession plan. Graham Manou had come in to work on the pathway in the meantime.

So when Pat called me in and said 'mate I'd like you to consider coming back onto the selection panel', I was somewhat taken aback. I said, 'I'll have to think about that and speak with Judy, because we've just re-organised our life around me travelling and working less.' Pat replied, 'I hope you can convince her, because we need you do to it.' That was the job interview, basically. It was clear that Rod Marsh had taken the panel as far as he could, and that they needed a different perspective. I also then had the chance to re-connect the panel to the wider talent network.

I could see that the team needed a wider perspective than the one inside the bubble. Rod had, at times, got too close to that bubble, rather than being able to offer a selection perspective from outside it. In previous years, I had seen Andrew Hilditch go through much the same thing. I'd told Pat that even on tour, you still need someone independent of the dressing room to give a view, because the perspectives from inside and outside are different. Trevor Hohns, who has been a selection chairman for almost as long as I've been a selector over a couple of stints, recognises this also. We've had numerous chats about not getting sucked into the bubble, needing to stand back and see what other people are seeing from beyond the team.

The coach, who has held selection duties since the Argus review in 2011, is too close to make those judgements effectively. Naturally, the coach forms relationships, which is what you want, but if you get a good coach, you don't want to lose them for being judged on the wrong things. Sometimes winning is out of the coach's control, and I would much prefer the coach's job be to coach. Develop players, be judged on whether you're bringing players through and helping them achieve the best of their potential. You may not be the No. 1 team in the world for this period, but you might be able to set yourself up for a future period where you can be.

The opposite view is that if the coach is to live and die by his win/loss record then he should be the sole selector. If it is a club team where the coach has access to all players at all times that might be so, but when he doesn't see all players for most of the year, I am not convinced. Equally, if the coach is seen to be making the selection decisions, many players will be reluctant to go to him with their problems. I think, in Australian cricket, that the coach has enough influence to not need to be officially on the panel.

My first selection meeting was for the day/night Adelaide Test against South Africa. A lot of changes were made to the team: Joe Burns, Callum Ferguson, Mitchell Marsh, Peter Nevill and Joe Mennie were all dropped, and Matt Renshaw, Pete Handscomb, Nic Maddinson, Matthew Wade and Jackson Bird were chosen in their stead. By far the most time-consuming discussion related to Wade. I had always been a huge fan of Wade as a batsman; he could have had a long career as a member of the Australian top six if he'd simply focused on his batting. He could play, but wicketkeeping was making his job harder, and his abrasive nature wasn't helping him either.

Suffice to say the team's leadership felt that a change of wicketkeeper was required and Wade was the preferred candidate; not because he was the best wicketkeeper, but because he was the loudest gloveman with the most 'mongrel', whatever that means. I stated 'that's never been a criteria for picking a Test team that I've ever heard of, and we shouldn't be starting that now'. As the idea developed in the meeting I just shook my head, saying 'no, we can't go down this path'.

Wicketkeepers are very important parts of the team; they're the glue in good teams. But not for their yapping; rather for their ability and their commitment. One of the best teams that ever played the game, the West Indies, never said a word: they didn't have to. We didn't need to be told by them or anyone else that they'd turned up to play – we could see it in their actions. That's what you need in a cricket team, but that's not what happened in that selection meeting. I shook my head again when the decision was made, and it's the first and only time I've walked out of an Australian selection meeting in total disagreement with what we'd just done.

I then walked into Pat's office and said, 'Mate, I just need to let you know that for the first time in my life as a selector, I've been involved in something that I totally disagree with. Every other selection meeting I've had my say, we've had a good discussion, a decision is made and we've all been comfortable that we've made the right consensus decision. We have just made the wrong decision, and it's going to end in tears, and I need you to know that from me right now.'

A year later, with the team for the first Test in the home Ashes to be selected, it did end in tears for Wade, because this time the leadership felt that a different wicketkeeper was required. Again I had a strong belief that we had the best wicketkeeper in the country staring us in the face: Tim Paine. We've got no other choice.

Strange as it may seem to say now, Tim was not everyone's favourite cricketer. His performances in 2010 in his first four Test matches had suggested a cricketer of real substance, and in 2011 he led an Australia A side to Zimbabwe and did a terrific job. He kept wickets well, led the side strongly, and showed he had the right personality for the job. Troy Cooley and I wrote a glowing review of Tim for that tour – on the field, off the field, and in relation to leadership. The following year, an Australia A side went to England, and Tim was chosen but not as captain. On his second comeback from the badly broken finger that nearly ended his career prematurely, the emphasis was very much on Tim to focus on his batting and glove work. But at tour's end the feedback was highly critical of how he had been self-involved.

Nevertheless, I had not lost my positive view of Tim, based on what I'd seen. As Ian Healy had reminded me of Rod Marsh, Tim reminded me of Ian Healy. He had something, and by this time he'd also been to hell and back. Earlier in 2017 I'd spoken to the Tasmania talent manager Michael Farrell, who told me that Tim was going to give the game away for a job with Kookaburra. Straight away I told Fazz: 'Tell him not to do that, he's only an injury away from playing for Australia. Unless it's been his life-long ambition to work for Kookaburra, have a rethink. He won't have to worry about a job in the future because plenty of people will employ him. But not many can play for Australia, and I don't think he's done yet.' That exchange led to a coffee with Tim at the Henry Jones Art Hotel in Hobart, but I made it as clear as I could as a friend, rather than a selector, that I didn't think he was done. I know he got very similar advice from Ricky Ponting among others.

Only Tim can say how dark it got for him amid all the finger problems and the struggles to rediscover his game when he came back. But there's not much worse you can do to a sportsman than to take away their ability to play the game. My experience, though, was that he was an exceptional human being, a really good cricketer and the right choice to be recalled. Yet it would take a good while before others were able to see the choice of Tim as anything other than a step backwards, to someone who had last played a Test match in 2010. For those who have contended that I'm obsessed with youth, Tim's tale can hopefully clarify that any obsession has much more to do with talent.

The selections for the 2017–18 Ashes took a long time: we had three attempts before finally settling on the combination. Initially, nobody really had any strong views about who the wicketkeeper should be other than that it was time for a change, so we parked it for a while. I'd had my say early in the piece, to the effect that Tim was the only realistic choice as a wicketkeeper batsman and a seasoned adult who has had to consider his life outside cricket and therefore he would bring some genuine leadership to the team. Eventually, after Darren Lehmann had excused himself for a while to go to the bathroom and presumably have a smoke, we returned to the topic, I reiterated what I'd said before about Tim, and that was the final decision.

There was plenty of disquiet outside the selection panel as well when the story got out that we'd chosen Tim. Most of it was along the same lines as the internal discussion: that he was yesterday's man, when in fact he was a mature cricketer with a lot still to give. Four years on, it is fair to say that Tim has not only performed his duties to a high standard, but he has also fitted in – with the occasional exception like the 2020 SCG Test against India – to the image of Australian wicketkeepers with a bit of an edge to them, but a humorous one. Moreover, as a captain, he has shown a breadth of life experience and perspective that had been lacking in his predecessor.

Paine got a second chance, after his first one was curtailed by finger injuries. I once asked the Australian football legend Ron Barassi about his views not only on spotting talent, but what to do once you've found it. In response to a question about how many chances you give someone to succeed, his response was succinct: 'It depends how much talent he's got.' Shaun Marsh had enough talent to warrant getting multiple opportunities. It is a disappointment, although not surprising in some ways, that he didn't consistently reach the heights that he should have. In the end, though he did make some progress over the years, Shaun never quite grasped all the elements required for success, especially in terms of mental and technical battles with opponents. The jury is still out, and may forever remain so, on his brother, Mitch, as well.

That is a shame, because both brothers had an inordinate amount of ability and could easily have been the marquee players of the era. In Mitch's case, there are not many occasions when you find someone who can bowl at 140 kph and bat in the top six. When you find someone like that who could one day do something along the lines of South Africa's Jacques Kallis, they can make a tremendous difference to your team. Some have contended that Mitch might have been better served by adopting a simpler method, akin to the sorts of innings once played by Andrew Flintoff as a hard-hitting all-rounder at No. 6 or 7. But we saw during the 2017–18 Ashes that he had the ability to be better than that, batting at No. 4 or 5.

There was also the conundrum about how many overs to realistically expect. For someone batting in the top six, around 15 an innings should be the top of the range. Once they start getting over 20 overs an innings it takes a lot out of a cricketer both physically and mentally, and it takes time to recover.

You get tighter around the lower back and the hips in ways that can affect your flexibility and suppleness for batting, which affects your footwork. Between the ears you're more likely to be fried also, from the mental effort and emotion expended in long spells. That was a constant debate with Shane Watson: he could offer some thoughtful and occasionally match-winning overs, but he was also better suited as a batsman to going in early, and had the capacity to take a quality bowling attack apart.

Sometimes I felt that Mitch's desire to improve, though well-intentioned, was actually to his detriment. He was constantly tinkering with his methods and listening to a wide range of voices, some of whom he might have done better to avoid. Mitch had a pretty natural set-up and a great ability to hit the ball with the power his physique gave him, an ability, by the way, that was somewhat miraculous in itself. When we did physical exams on Mitch when he first came up to the Centre of Excellence, eye testing indicated that his vision was extremely poor: bad enough to affect his ability to get a driver's licence without glasses. But it was amazing how well his instincts filled the gap, taking cues from the bowler and the environment.

Mitch had contact lenses fitted in the end. Barry Richards had his eyes tested late in his career and discovered a similar thing about his eyesight. So he got contact lenses and had a huge re-adjustment to make because he had too much information rather than the strictly limited, but perhaps simpler, feed of visual cues he had been getting before. At times, particularly when he started an innings, Mitch's hands could be too firm on the bat handle, apt to draw edges or even a return catch on a slow pitch. That generally tends to be a mental thing, as anxiety and fear of failure have someone strangling the bat and trying to get at the ball as soon as possible. He also had a widened stance at times that would only make him more immobile, rather than feet closer together that might've given Mitch the chance to react, forward or back, to the ball.

I had a chat to both Mitch and his father, Geoff Marsh, during a Sheffield Shield match in Townsville in late 2016, just after I'd returned to the selection panel and he had been dropped from the Test team. Early in the game I spoke to Geoff and said that while I didn't want to impose, I'd noticed a couple of things and if he was interested in having a chat, I'd be more than happy to. Sure enough the next day WA were batting and Mitch was out cheaply, so they came up together and we chatted for an hour or so.

Basically I said, 'I'm not a selector talking to you here, I'm doing this as a friend and a former coach. I'd love to see you having more success and I think what you're doing at the moment with the wide stance can't work. It's not efficient, it's not going to help you become the player you want to become.' I talked through a few things like the active neutral position and things aimed at lightening things up mentally as well as physically, to become more relaxed and better able to concentrate on what's important at the right times. Mitch went away and did some more work with the Perth-based coach Scott Meuleman. They concentrated on things like getting him playing off both forward and back feet, and during the following Ashes summer and the start of the South Africa tour, Mitch batted as well as he ever has or probably ever will.

That could, and perhaps should, have been the start of Mitch's evolution into a truly successful international player. Sadly, it looks more likely now to have been the peak of a frustrating career for one so gifted.

17

NEWLANDS NADIR

Australia, 2018

WHEN DID PROBLEMS in the Australian dressing room that ultimately bloomed into the Newlands scandal actually begin? Many contenders have been suggested, from the ultimatum to the team to improve its performance after the bad Bellerive loss of 2016 to the heated scenes in Durban at the start of the 2018 South Africa series, and others in between.

While it needs to be stressed that they had nothing to do with putting sandpaper on a cricket ball, my firm view is that there had been cultural problems evident in the national team for quite a few years prior. When I first experienced the Australian team environment on my return to work for Cricket Australia in 2007, I couldn't believe how the dressing room environment had changed. Things like blokes throwing bats in the dressing room or having extensive temper tantrums were commonplace. I also heard all sorts of allegations flying around inside the room about the amount of reverse swing being obtained by opponents after the Australians couldn't move it off the straight. Fires of this kind were left to blow themselves out, but quite often that would take a long time.

While I view what happened at Newlands as being different to what I witnessed in earlier years, the through line is about how important the dressing room is to cricketers, and how vital it is to manage it well as a team leader. I'd always seen that environment as sacrosanct, and critical that it be a safe environment where you can let off steam – as long as that outburst isn't so prolonged that it can bring the dressing room down.

Throwing bats in that room should never be acceptable, something I learned at school. After one dismissal that riled me more than usual, I walked back into what I thought was an empty dressing room and threw my bat. Immediately I became aware of someone else's presence and turned around. Our coach, Chester Bennett, stood there impassively as I braced for a dressing down. With a look of disappointment on his face that said far more than the words, he remarked, 'Greg, I'd look after that bat if I were you, you might want to use it again.' With that he turned on his heel and walked out. That had a bigger effect on me than if he'd picked the bat up and hit me over the head with it. I never threw a bat again and discouraged anyone else from doing so.

Even swearing and carrying on after your dismissal – if it lasted more than a few seconds, I saw it as important to intervene and settle someone down: encourage them to go for a walk or chat about how they're feeling or whatever else is needed to calm the room. You never want a room that is jolted by the fear and anxiety automatically built up by seeing a teammate losing their rag after dismissal. To see a dressing room that was the antithesis of that in 2008 was a shock to me.

A few years later I was a fair distance removed from the 'Homeworkgate' dramas in India, when the team management chose to ban four players from a Test match. They did so for menial reasons that demonstrated the pressure the coach Mickey Arthur was under more so than anything else. It stands as another reminder that when you're touring overseas you live in a bubble, removed from the real world and with a loss of perspective.

On one occasion when I was coaching India, we were playing in South Africa and all of a sudden there was an eruption of 'look at that'. We had got ourselves into a collective mindset where all our blokes were seeing in the game were the bad decisions going against us. Eventually, at a break in play, we had to sit the team down and say, 'Look, if you sit here just looking for bad decisions against you, then that's what you'll see. There are plenty of decisions where if you were sitting in the other dressing room, they would be saying they're going against them, so let's forget about that stuff, we've got no control over it. Let's focus on what we can control, and I don't want to hear any more of those comments about the umpiring. If you feel that way, keep it to yourself.'

Earlier when I was coaching South Australia, our left-arm spinner Brad Young had a propensity for playing bands like Nirvana as loud as possible in the dressing room before a day's play. He'd arrive early and take control of the playlist, turning the Nirvana up loud and clear. Apart from the crunch of the music, the lyrics of Kurt Cobain may have been poetic, but they were also dark as all get out. Eventually I had to pull Youngy aside and say, 'Mate, I know you love the music, but if you want to listen to it to rev yourself up, please put your headphones on, because it really puts a heavy pall over the dressing room.'

That's the delicacy with which I viewed the dressing room. It is very easy for groupthink to take over, and all of a sudden something that others would barely see as a blip on the radar becomes an all-consuming issue. If you're in the bubble you're too close to make some assessments and decisions, and guess what, that's where Cape Town ultimately came from. That team and touring party were all talking to themselves, so they started to believe their own publicity, not letting anyone else in.

We all knew that Australia and South Africa had had some really hard, combustible series against each other over the 25-odd years since the Proteas came back into international cricket, with plenty of feeling between the teams. In more recent years that had been building up over two or three series – 2012, 2014 and 2016 all had bust-ups of one kind or another – and so the 2018 Australian touring team went to South Africa spoiling for a fight, to the point of planning for it.

One of the discussions I had with the coach Darren Lehmann prior to the series was about dragging David Warner back in from being the attack dog. A couple of years earlier, David had moved himself out of that job after getting into a position where any further missteps would have meant suspensions under the ICC code of conduct. In the intervening period he focused on his cricket and was going well, at least individually. But there was a feeling from the team's management and leadership that an attack dog was needed, and that haranguing opposition players and getting in their faces was part of how the team won.

I disagreed totally, but the counterview from Darren was 'that's the way we've always played cricket'. My response was, 'No Darren, maybe that's the way you've played cricket, but it wasn't the way I played.'

'Oh mate, but you blokes sledged other teams.'

'Mate, banter went on, the odd bit of sledging went on, but not haranguing opposition players and certainly not doing so in a premeditated way. It's never been acceptable in any workplace, let alone on a cricket field, and it shouldn't be acceptable now.'

'No mate, you've got to do this to win.'

Why did Darren think that was the way Australia always played? Probably because of the emphasis on 'mental disintegration' when Darren played most of his international matches, during Steve Waugh's wildly successful period as captain. While this sort of thing was occasionally seen under Allan Border and Mark Taylor, in Steve's time it became acceptable to stand there and harangue an opposition player as a commonplace tactic. Over succeeding generations it went from a necessity to something like a badge of honour to be able to get up the opposition's nose faster than they could get up ours.

And so that was the attitude, 'we've got to get in their face'. Different era, different game was the excuse, but is it really that different? Sure it is a fully professional and highly paid career, and if you get dropped you've lost your job, whereas we went back to work. But I think the biggest difference was that we went in the opposition dressing rooms on a regular basis. At the end of a day's play we had to front up in the opposition rooms or welcome them into ours. If you made an arse of yourself on the field, you had to face the music that night. Young player or senior player, you were never allowed to dodge it. Basically you'd have to stand or sit in the middle of the floor and explain yourself. Usually it was a bowler getting frustrated and lashing out.

Sometime between then and the present day, starting perhaps in the 1980s, those shared conversations became much less common, and teams did not mix anywhere near as much. As a by-product, the general discussions about the game became chatter exclusively among teammates, and one of the topics was 'how do we get under this player's skin'. That's an environment that quickly becomes very dangerous. Whereas on-field confrontations were once sorted out on the day by two groups of peers, meaning the next day began as a clean slate, by the time of South Africa in 2018, these guys weren't interacting in a human way with the opposition until the end of a series – if they were lucky. Before that point, most exchanges would be on the field, and of the unpleasant variety.

There was a period leading up to Cape Town where quite a few of us had the same feeling. We couldn't tell you what the problem or the blow-up was going to be, but we knew that something ominous was around the corner. In essence 'this is not going to end well'. As a selector, subject to more advice than just about any other job in cricket, wherever I went about my daily life I copped it every day about the behaviour of the team. People were turning the TV off in droves, incensed at some of the things they were seeing. The alarm bells were ringing.

In the whole time I was involved in the pathway of under-age, domestic cricket and the development of players, the ethos was very much about us playing the game in the right way. That is, showing by our actions and not by our words that we were there to play good cricket. Having the national team obviously doing something different to that caused problems for us, because people were seeing that, and deciding that was the way it had to be played in lower grades of cricket.

We've heard that James Sutherland and the CA board counselled the team to calm down at various points earlier in the series. We also know that the chairman David Peever was making threats for the tour to be called off if Cricket South Africa didn't do something about the ugly personal abuse being delivered to the partners of some of the players. But an immutable truth of cricket played on the biggest stage is that while things invariably drop back onto the players, often it is an administrative error that causes things to develop in the first place.

The pay dispute in 2017, which itself escalated to the point that players went unpaid for a month after the expiry of their existing deals, while an Australia A tour of South Africa was cancelled, was a factor here. It contributed to an environment in which players were even less likely than usual to accept correction from the same authority that had pushed them and the Australian Cricketers' Association over a long and ugly row. The 'us versus them' attitude that has always prevailed in Australian cricket was back in a big way in the winter immediately prior to the Newlands blow-up.

As a former member of the ACA executive, I was conscious too that over the years the players' concerns had grown more selfish with time. Their attitudes towards CA and the game were becoming increasingly ignorant of the levels below the elite, not least around club cricket. Add to that the fact that the players had demonstrated their power in the dispute's ultimate resolution, complete with backpay and the retention of a revenue sharing model, and so maybe they were feeling a bit cocky. The administration had, unfortunately, only exacerbated the disconnect by using blunt force in the 'negotiation', falling prey to its own example of groupthink that this was the only way it could be done.

I'm a friend of James Sutherland and I think he was a very successful chief executive of CA over many years who worked assiduously for the benefit of the game. But there were certain things on which we did not agree. I spoke to him about the behaviour of the players on the field, and it is safe to say that he didn't see it as anywhere near as much of an issue as I did. When Tom Veivers and Brian Booth, who between them played a heap of Tests for Australia in the 1960s, wrote to James, questioning many of the same issues I saw, the response was that 'it's a different game today'. That, to me, was a misunderstanding of the complaint. It may well be a harder game, with higher financial stakes, but bad behaviour is not acceptable whatever the era, or the stakes. Racial, religious or personal abuse is never acceptable in any environment. The sporting field is no exception. It's never acceptable – but it was being accepted.

The other contributing factor in early 2018, critically in terms of the team's leadership, was that Steve Smith was a shell of his former self. Having taken on the Test and ODI captaincy in 2015, Steve was also handed the T20 leadership for the World Cup in 2016, even though Aaron Finch had been doing a more than serviceable job. It's particularly hard to captain a country in all three formats, and it is also extremely tough to do it as the coach. Yet Steve, a young leader, was having his mental and physical reserves drained away at a rate of knots. You need downtime to step back, clear your mind, and make sure you've got a clear perspective on what's going on. I don't think it's good sense to have someone captain or coach all three forms – you'll lose them pretty quick.

During the preceding Ashes in Australia he'd had a big series, put a lot of effort into it and was clearly drained. In part, this was because he wasn't hitting the ball well, so needed to spend a lot of time over his runs. Exactly how drained wasn't clear to me until I spoke with him in Perth towards the end of the third Test at the WACA Ground, where Australia regained the Ashes. Steve was sitting on one of the physio benches staring into space; I walked into the room towards him and he didn't register that anyone was there. I said 'how are you going' and he blinked and said, 'Oh mate, I'm gone. I can't sleep, I'm not eating … during a Test match I can't do anything. All I can do is play cricket and stagger back to my room.'

I could relate to that, because there were times when all I could do from one day to the next as captain was just go to my room, have something to eat and go to sleep as early as possible to conserve enough energy for the next day. But he had gone beyond that, because he was so strung out he couldn't even rest his mind without sleeping pills. So he was a shell of a man by mid-December, and that was a contributing factor to what we saw in South Africa a few months later. It basically meant there was one less adult in the room. I've no doubt that whatever went on at Newlands went on around Steve, because I don't believe he was even capable of participating in any kind of plot. He had become extremely fatigued and withdrawn.

I had a huge degree of empathy for Steve. Just as he had his meltdown in South Africa, I had mine at the MCG in 1981. I didn't see it coming, and I don't know if anyone sees it coming. I didn't realise until that day just how strung out I was. And I don't think anyone around me knew it. So it is a bit hard to see it coming when you're right in the middle of it. I think I could see it coming for Steve, particularly after that day in Perth, much as I had seen it coming for Kim Hughes 33 years before.

The renowned sports psychologist Rudi Webster walked into the dressing room during the 1981–82 season, right at the end of my lean run. I sat down in the old MCG dressing room, Rudi walked through the door and said, 'Greg I don't want to add to your problems, I'm sure you're getting lots of advice from others, but are you watching the ball?' I said to him something along the lines of 'what do you f***ing think I'm watching', to which he responded, 'No, are you really watching the ball like you usually do – don't give me an answer now, but when you calm down it might be worth reflecting upon.' When I got back to the hotel and thought about that, I did realise that there had been moments, walking off after dismissals, where I'd looked back at the sight screen and thought 'I didn't see that ball'. When you are that far gone, it's also difficult to see, or hear, good advice.

Players have also found it easier to become isolated even within the team environment for other reasons, making it harder to pick up how they are really doing. In the years before players had their own individual rooms, you were pretty much never allowed to be on your own. That made it very hard for some-one to withdraw and hibernate in their room for days on end, because your roommate and others would be saying 'come on, we're heading out' for this or that. There were times when you didn't feel like going out, but you did because no-one would let you stay. Going to single rooms has made it much easier for guys to retreat into themselves, particularly with the onset of physical and mental fatigue from constant touring.

We had also seen an increasingly cavalier attitude to the way the ball was being 'managed', not just at international level but in the Sheffield Shield. Over many years, the practice of scratch-ing the ball had been going on in close to plain sight. Everyone knew about it, but no-one did anything much about it, and when anyone got caught they received a slap on the wrist.

During the Sheffield Shield competition final in March 2016 at Glenelg Oval, Victoria bowling coach Mick Lewis had been caught on camera scraping the ball on the gutter before throwing it back. Mick's head coach with the state team, David Saker, was elevated to the role of Darren Lehmann's assistant a few months later. By the summer of 2017–18 it was increasingly clear that numerous states were worrying very little about trying to move the new ball, and instead were doing all they could to turn it into an 'old' ball as quickly as possible.

As bad as the Newlands ball-tampering incident itself looked on the field, the press conference afterwards was just a train wreck. As the coach, Darren Lehmann really should have gone into that press conference and said, 'It's under investigation, we can't say anything at this stage, we'll talk more once the finding is handed down.' Instead, Steve Smith thought that in line with previous ball-tampering penalties, he'd just own up to it, they'd get a slap on the wrist and get on with it. But that mis-read the situation, and served ultimately to fuel the flames already burning. I know the team was advised not to tackle the press conference in the way that Smith and Cameron Bancroft did. Ignoring this advice was yet another symptom of the bubble. The team was separated not just from the outside world, but even from members of staff supposedly on the inside.

Pat Howard asked me after Cape Town whether I thought we had a 'win at all costs' attitude. I said, 'Mate, if you stood back from it for a little while, you'd see that we did, and it led to what we saw at Newlands.' Pat was shattered by the whole thing, and the fact that maybe he had unwittingly played some part in it.

Pat, of course, was trying to hit certain targets from day one of his job in 2011, and those were to have the Australian team ranked No. 1 in all forms of the game while winning World Cups at the same time. We were following Tiger Woods' old line that 'second sucks, and third is even worse', irrespective of any other factors that might be at play. It has to be said now that there were people within CA who felt, and made it known, from day one that this was wrong and that it was going to lead to problems.

The counterview was that all we can hope to do is to be competitive in every game we play, and the ranking will be what it will be depending on the talent we have coming through relative to the rest of the world. I certainly made my views known at the time that if we do this, there will be side effects and ultimately consequences. The tack CA took also ran contrary to all that we knew increasingly about the way that the best performers in elite sport went about their business: a process-driven approach that takes the pressures of outcomes out of the picture as much as possible. An outcome-driven approach, by contrast, created a sense of pointlessness or failure to anything but ultimate success.

If you aim for No. 1 in all formats, then it's going to impact everything you do, not least of all selection. You will start doing things for short-term reasons when there is a chance to fleetingly hold that No. 1 ranking, and we saw that happen on multiple occasions. One such example was the selection of Rob Quiney to bat No. 3 for Australia against South Africa in 2012, a series where, if Michael Clarke's team had won, they would have taken top spot on the rankings. Nothing against Rob, but I felt that aiming so nakedly for No. 1 in all formats was sacrificing the future for the present.

I have to say that I think time has borne out the concerns that a few of us had a decade ago. To have that aim of being No. 1 sounded very clear and bold is all well and good – it is a sound objective to have. But when you set it in stone and then put it at the top of the agenda every day, it affects every last bit of your business. Then it affects the coach, the captain, the players, the selectors and everyone down the line. Sadly, that contributed to what we saw in South Africa.

No matter what KPIs you give coaches of teams, they know they have to win. But when you employ coaches on explicit KPIs to win matches and series, you are providing them with far too much incentive to think about the present at the expense of the future. Hopefully there will never be another decision made in Australian cricket that is as short-term, as focused on winning at the expense of all else, as the call to sandpaper the ball.

As for legacies, it is unfair to dump it all at the feet of the players. Cameron Bancroft may never recover from his involvement. Smith has been able to get over it through the weight of runs, and Warner has too to a similar extent. But Bancroft may never get over it. He doesn't deserve it; you would hope if you'd been in his position you'd be aware enough to say 'no, I don't want to be involved in that'. But the trouble is when the whole dressing room's moving in a win-at-all-costs direction it takes a pretty seasoned character to swim against that tide.

Ultimately every one of us in the organisation was guilty. We all walked past things we shouldn't have walked past, from top to bottom. There were opportunities to speak up as an organisation and we didn't do it. One of the realities of such a long lead-up is that it may take another generation or two before the crutch of nasty, premeditated sledging is fully abandoned by Australian players. I am not completely convinced that the good work of the past three years has fully stamped it out: undeniably there are some cricketers who still reckon it is a competitive advantage worth having.

New Zealand, now the reigning world champions of Test cricket, have proven beyond any doubt that it just isn't something you need in your armoury to succeed. In many ways, the type of cricket played by Kane Williamson's team – sound batting with proactive running between the wickets, sharp fielding and precision bowling with a combination of speed, bounce, swing and seam – is the kind Australia made their own over many generations before sledging emerged as a tactical weapon.

I noted with interest when Justin Langer spoke about how difficult it would have been for him as a young player, had someone like Allan Border fronted him with a similar suggestion to the one taken up by Bancroft. Of course Border, and the other senior players around him in that side, were the kinds of characters who would not have countenanced such a thing.

It had been those solid characters who we, as a selection panel in the mid-1980s, tried to choose and persevere with around AB when regularly winning matches was nigh on impossible. We had a generational benefit from that decision; it remains to be seen whether the dressing room problems that grew over the years leading to Newlands will ever rear up again.

18

AN ENDURING PARTNERSHIP

by Judy Chappell

M Y EARLY LIFE was very different to Greg's. My sister
Libby and I grew up with a father and mother who played
competition tennis, so we got dragged around on Saturday
afternoons to watch them as we were growing up, as opposed to
Greg, Ian and Trevor doing the dragging themselves. I was very
involved in sport, generally, but with no specific focus. I played
a lot of tennis, a bit of softball, a bit of golf, and I swam and ran
in school carnivals. While quite competent, I was never going
to be a star.

Then there was the singing. It started with church choir
singing. Mum had the most beautiful soprano voice, Dad also
had a go, and my sister and I followed suit. As we got older we
joined a group called the Katandra Singers in Sydney, 'katandra'
being the Guringai word for 'songs of the birds'. A person known
to my parents in their younger days had started the group
a few years earlier with a group of high school boys and girls.

We sang at a lot of fabulous events, even on the stage of the Sydney Opera House. The couple of outstanding male singers, tenor and baritone, left the group when they went to university, but the remaining members of the group sang at our wedding, and that was really special.

I have fantasised at times in brief moments about being a soloist in an opera on stage. In my late 20s I did sing with the Brisbane Conservatorium, and Brisbane Light Opera Company and the Lyric Company, among others. We sang beautiful choral music and a couple of light operas. I really enjoyed those. I sang alongside Lisa Gasteen, a world-renowned opera singer who specialised in the works of Wagner, so I knew that my voice, while pleasant, was not so outstanding that I would have a future on the stage. That experience, loving music but figuring out where I stood, helped to clarify that my life had another purpose.

The Methodist Church featured quite strongly up until I was about 18. I started to notice there were a few inconsistencies between the words and deeds of a few church friends, and I came to the realisation that I didn't want to be part of that anymore. One Sunday morning I just said to my parents 'I'm not going anymore', and that was it. But at the same time I always knew there was something deeper going on than the straitlaced religion we saw in church. There was a spiritual aspect to life that I felt strongly connected to. If you'd asked me to explain even then what it was, it was really around the word love.

I'd hear people say, across Christian denominations, this word 'love'. But my main experience of it was through family friends who took on leadership positions in the community. Whenever I was with them, for a Sunday afternoon gathering after church or a monthly dance at Arncliffe Methodist Church or in the church hall at Bexley, where we lived, these people took it upon themselves to be like my grandparents. I only had two surviving grandparents past the mid-1960s, and other relatives did not live near us. So these people were so loving and caring, always asking after you and how you were, that I came to understand that was the essence of what religion really is about.

Everything afterwards was informed by that, especially my relationships with people. The most significant relationship I was to have, of course, was with Greg. But that same quality came to the fore, because my experience of life had brought me there. Whereas Greg and his family had been so focused on cricket in every respect, which had nothing at all to do with me. We met because my sister had asked our father to take her to the cricket, and he was so surprised and thrilled that one of his daughters would want to go watch. The match happened to be New South Wales versus South Australia at the SCG, and it led ultimately to her meeting Greg.

By the following season at the corresponding match, we were invited as a family by Greg to spend the day at the cricket. We took Greg and the opening batsman Ashley Woodcock on a drive down to Bulli Pass, overlooking Wollongong. It was a lovely evening, but very chaperoned! That was how we first met, and the first impression was one of physical attraction for each of us, but there was also more to it. We both realised and said so, not that much later. We saw each other again late in 1969 following his return from his second season with Somerset, about seven or eight months after I'd met him, and went on our first date – driving down in Dad's car to the drive-in theatre at Woolooware near Cronulla. Greg drove over a 'silent cop' traffic dome and was pulled over by a real cop! He told me later that he was so smitten with being in my presence that he was just driving on instinct and didn't realise.

When we arrived home, we sat in my parents' living room for a while, just the two of us. He was leaving to go home to Adelaide the next day to belatedly celebrate his 21st birthday, and he just said to me 'I would like one day to be able to ask you to marry me', and I just felt 'oh, that's interesting'. We realised that we'd been attracted to each other's souls. We just knew there was more to each other than the physical; it was something we recognised and he actually gave voice to it. I felt it was quite interesting at the age of 21 that he was able to say I'm attracted to your soul. So it was really lovely, and that then helped us in a way to inform how we then grew together as a couple and faced the challenges that were to come.

For most of the intervening couple of years between 1969 and 1971, our relationship was maintained mostly by letters and aerograms. (We even shared cassette tape recordings, as was the case during Greg's Ashes tour of England in 1972. When in Worcester for a county match, he recorded the sound of the bells in the Cathedral in which our family friend had learned to play the organ. She played the Widor Toccata on the late Ron Sharpe-built fine organ at our Bexley UC wedding in November 1971.) Very few people could afford long long-distance phone calls that were charged by the minute. Having had Greg say to me he would like one day to marry me, there I was a couple of years later still knowing we were the ones for each other. We could either faff around and date other people, or realise that this was it. Looking at the cricket program, Greg had a full summer coming up in 1971–72 and then a tour of England: almost two more years of him being away. So I just said to him 'why don't we get married sooner rather than later'. In August 1971 we announced our engagement, and then were married in November.

Those early few years were a struggle. I really enjoyed having Greg around, but immediately after we were married – literally the next morning – we flew from Sydney to Adelaide and that was the beginning of our life together. It was such a sudden removal from my whole life and family in Sydney, and suddenly here I was in Adelaide. For the first couple of days we lived at his parents' home while they were away, and when they got back we moved into a motel in Glenelg. It was quite confronting at times for me, learning to live with a man after not even growing up with a brother.

We were married on a Tuesday night, and by Saturday morning, Greg was playing a club cricket match for Glenelg! He had bought a little house in Novar Gardens, formerly used as accommodation for immigrants, and once we moved in there I taught at Mitchell Park Primary school. In those early days I felt isolated from everything I knew and the comfort of those things, even as I had an interest in cricket and in Greg's career. I think it was my own spirit of adventure and interest in the unknown that helped me to cope with all of that.

I have to admit that it was a challenge too, in terms of some of my own dreams and passions, to live with someone who was so very outstanding in his chosen path. Perhaps I didn't quite have the same passion and self-belief to do the same in areas like singing or writing. But what I did always have was a strong level of self-belief and self-knowledge to know that I had value, and having that makes you so much better at being able to care for others.

For a while a difficult aspect of our married life was that I wanted to receive as much affection as I was giving. It took some time, but eventually Greg learned to relax a little more, to unwind and also to value more about himself than just the cricket. There was a lot of reward in being beside him as he came to value himself more broadly as a husband, a father and a human being, rather than just as a cricketer.

In moving from Sydney, to Adelaide, to Brisbane, to Canberra, Greg and I had plenty of conversations that helped to shape our life. In 1998, when he was offered the role as coach of South Australia, I was quite eager to remain in Canberra, which we had moved to when son Stephen was studying at the Defence Force Academy. My sister was there, and I'd really loved the six years we had there. I had found a role in which I was beginning to use my personality, my words and intellect – an offer to chair the Women's International Network in Canberra, largely composed of diplomats and/or their wives. So it took a bit of convincing, and I remember having a few anxiety attacks at the time, worrying about it.

In Greg's mind, he had the idea that there were a whole lot of different things to do, and he was so excited about the opportunity with SACA, after some years of commuting between Canberra and Sydney. By contrast, I felt I was going backwards, and I had no really close friends or family there who I could spend time with. So initially there were reservations. But by August 1998, all our children had left home, and I was feeling fairly bereft that the one thing that had now been offered to me was not going to happen. I started to feel strongly that I was able to do the WIN job, leading a group of eminent people. Looking back from a distance of more than 20 years at why I didn't take the job, which would have led to us leading two separate lives or not being married anymore, it was really a matter of valuing the relationship above all.

After a little while in Adelaide, I realised that the change of location and job meant that we could spend so much more time together. In that sense, what had initially been a move for a job for Greg became a great relationship builder for the both of us. Things like sharing lunch because we lived quite close to Adelaide Oval, or being able to go down to the No. 2 ground for trial matches and training and sitting with the wives and partners of the players. They welcomed me with open arms, and the ability to share my own experiences helped them a lot with where they were at in an earlier stage of life.

What this is all to say is that we have trusted each other in our decisions, and shared the strong sense that whatever we did there would be life lessons in it. Going to India in 2005, for instance, seemed at the time to be very Greg-driven, rather than by both of us. But when I looked at it and we discussed it, Greg said 'let's treat it as an adventure', and that is really how it was. I threw myself into that time in India, to the extent that I frightened the life out of some of our security with the degree to which I'd follow my heart into out of the way places in India and Pakistan. But by following my natural optimism, I found overwhelmingly more pros than cons.

The failure rate of cricket marriages is pretty high. But what has sustained us in large measure is always feeling that there was something extra that we drew from to maintain the relationship. Certainly we've had huge challenges, and you could easily walk away from each other, as many people do. We've both sensed in ourselves and in one another that there is a commitment to each other and a deep inner knowing that there's something between us that connects and is meant to be together. As a team, you can accomplish more than you can individually; as a couple we are greater than the sum of our parts.

One little thing is that I have a great knack for remembering names. It may be my musical background – I see patterns in language and in names that make it easier to recall them. Greg will often say to me 'if I don't introduce you to someone, it'll be because I've forgotten their name and I should know it'. So we'd walk in and someone would appear, I could sense the hesitance in Greg, and so I'd introduce myself as Judy Chappell '… and you are', and we always seem to get around it! That's what I mean by working as a team.

Something else I have always encouraged in Greg is a willingness to show his emotions, especially towards his mother and our children. I remember in the last couple of years of her life, Greg's mother was in aged care, and I would hear a bit of their conversation together. What was interesting was the signing off – the same with his brothers really. One day I told him 'tell your mother you love her, because you can't know how much it will mean when someone says I love you'. That was really a turning point for Greg in terms of expressing his emotions.

At one point in his childhood, our eldest son Stephen went on a Brisbane Grammar School camp, and one of his activities for English was a writing assignment. They were asked to write a story about their relationships. He wrote about his relationship with his father, why Greg didn't go to see Stephen play cricket and sit with the other parents, and how hurtful that was. It wasn't until a parent–teacher night following that camp that the English teacher said to Greg 'have you read Stephen's piece', to which he said 'no, I don't know about it'. The teacher said 'well I think you should read it'.

So we did, and then Greg was able to have this incredible conversation with Stephen at the age of 16. He told Stephen that he didn't sit and watch because that would have made him the centre of attention, all of them asking questions about cricket, and not focusing on you and your team. This was history repeating really because Greg's grandfather Victor Richardson had done exactly the same – going to Prince Alfred College and hiding behind a tree so others wouldn't see him there watching his grandkids play, because he knew what would happen.

It was a really good and open conversation for Greg and Stephen to have to start to repair some of their relationship. It had never been easy because of Greg's frequent absences, but it helped Greg make up his mind to reduce his commuting between Canberra and Sydney to spend more time around our younger children Belinda and Jonathan. 'If I hadn't made time for Stephen,' Greg said, 'we might never have had a good relationship.' So he felt he had to make sure he avoided that with Belinda and Jonathan. That was a turning point.

I remember with Stephen, either late in high school or early in his flying career, and Ian happened to be with us. Stephen came up and gave him a handshake and a hug, and Ian was so taken aback, 'what's this, where did you learn that'. And Stephen replied 'that's what we do at home', which impressed Ian. I think my parents showed my sister and I more visible signs of affection, whereas Greg instinctively knew how much his parents loved him through their actions – particularly all the driving to cricket! – rather than things like hugging.

Sometime later I noticed Greg signing off emails and texts to Ian and Trevor with 'love you, Greg'. I thought, 'This is fantastic, I'm sure this is my purpose in life, to help people express love!' It has been a joy to see the evolution of Greg, Ian and Trevor together. When we lived in Sydney in the early 2000s, we would get together regularly at an Indian or Thai restaurant for dinner. Ian would dominate the conversation, Greg came in a close second, and Trevor and I would sit there pretty quietly. However, over the past 20 years, I have seen Trevor really start to come out of his shell and not be reluctant to voice his own strong opinions. I was so pleased when I saw that happening, as the balance shifted into something more equal than it once might have been.

We like to think that our example can and has helped others. You see it in people around you. They may not even voice it themselves, but you know that by seeing an enduring relationship it helps them – either to stay together or conclude why they should not. Back in the late 1980s, a friend of mine said to me 'I've met somebody else'. We had been good friends with her and her long-term partner, and I said to her, 'Go back and think about the beginning of your relationship with your partner, and look at the qualities that drew you together in the first place. If they're still there, and they really mean something to you, then it's worth fighting for or working on.' Her answer to that was 'no', to which I replied 'well there's your answer'.

There have, of course, been times when Greg has struggled with the adversity of various moments, whether it be World Series Cricket, his long run of ducks or more recent episodes. The best way I can summarise how we are with one another in those moments is to recall a comment I made to a newspaper journalist on the front lawn of our home in Brisbane after the underarm incident itself. I said: 'I'm sure Greg did the best he could, with the knowledge he had in him at the time.' That, really, is the only way we can live our lives. When I think of all the different roles and the times he's come home and discussed various things, the conversation invariably comes back to that.

Another thing I've always been a big believer in is that so much of our lives are about asking the right questions of people to bring out the knowledge they have in themselves. The sign of a good leader is asking those questions of people under your leadership but then leaving room for them to find the answers from within. I keep reminding myself and Greg that sometimes leadership or mentoring isn't about telling or instructing other people, it's about asking them to find an answer from within their own knowledge base. Right to this very day I have enjoyed those conversations, and I hope they continue for quite some time yet.

A tale that demonstrates our connection over all these years goes back to another time early on, when we were apart for many months during the 1972 Ashes tour. As I have said phone calls were very expensive, so only made sparingly. They also needed to be booked in advance. But if the phone would ring at home, I'd pick it up and I would say, 'Gosh, they were quick connecting us tonight.' Greg, at the other end, would reply, 'No, I'm ringing you!' That happened quite a number of times on that tour. What was going on between us, then and now, was an intuitive connection, a need to speak to each other at the same time. There might be weeks between phone calls but somehow that connection was there.

19

BROTHERS

I'VE REFLECTED OFTEN on Ian and Trevor and our lives together. In a strange way, each of us was an only child. There was a five-year age gap between Ian and me, and four and a half years between Trevor and me. That meant when I was born, Ian was already at primary school. So my first five years of life were at home, while he spent much more time away. Then, as I've joked more than once, I was nine years old before Ian actually noticed I was alive. Eventually he ran out of other mates when he was about 14, and all of a sudden I got dragged into playing Test matches in the backyard. I was still only 13 when Ian started playing Sheffield Shield cricket for South Australia.

Trevor had a similar experience. I was pretty much at primary school by the time he was born, and so he went through the same process. He had very little time with me until he was nearly 10 years old, and even less with Ian. We didn't have a lot of time together – we were never at the same school at the same time, and we never played junior cricket together. Playing cricket together was all in the backyard, and as opponents rather than teammates. Ian's often said we only played together when we were adults, and that we were lucky to build a relationship as adults through cricket, because we really didn't have much of a relationship as kids.

It took us a bit of time, then, to build the sorts of relationships that you'd expect from siblings. And without sharing cricket, we may never have done that building. Eventually, as we all grew older, the age gaps no longer made much difference. But for a long time there was not much in the way of overt signs of affection between us. This was as much a generational thing as anything else. It was only through education, a lot of it through Judy and our family, and the realisation that I didn't want my kids to grow up in that austere sort of environment, that I really made an effort to express my love to our kids, both physically and by word of mouth, and also to Ian and Trevor. Thankfully this was reciprocated with enthusiasm.

We all speak regularly, sometimes up to two or three times a week. Trevor was up in Brisbane this year for a few weekends together, and we also spent time together down on the Gold Coast. We had a big family reunion in July 2019 to celebrate the centenary of our father's birth, and we were meant to have one in July this year for the centenary of our mother's birth, but the lockdowns got us. We all see each other quite a lot during the summer months when we're all working in cricket one way or another. I'd get to Sydney regularly and would always see Trevor, and I'd see Ian regularly around the country through his work in TV and radio.

Those who know us have heard us finish each other's sentences. Ian and I have conversed, debated and argued all our lives. But the most marked change in recent years has been Trevor's increasing contribution to these exchanges, having always been very much the quiet one. Overall it is a pretty good bond between us, and one that I'm proud of, in particular because of how we had to work at it. Equally, I'm proud of how our three kids have wanted to be close to Ian and Trevor, just as we are close to Ian's daughter.

My charitable partner in crime, Darshak Mehta, has spent more time together with us than most:

I often get asked what are the Chappells like? What is Greg Chappell like? Are the brothers close? The Chappells are a close family unit and incredibly fond of each other. On cricket matters, they are almost like one voice and can finish each other's sentences. And, there is not a defensive bone nor malice in them. Direct and honest. I learnt a long time ago to minimize cricket discussions with them. That way, I would miss out on a free and unflattering character assessment.

An inherently reserved though highly articulate man, Greg handles fame with aplomb, but does not seek it or relish in it. A wicked sense of humour is not obvious and reserved for people he is comfortable with. Greg is the most tactful of the three, so you can imagine Ian and TC in full flow!

Over a decade ago, my wife and I were invited to a family Dinner celebrating Greg and Judy's anniversary, in a Vietnamese restaurant in McMahons Point, Sydney. TC, GC, Judy, Ian and Barb. It was a memorable evening. At the end of the night, my wife thought she had been to a Billy Connolly show. Not, simply because it was funny, but the language ... Yes, they are themselves at all times!

More than anything, people have wondered about my relationship with Trevor in the context of the underarm and its aftermath. It was quite some time after the event itself that we actually spoke in any depth about it. The conversation was driven by how I gradually became aware of the fact that others were making comments about the repercussions it had for Trevor, and that I had put him in a difficult position where he was typecast as 'the underarm bowler'.

I've always said that had it been any bowler other than Trevor that day, I wouldn't have done it. There was an unspoken understanding where I knew that he'd get why I was asking him – and that he'd just get on with doing so. Had I asked Dennis Lillee to do it, we may well have had a stand-up argument in the middle of the MCG.

Had the underarm been a wide, giving New Zealand another ball and one run less to make, I'd have been in deep shit. I can't imagine I'd have asked Trevor to do it again. Of course, I knew he wouldn't bowl a wide – but it's harder to bowl an underarm than you might imagine. Some years later I played in a charity match where Sir Richard Hadlee, no slouch with the ball in hand, greeted my arrival at the crease by bowling a light-hearted underarm. In much less pressured circumstances, he missed the mark and it dribbled away for a wide.

So when Trevor and I got together I said to him, 'Mate, do we need to have a chat about the underarm?'

'No.'

'You're fine?'

'Yeah I'm fine.'

'Do I need to apologise?'

'No, not at all.'

'Ok, fair enough.'

We have had some more extensive conversations since then. For a while Trevor did get pissed off about how everywhere he went, that was the only topic of conversation. But he's worked through it in his own mind, and I eventually started joking to him about how I'd made him famous. He's been invited across the Tasman on several occasions to celebrate the event that helped put New Zealand cricket on the map. In 2019, the majority of the team from that game were in Melbourne for a 40-year reunion of that tour. During that week, their captain Geoff Howarth and I had another discussion about the whole thing and he really brought home how much it enabled the game to gather a level of prominence much closer to that enjoyed by rugby.

We were lucky, in a way, that it happened against New Zealand, a nation known for its forbearance. Trevor is very good mates with Brian McKechnie, who he bowled the underarm to, and Bruce Edgar, who was at the non-striker's end. Sydney's Gordon Cricket Club, where Trevor has played and coached for decades, scheduled a celebratory dinner for this year to mark the 40th anniversary of the event, and Bruce and Brian were invited to travel over.

Feisty is the word I'd use to describe Trevor. He's got a very good, dry sense of humour, is incredibly competitive on the sporting field, and a very loyal friend. It was a pretty tough road for him to take, coming into the world behind Ian and me, certainly from a cricket point of view. For me, Ian was a flag-bearer when I was a young player. He led the way and left footsteps in the sand for me, playing Shield cricket as a teenager, and then his first Test match when I was 16. By the time I got to the Test team in 1970 he was not quite established himself, and has often said that my arrival gave him the kick-along he needed to make the most out of his batting and, in turn, captaincy.

But by the time Trevor was on the scene, we were both well entrenched at the top of the game. Trevor was an exceptional baseballer and a better Australian Rules footballer than either of his older brothers. Fast, skilful and fearless, he would almost certainly have made it as a player of distinction in the SANFL. Had he pursued either of those sports, it would have been a lot easier for him to make a mark. One day I asked Trevor, 'Why the hell didn't you pick something else?' Came the reply, quick as a flash: 'Because I love cricket.' The Richardson and Chappell blood courses just as strongly through Trevor as it does through Ian and Greg.

20

RECOVERY, REINTEGRATION, RETIREMENT

Australia, 2018–2019

A T THE END of the bitter World Series Cricket split in 1979, the sum total of my 'reintegration' to the establishment was as follows. Norman McMahon was the chairman of Queensland Cricket and he rang me up at 11 am one day shortly after the peace deal between Kerry Packer and the ACB had been announced. My business at the time had an office in Spring Hill, a 10-minute walk from the centre of Brisbane, and Norm was with the tax department in its office just next to the Brisbane Hotel. 'I guess we need to have a conversation,' Norm said. 'Would you like to have lunch today?'

'Oh yeah, where would you like to meet?'

'How about the Brisbane Hotel.'

So I got down to the front bar of the Brisbane Hotel about 12.15 pm, and it was jam-packed, largely with staff from the tax office. Norm met me and ordered a couple of butchers, small beer glasses. We were shoulder-to-shoulder, you couldn't hear yourself talk, and I said, 'Norm, why don't we go into the lounge bar.'

'Nah, the beer's two cents more expensive there.' Forever the accountant.

After we'd had about seven beers, he said, 'You don't need any food do you?' And I said 'oh no Norm, I never eat at lunchtime', thinking he was joking. In the end I had 11 beers and he had 15, for lunch. To this day I don't remember what we discussed, because when I walked back up the hill to the office, my head was swimming. But that was the extent of efforts made to patch up the schism from WSC, the only conversation I ever had about it, and I haven't a clue what we talked about.

Undoubtedly, a lot of the pain experienced in the years after WSC could have been lessened if we had made a more serious effort at getting together and discussing our differences. Fortunately by 2018 such matters are better understood – credit needs to be given to Cricket Australia for the reintegration work that was done among the players after Newlands. Belinda Clark – the former Australian captain who later managed the Centre of Excellence and headed team performance after Pat Howard's exit – was heavily involved. I believe the process was exceptional and probably made the reintegration of Steve Smith and David Warner the success that it was. No doubt, without that, it wouldn't have worked as well as it did in England in 2019, because there was some damage done and some scars needing to heal. Relationships had been cracked and needed to be dealt with.

It was explained to us as being like a marriage breakdown, where the two parties have some time apart and come back to try again. If the two groups come back with the same thought processes and attitudes they had when they parted ways, that's probably not going to work. So the groundwork done there, also involving Tim Ford – a leadership consultant who'd won silver in swimming at the Commonwealth Games – was critical.

James Erskine, who once managed Tiger Woods and has long been with Shane Warne, took over the management of David Warner in the middle of 2018, which was another important piece of the puzzle. I spoke to David during that period because I was concerned that he was going to come out with his tell-all story of South Africa. Such an account released at that time might have made him feel better in the short term, but it was going to destroy his chances of coming back. What I found in conversation with David was that Erskine had well and truly talked him away from that particular precipice, advising him against anything like that, at least until the end of his playing days.

So the discipline of Smith and Warner was also important. They realised they had to take the penalty on the chin, swallow the pride and ego a bit, and admit to themselves and their peers that they'd made some mistakes, before they could come back. This they did in a team summit in the UAE during a series against Pakistan in early 2019. It wouldn't have worked without the amount of preparation that went into it behind the scenes, and things played out over a period of months. It was well thought through, well planned and well executed. Proof of its worth came in the fact that the team did not fracture under the pressures of a World Cup and an Ashes away from home.

Tim Paine and Aaron Finch as captains and Justin Langer as coach were all involved, as were the support staff. It was terrific to see as an exercise in people management getting all the parties on the same page. Everyone had the opportunity to say their piece and be heard, and that was an important part of the healing process. They were heard in a safe environment. They were able to say things face to face, which was important, and the great courage and humility Dave and Steve showed was essential.

Cultural questions about Australian cricket were being asked pretty broadly throughout 2018 and into 2019. The realisation had come that things needed to be cleaned up, and Justin Langer, as the new coach, was very firm about that as well. It had already been factored in before the cultural reviews hit the public sphere – one by former Test bat Rick McCosker, another by Dr Simon Longstaff at The Ethics Centre. Those within the game already knew what needed to happen. If anything, it meant we were going to make fewer apologies as selectors for seriously looking into things like character and off-field behaviour as criteria for selection. We had always done this, but it was useful to have a reminder as to why it was so important.

Choosing Justin as coach of Australia following Darren Lehmann's resignation was a move that suited the times. Had he been handed the job a year or two before, in a much less humble environment, it is quite possible that Justin would have struggled a lot more than he had to in the first couple of years after the Newlands scandal. Justin is a very compassionate man, who knows he has to have a tough persona as the head coach and selector, but struggles with the inherent contradictions of those two extremes. As a coach and mentor you don't want to be all tough, all the time, but you don't want to be too soft-hearted either.

Wayne Bennett, the legendary rugby league coach, is also the greatest pragmatist I've ever come across. He knows what works, he knows what personalities work, and he's happy to appropriate ideas from anywhere. A bit like Sir Alex Ferguson, who seldom had an original idea, but was able to synthesise a whole lot of ideas and concepts from others into a Manchester

United dynasty right at the time the Premier League was turning European football on its head. Once asked, after their pre-eminence was well established, why he didn't simply buy the best players, Ferguson replied that he was looking for a particular type of player. If they don't fit what we know works, they don't come here. And if they get here by mistake and we find out they don't fit, they don't stay. We aren't going to deal with people who are going to try to change us and our system.

At a forum a few years back, Bennett was asked by a fan of St George why he didn't make a certain change to the club. Bennett fixed the guy with a long Bennett stare, and said: 'Because it doesn't work. I've survived 25 years in this game, because I tend to focus on things that work.' After you've been in the game for a while, you do tend to know what works, and that is where the toughness can be required if you're dealing with players who don't swim between those flags.

For all that, the difference between coaching a domestic side to coaching a national team is enormous. For one thing a domestic coach gets to sleep in his own bed for half the season, and probably three-quarters of the year. The international coach is on the road – and in a foreign bed – about 300 days a year. That's a big adjustment, even if you've done it as a player. In some ways it can be even harder for a coach, because unlike a player you never really get the chance to switch off, and nor do you get the pure enjoyment of actually playing. I spoke to Justin about needing to have days off and also picking up things to take your mind away from the coaching role: golf, fishing and the like.

The other thing I advised was that Justin couldn't afford to get caught up in what the members of the press were writing, or what broadcasters were saying. If we have a very strong philosophy on how we want to play the game and we're adhering to that for the most part, the winning and losing is not the be all and end all. As long as we are tracking towards becoming a better team in the medium and long terms, then we've got to be accepting of that – and the administration needs to back that up. By the same token, Cricket Australia needs to be assessing the coach on whether we are happy with the style of cricket, getting better as a team and seeing players develop, rather than solely on wins and losses.

One of the challenges I saw for Langer was that, in part because of his place on the board of the West Coast Eagles in the AFL, he thought of himself in terms of a football coach. That thinking can be very dangerous, because cricket coaching and football coaching could hardly be more different. For one thing, the captain should be the leader of a cricket team, whereas in football the coach has long since become the most dominant person at a club. The coach of a cricket team, then, needs to see himself as the key support person for the captain, rather than the master string-puller of the whole set-up.

Langer and Tim Paine were at least on the same page in terms of sharing responsibilities between them, an arrangement Tim endorses, and have been able to form a functioning partnership. But I'm not convinced that it is a long-term option. We're in a bind if we haven't got captains who are demonstratively the leaders of their teams, because it is impossible to make the pro-active decisions that influence the outcomes of games if you're waiting for off-field confirmation of your thoughts.

Langer had a fiery baptism in England during the limited-overs tour in June 2018, when there appeared to be such an enormous distance between the teams that we should reconsider even turning up for the World Cup the following year. But with numerous players out, not just Warner and Smith, it wasn't so much about winning games as getting the personnel, team balance and style of play figured out for the conditions we would face in 2019. While England scoring over 400 at Trent Bridge was not a fun day for anyone, the availability of some of our better bowlers plus the greater pressure of the occasion meant that we were able to find a happy medium between attack and defence for the Cup itself.

One of the more criticised calls we made in 2018 was to not select Glenn Maxwell for the Test tour of the UAE to face Pakistan while Smith and Warner were suspended. Instead we picked Aaron Finch at the top of the order and Travis Head and Marnus Labuschagne in the middle. In part, this was a case of miscommunication to Glenn and his management, because he was initially counselled not to overcommit to Lancashire in England so he would be free for Australia A and then potential national duty. But those communications – which fly around with extreme frequency – should never be taken as a guarantee of selection for international matches.

Glenn's only previous Test cricket had been in India and Bangladesh in 2017, and he was called in as injury cover for Shaun Marsh on the eve of the 2017–18 Ashes series in Brisbane. There is something of the genius about Glenn at his best, and we debated his place in the scheme of things at some length. But the decisions to make investments in Head and Labuschagne in particular were made with a long-term view to life after Maxwell's generation was no longer around, and in the short term to making sure that the team Smith and Warner returned to was tracking in a positive direction.

In a way it was about looking at a period of adversity as one of opportunity – you don't often lose two players that good for that length of time together. We had to come out of that ban period with a better team than when we went into it, and so the selection conversations became very much along the lines of needing to find out about players we hadn't yet learned enough about. In the case of Aaron Finch, we wanted to find out if he could make the transition from limited-overs to Test cricket: there was enough in the package to try it. While he made a decent start in the UAE, he struggled in Australian conditions against a high-quality Indian attack, and it was a very good effort on his part to come through and recover his white ball game in time for the World Cup campaign the following year.

What we liked most about Marnus and Travis as younger players was their love of a contest. As a Test batsman you've got to like putting yourself in danger, you've got to like putting yourself up against the best the opposition can throw at you, and come out of it the other side with success. But if you're dodging that contest, to avoid the best the opposition can hurl at you, and you keep saying, for instance, 'this is the way I play', that's not looked upon as kindly. That sounds very much as though you don't like the contest, and your idea of a level playing field is when things are actually on your terms.

Out of the 2012 Under-19s cohort, Travis would not necessarily have been the one I'd have picked out as a future international cricketer. But one of the big differences between him and the rest was that he went almost straight from that Under-19s side and started playing for South Australia. In turn, that meant he was building experience and learning how to make hundreds – with plenty of trial and error before he figured out how to do it – in his late teens and early 20s, a time when most cricketers in recent years had been stuck in limbo between under-age cricket and first-class ranks.

By contrast, Ashton Turner was a young cricketer who had tremendous qualities evident at a very young age. I saw him captain the Western Australia Under-17s team in Adelaide, and they won the championship on the back of his performances: batting, bowling, fielding and captaincy. When they needed a wicket, he would come on and get them one; he batted in partnerships when they were needed; his captaincy, field settings and bowling changes were terrific. But next year at the Under-19s championship, probably because he was younger by a year, Turner was passed over for leadership of that side, and then found it tough gaining opportunities at state level.

On his debut, Travis had a poor first innings but then put together a critical contribution in the fourth innings as Usman Khawaja helped Australia escape with a draw. The following year, Marnus walked out as the first concussion substitute in Test match history after Steve Smith had been rocked a shocking blow by Jofra Archer – and went on to save a Test match for Australia, on the final day at Lord's against England to preserve a 1–0 series lead. I'll never forget the sight of Marnus being whacked on the helmet himself by Archer as soon as he got to the middle, and jumping straight back up as though he was spring-loaded. In both cases, the contest was stacked against them, in terms of the opposition, the conditions and the game scenario. But in both cases Head and Labuschagne came through.

In some respects Labuschagne is reminiscent of Allan Border: not the most obviously talented batsman around, but chock-full of desire to be a good player and willing to do absolutely everything in his powers to get there. They're the sorts of things you consider as a selector. As I've said to many young cricketers over the years, don't ever think that someone's not watching you.

As a selector I'm watching you off the field as much as I'm watching you on the field. If I wanted to know how good a cricketer you are, I could stop at the scorebook and some match footage. But I want to know who you are and how likely you are to cope with the extraordinary demands of being an international cricketer. What you're like when things are going well, what you're like when things are going badly. I want to know what you're like when you get dropped; how do you react to that. Do you go and sulk, sit in the corner and suck the oxygen out of a room, or do you jump up and run around and ask blokes if they need a drink or want their shoes cleaned? Being disappointed is not a problem in itself, but how long you are disappointed can be – after a time you need to find a way to channel that into your next positive actions. All of those things are important.

How you deal with failure defines how successful you're going to be, because cricket is a game of failure. Sir Donald Bradman batted 80 times in Test cricket and only made 29 hundreds. So he had 51 failures. If he's failing that often, guess how many failures the rest of us are having. If you can't deal with failure, you can't succeed, because you won't be able to go back for your next visit to the crease with any confidence. If you can't trust your training and believe in yourself, you're not making it.

As a young player coming into first-class ranks, Labuschagne looked very manufactured, someone who had been heavily coached. He appeared very committed to having shots that mirrored what you might find in a coaching manual or video, with a very tight grip on the bat handle. He had limitations – but there was an energy about him. In the field you could see how passionate he was. So while I had reservations about how stilted he was in some of his movements at the batting crease, there was something about him that made me want to keep watching for how he developed.

Queensland had a fairly settled batting order and it wasn't easy for him to break into it, but he got opportunities in limited-overs games that perhaps helped him to free up a little. Over a number of conversations I had with him, I could also see how much he loved the game and also the fact that he possessed a strong degree of self-belief: not only as batsman but also as a wrist-spin bowler. Where some others might shy away from articulating these thoughts, Marnus wanted to be a good player and genuinely felt that he could be a good player; however much talent you might have, that is the right place to start. There was no false modesty there – a quality I had also seen in a young MS Dhoni.

We took Marnus on the Australia A tour to India in 2018 that was blighted by bad weather. When I saw him around a team, around hotels and training, he was totally relaxed. He's got great hand–eye co-ordination, as seen when he and Matt Renshaw basically turned the team room into an indoor sporting area. They shifted all the furniture to have indoor tennis, indoor golf and other games. Marnus absolutely loved it, while also showing skill and competitiveness that saw him win far more often than he lost, but also cope well with defeat when it did arrive.

If he wasn't able to go out and play cricket, he would invent something else to play until he could do so. That left me to conclude that if he could relax a little in the middle and learn to play an innings, he was going to be a good player. Looking now at the cricketer who has leavened out some of the more studied elements of his method with genuine know-how about how to make hundreds, Marnus has demonstrated a very high level of aptitude and adaptability to cricket's various challenges. That made it altogether fitting for the YouTube whizz Rob Moody to share a video in which Marnus compared quite favourably to a mirror image of Michael Hussey.

~

Everyone has, and is entitled to, an opinion as far as selection is concerned. Some, though, reach further than others. When Shane Warne sits in the commentary box on Fox Cricket and argues that D'Arcy Short should be opening the batting for Australia in Test matches, you know as a selector it requires a clarifying conversation. Warne has a big enough reputation, and the megaphone to go with it, to change public opinion. I know Shane well enough to be able to have that conversation, and in January 2019 during the Sydney Test that's exactly what I did.

During a rain-interrupted match in which Australia were sliding inevitably to a series defeat against India, Shane was seemingly picking a new Test team every day, amounting to about 25 players who he thought should all be fitting into the same 11-man team. We had no Smith and no Warner for obvious reasons. Take your best two players out of any team and it makes a difference. What I bridled at with Shane was that I know he's got a good cricket brain, but he seemed to have a small group of players he seemed to be deliberately promoting as a point of difference.

'Warney, give us a break, you've picked 25 blokes, we've got to pick 11. You're not doing yourself any favours and you're not helping Australian cricket.'

'Oh mate, I'm entitled to my opinion.'

'Yes you are entitled to your opinion, but you've got to understand the impact that you're having. I can cop it from anywhere, but I don't need you piling on as well.'

In the middle of that night I woke up and gave him a few more choice thoughts. Next morning, I get a response from

Warney. 'Mate I've just got off the plane in Melbourne, obviously this means a bit to you, can I give you a ring when I get home?'

We ended up having about 90 minutes talking on the phone. At one point I asked him how many Sheffield Shield games he'd seen in the past five years. When he replied 'none', I told him that the selectors were, between them, seeing every ball bowled and if someone's done well you replay the whole thing, often more than once, to take a closer look. It was a really good discussion. We've both got strong opinions and we agreed to disagree on some things.

Importantly, he accepted the point that he wasn't help-ing by pulling so many names out of the hat. We know we've got a problem, we've got two of our best players out of the team and we can't pick them. But what we're trying to do is to make sure that during this period we actually finish up with a better team when they come back into it. There's no point in us rotating the chairs and giving everyone one or two games and then dropping them again. That's what we'd done for a couple of years in the 1980s before we realised we had to pick and stick.

Something that helped us here was the fact that in Trevor Hohns, Australia had a selection chairman not too far short of Laurie Sawle's class. Known universally as 'Cracker', he managed to do the job over a couple of stints, until recently deciding he'd had enough. He did it with a combination of passion and resilience that you can only admire. I struggled at times with watching the volume of cricket that we had to as selectors, but Cracker could at times remind me a little bit of Bill Lawry in the commentary box in his eagerness to get to the ground. This is not to say Trevor is as demonstrative as Bill! Highly phlegmatic, a quality that helps him in the many awkward conversations a selection chairman must have, Trevor doesn't always say a lot, but makes sure that whatever he says has meaning.

He too had strong views, but didn't impose them unless he felt he had to. In that, he reminded me of Sawle's ability to steer a selection discussion towards consensus, with the occasional intervention that still left everyone feeling their views had been heard. No selection chairman I know particularly enjoyed the media component of the role, but Cracker invariably did it well: measured commentary that is forever respectful of the many delicate matters at play. I certainly felt that Cracker and I were complementary forces on the selection panel, particularly given my link to the junior and developmental levels of the game that allowed me to see outstanding talents coming through. One of these was Cameron Green.

I've never seen a six foot seven batting superstar before, but Cameron is it. He's the bloke who has the chance of being that player. Clive Lloyd was probably the tallest batsman I played against, and Kevin Pietersen is another of the tallest players of that talent and performance level. Green, though, could be anything. When I first saw him in 2016, he wasn't really on anyone's radar, he wasn't making a lot of runs, but I told anyone who would listen that this kid was our next great batsman. And he can also bowl at 140 kph, and he's threatening.

Bowled sparingly but played primarily as a batsman, Green will be able to develop rapidly in the top six and by the time his body is mature enough to cope with greater bowling loads he will be churning out quality runs on a consistent basis. Frontline bowling use on the other hand will see Green face the likelihood of overuse injuries that can take 12 to 18 months of recovery time, robbing him of batting growth and leaving us to wonder how good he might have become.

His best fit is doing the Shane Watson or Jacques Kallis role of batting in the top six and offering 10 to 15 overs an innings depending on circumstances and conditions. But he can bat anywhere in the order, and, given how hard it is to find exceptional batsmen at the best of times, that really has to be the priority for him.

What gives me most comfort about Green is that he sees himself as a batsman. Often those sorts of conversations can be taken in another direction by coaches, who can win those arguments over young players unless they're particularly determined. As selectors we were endlessly grateful that in his early 20s Steve Smith put his foot down over the fact that he saw himself as a batsman first and a wrist-spinner much, much later. We knew that was where his greatest talent lay, but it was vital that he believed it too.

~

When James Sutherland flagged in the middle of 2018 that he was finishing up as Cricket Australia's chief executive after 17 years, that was when I really started to solidify in my mind that it was time for me to go also. I didn't really have another battle in me, to re-argue the various cases that we had been arguing for years, with a new CEO, a new chairman, and a couple of new high-performance managers. A few times I found myself thinking 'I've sat in this meeting too often', and almost lost track of the number of times I'd retraced familiar ground with different people. It also felt like a good time for someone else to have their say and influence on the direction of Australian cricket for the next 20 years.

There were also a lot of people coming into the organisation who had little or no knowledge of the game, and certainly had no knowledge of the history of the game. While it has changed enormously, there is still value in understanding where the game has come from in order to inform where the game might go next. And I was meeting people who had no idea where the game had come from and I got the distinct impression they had no idea where the game should be going. Those experiences made me feel like something of a tired revolutionary, who didn't need the stress and strain of fresh arguments over old ground. I was still loving the nuts and bolts of what I was doing. Less so the travel, an increasingly corporatised environment, and a lot more concern about perceptions than whether we were actually doing the right thing.

At the start of 2019 I made the commitment to Cricket Australia that I would be finishing up before the start of the next home summer. By the time I returned home from the 2019 World Cup and then sat through the many late nights of an undulating Ashes series, I knew I was done. In a way it was a bit like the conversation I had with Ian when he retired. 'You're mad, you've got plenty of cricket left,' I told him. 'No mate, you'll know,' he replied. 'When the time comes, you won't need anyone to tell you.' And he was pretty much right. I'd got to the point where I knew the travelling was no longer a realistic option. I could have done more from home maybe, but not on the road.

21

THE AUSTRALIAN SYSTEM
AND ITS DISCONTENTS

GOING OUT ON the field every day, giving 100 per cent effort and doing your best, day after day over a long sporting career, is what I think of as being professional. Every bloke I played with over the long term was professional in their approach to what happened on the field. Occasionally, one or two of them let themselves down in preparation – there's a big difference between three beers and 10 – and maybe didn't perform as well as they might have, but from an effort point of view they gave everything they had. We weren't well paid, but I'd put the professionalism of the players who performed over long periods in my era up against any. Those who came into that environment and prioritised the off-field fun over the on-field fun generally didn't last too long. What you had to learn early was that if you did well on the field, there were more than enough opportunities to enjoy yourself off the field. But if you focused off the field, you were eventually going to run into problems.

I tried, briefly, to follow Doug Walters' example in terms of beers and smokes, but I quickly learned that it didn't suit me. I simply didn't have his constitution. But if we'd locked Doug up at 8 pm every night and told him he couldn't have a beer and a cigarette, I doubt he would've been the player he was. That was his way of dealing with whatever he had to deal with. Forced to go to his room early, he would have endured sleepless nights and been more exhausted the next day than he was with far fewer hours of much more restful sleep. Doug was an extreme case, but the point is, there needs to be flexibility.

On one occasion my brother Ian was commentating during a tour of Sri Lanka when the island was still in the grip of civil war, which meant the Australian players were pretty much confined to their hotel. After a little while he asked me, 'how do you reckon we would've gone like this?' I replied that I thought there would have been at least two or three escapees from the security cordon every night, because guys would have found a way to get out and have a break from the environment. Thinking cricket 24/7, taking kids out of school at an age where they don't know how to do anything else, and then paying them so much that they don't need to, is a dangerous path. Thinking about cricket for that long at a time will not make you a better player.

Like everybody I've had setbacks in life and any number of them could have undone anything and everything. We've all had them. But how long you stay there can determine how much damage those setbacks do. My 1981–82 long run of ducks went as long as it took me to work out that it wasn't the physical level but the mental level that was the problem. At other times in life outside of cricket I've allowed myself to wallow for a period, but thankfully not for long, because of the understanding I had that I am more or less the creator of my own world.

That sort of perspective is harder to have if all you know is cricket. An example of behaviour that has arisen through players only knowing cricket, and not thinking about how such things might transpire in any other career, is in bat sponsorships. It started with conversations I had towards the end of my playing career, when bat contracts started to get a little more lucrative. Often I was asked 'which bat contract should I take', to which I would reply, 'Mate, take the one that's got the best bat, because that's what's going to make you money. An extra few grand on your bat contract is not going to make much difference, but an extra few thousand runs will make a big difference.'

Flash forward to the contemporary era, and players have the best of both worlds in a way that is completely devoid of reality for most people. They get the best contract and the best bat, by finding their own favoured manufacturer and then applying the stickers of their bat sponsor to the clean skin. I could never have signed a contract with Gray-Nicolls and used someone else's bat with Gray-Nicolls stickers, because it would not have sat right. But present-day players have long since got over that conundrum and found that they can feel right about doing that.

~

Any reassessment of the Australian cricket system should always begin from the simple point of asking, what do we want out of it? The answer to this is players who will take the game forward and play the Australian style of cricket. Briefly defined, that is by looking to score runs with the bat, run hard between the wickets, then look to take wickets with the ball, by genuine fast bowlers, swing bowlers and wrist-spinners and the occasional finger spinner. All backed up by players who can field and catch.

If we can develop those sorts of players, then we will always have a pool of talent from which we can choose. But if we're producing one-dimensional players with an accent on safety-first ways of playing the game, we will fall by the wayside very quickly.

A lot is made of facilities and the disparities between schools, clubs and different parts of the country. A good thing to remember here is that whatever the facilities on offer in Australia, they will invariably be better than what was available to the likes of MS Dhoni in India, or a host of brilliant players from Pakistan. The best players don't come out of academies; they come out of the school of hard knocks. What Dhoni got that he would never have got at Prince Alfred College was to play endless pick-up matches against other kids.

On one India camp we got all the guys to share a little of their backgrounds. I particularly wanted the coaches to know where the guys all came from. Dhoni told a great story about how he wasn't particularly fussed about cricket when he grew up, but he started playing with his mates after school on the streets, and graduated from one game to another game, one group to another group, to the point where he was recognised to play in a representative game. From that point he had to re-establish himself again, always being the outsider. Each time he got selected to go to a different level, he was the kid who had to prove himself all over again. Over time, that made him the player he was, not only because it bred toughness, but also courage to be aggressive because he knew he needed to show sceptical groups that he could play.

One thing I said to the BCCI when I left was that you have so much money that it would be easy to build academies everywhere, but it won't necessarily be the academies that will produce your best players. What you need to do is to provide opportunities for kids to play as widely as possible, but not necessarily with the most luxurious facilities. You need a lot of scouts who understand the game, to go to the centres where kids regularly play and just watch them. Don't coach, watch. It won't take long to identify who the best kids are: the athletes, the hand–eye skills, the competitors, the resilient ones. That's all you have to observe, and then give them opportunities to play.

Ian Frazer and I said that to Lalit Modi in Rajasthan. Just provide these kids with opportunities to play. Make sure they have enough bats, balls, stumps, pads and helmets. They don't need an academy per se, but they need somewhere safe where they can play and learn by playing, rather than being over-coached. Film these sessions with cameras, and then feed that footage back to base in Jaipur where you've got people to assess what they're being sent from scouts on the ground. From there we get the best kids to Jaipur, run them through programs and sift through them again. We didn't quite get to that stage, but that would have been the long-term plan.

The last thing you want is to have a coach who will try to turn MS Dhoni into Dilip Vengsarkar, because you'll be taking a silk purse and ending up with a pig's ear. Let's not interfere, but let's make sure that in every region in Rajasthan you've got an area where kids can go and play, with people to supervise it and make sure it's safe. If you teach a kid the 'correct' way of playing a cover drive, you've put a lid on how well they can play the cover drive. Whereas if you tell the same kid I want you to hit as many balls as you can through that gap over there, they work out how to do it, then you get MS Dhoni.

One of the biggest things in Australian cricket is that we've over-structured it. The interlinking systems of contracts, enormous numbers of support staff and muddled incentives – where becoming a quality performer in a united and successful Australian team should be the overarching ambition – make it harder for CA than it should be.

What could be done instead? The best answer would be to reduce the number of domestic contracts on offer per season to something like 10 per state, making them sought after but not so numerous that anyone could afford to coast. The next group of eight or 10 could be given incentives to allow them to get to training and games, but also encouraged to put time into jobs or tertiary study and so grow as a person as well as a cricketer. There could also be incentives offered to select seasoned players who you wanted to keep involved at club and second XI levels while also holding down careers, rather than seeing them do that in sub-district or regional competitions. Living and breathing cricket 24/7 will never be the best environment to develop hungry cricketers.

For a young cricketer, say one of university age, coming to cricket training three times a week and really valuing that time will be enough to keep them developing but also hungry. Coming in to train five days a week and doing nothing else, by comparison, is likely to burn out the interest and enjoyment of far more young players than it helps. I've never believed that more sessions necessarily mean more improvement. Short, focused, intense sessions will develop talent far more readily than long, interminable sessions at low intensity – those sessions work more to fill time and justify support staff jobs.

Once players have established themselves and graduated to international level, I favour the top echelon being rewarded with an even greater slice of the player payment pie than they do now, rather than spreading it down the list. Even now, looking at the annual CA contract list, there will invariably be numerous players who will play very little for Australia over the course of the year. I'll never be convinced that professional cricket for every player in domestic ranks is in anyone's best interests. I say that regardless of arguments about the share of the pie that goes to the players, and the competing demands from other codes for the sporting talent pool.

Obviously this scenario would cause headaches for those administrators conscious of the opportunities on offer in other sports, namely the winter football codes with playing lists closer to 40 per club. 'The war for talent' was a phrase I heard a lot over the past decade at CA, but cricket really needs to back itself in, by concentrating on developing the committed kids as well as it possibly can. If we generate enough great players to lead the way at international level, and the spread of those players reflects the changing cultural mix of the country, then we will gain a lot more followers and players than we ever lose.

Historically Australia has been one of the best at developing young players and keeping them in the system, but I think that's changed. I'm seeing a bunch of young players with great potential who are in limbo. That's unacceptable. We cannot afford to lose one player. India have got their act together and that's largely because Rahul Dravid has picked our brains, seen what we're doing and replicated it in India with their much larger base. I think we've already lost our position as the best at identifying talent and bringing it though. I think England are doing it better than us now and India are doing it better than us also.

Look at the Indian team that won the Brisbane Test in 2021, clinching the game and series with three overs left in the last session. Decimated by injuries, they had six players in the team who had made their debut in the series – two in this very match. 'This is India's second XI,' people said. But those same guys had played a lot of games for India A in all sorts of different conditions, not just in India. When they get picked, they're not tyros at all, they're quite hardened international cricketers. We picked Will Pucovski out of Shield cricket, but Will has hardly played a game outside Australia. That's the difference.

There is also a reasonable argument for having more domestic teams than the six we have had since the start of the 20th century. That's because we can't afford to have the bigger states warehousing kids just because they might need them at some stage. I think that's dangerous. If we were designing a structure from scratch now, we wouldn't design it the way we have got it. I think New South Wales could possibly have a second team. We need to disperse the talent a little bit more evenly, rather than having good talent sitting on the sidelines in Victoria and New South Wales when they could be playing really well.

One scenario that could work would be to move to using the eight Big Bash League teams as the first-class cricket entities in this country. Such a change would mean severing the link between the Sheffield Shield and the six state representative sides that have competed for the title over well over a hundred years. But if it allowed for more quality Australian players of the future to come through the system, it would not be looked upon too unkindly by the many legendary cricketers who forged their path in the years when the six teams were drawn from a population far smaller than it is today.

We've also got full-time cricketers, so why do we have to be constrained by the timing of our cricket season? We've got access to these guys for basically 10 months of the year. One of the things I believe would make a big difference would be trying to play a full block of Sheffield Shield cricket in the early part of the season so that guys get a run at red-ball cricket. Playing five Shield games and then 50-over cricket and then BBL and then finishing the end of the Shield season just breaks up that opportunity to develop long-form batting, which is a good foundation for the other formats anyway. Marnus Labuschagne wasn't the finished article until he got that sort of continuity with Glamorgan in 2019, just in the nick of time for our Ashes campaign.

It's harder for a young batsman to develop the basics of long-form cricket than ever before. We've got to accept we're not going to be playing on traditional Test grounds for the whole season, but we're not doing that anyway in the back-end of the season. The back-half of the season I would use for Australia A games. Then I'd also have an Australian Under-23 team either touring or having other teams visiting Australia, just to get another level and a higher standard between Shield cricket and Test cricket.

New Zealand's triumph over India in the inaugural World Test Championship final was another moment in which sound planning and a focused cricket system came to the fore. Without anything like the same talent pool as most of their rivals, given their much smaller population, the Kiwis have always had to make the very most of their resources. Over the course of a decade now they have been almost constantly improving. The team that won in Southampton was running in the slipstream of another good team that had performed in World Cups in particular, Ross Taylor and Kane Williamson providing the main links between the two.

It may be a blessing in some ways that New Zealand haven't got too many players to pick from. It means they have to identify the ones who have a chance and give them that chance. I don't care whether it's New Zealand or India, that's what you've got to do. We always used to laugh at England's tendency to think players needed close to a decade in the county system before playing Test matches, and then to discard them willy-nilly for whoever was making timely runs at the lower level. But the unfortunate reality is that Australian cricket has veered that way in recent years, leading to inferior results a lot of the time – especially given the battery of fast bowlers we have. Performance at first-class level is an essential part of any player's education in a functional cricket system, but it is far from the only defining factor in whether they can go on to achieve great things at the next one.

All of these conversations, which might once have been pushed through by a barnstorming Pat Howard, have been given fresh impetus by the questions raised through COVID-19. It would be a shame if CA was not giving them serious consideration, the better to preserve the game and the national team that we love so much.

22

LOVING CRICKET BUT
NOT BEING DEFINED BY IT

I'M OFTEN SURPRISED, sometimes humorously so, about how other people perceive me based on what they've seen through the media. Terms like 'tough', 'uncompromising', 'intimidating' and 'my way or the highway' often come up. At the same time, you never truly get used to how deferential people are when you walk into a room, or whenever the conversation turns to cricket – I need to be conscious of making sure other people get their say. People who know me well, particularly those who have worked closely with me, see me differently. What they found was a very different person to what they expected.

This is pretty common among public figures, and we all do it, forming a view of someone based on very limited exposure. That's always amused and frustrated me in equal measure, because although you can brush a lot off, sometimes it does still sting. I'm extremely grateful I didn't play the game in the social media era, although I'd like to think I would have been able to filter out any useful observations and discard the rest.

No-one owns all the wisdom around a subject, whatever it might be. I know there will be a few people I've argued with over the years who may have got a different impression. I know Rod Marsh, for one, will recall we've had some really robust discussions over the years, where we've both been forceful and not given a lot of ground. But cricket, particularly other roles around the game apart from playing, has taught me that there's no real future in being that strident. You learn far more from listening than from talking.

My father, Martin, imbued me with a strong sense of wanting to learn my own lessons, and I think that has stood me in good stead as a leader and a mentor. If you're going to employ people, there's no point doing so and then trying to do the job for them. In parenting, Judy and I were very conscious of ensuring our children became independent as early as possible. Perhaps we went a bit too far – they all left home as soon as they finished school to pursue their careers. Stephen and Jonathan went straight on to work and study away from home as soon as they were out of school, and Belinda was more or less the same.

Something we always worked on was ensuring that our children's lives were as private and normal as possible. Belinda, in particular, struggled to understand as a child why whenever we went out for dinner, or anything else for that matter, we were always being stopped by people for a chat. As a consequence we spent a lot of time with friends and within our social network, and we were quite choosy about the invitations we accepted: it was never in Judy's or my idea of life that we would pursue status as celebrities or socialites. We had a holiday house in Caloundra on the Sunshine Coast for many years, and whenever possible we headed there. The moment the kids finished school on a Friday, we'd drive off to escape, and not return until it was time to drop them back at school on the Monday.

My father's early death was a seminal moment. At that point I realised that I had to take responsibility for my own health. I couldn't rely on somebody else looking after it. I was 35 years old at the time I lost my father and I realised I didn't want to get to 50 and then be told by a doctor that I had to change my lifestyle. I read and studied as much as I could about good health, which led me as far as being a vegan for more than a decade. This wasn't to live longer, but to live *well* for as long as I do live. I copped a lot of piss-taking from friends about all of this. Over time I have moderated a few things, and now, in my 70s, I feel more than comfortable with my choices.

I'm not a natural extrovert. Cricket forced me to become more outgoing and gregarious than I think was going to be otherwise. That is why I need time away from cricket and the public eye to regenerate my energy, because that has never been a totally natural experience for me. This is not to say it was all draining: I was able to use the energy of playing or speaking in front of an audience to get me going. While I had an inherent shyness about speaking, it's fair to say I also had a streak of the show-off about me, in that I enjoyed the experience of putting my skills on display. Had I been able to do that without speaking too much, it might have been the perfect balance, but you can't have everything!

Cricket has been the vehicle through which I've learned most of my life lessons. It also gave me opportunities beyond the game that I would never have glimpsed otherwise, particularly in the business world. Moreover, the fact that players in my era had to work for the majority of our careers meant that it enabled me to learn more widely than the current generation of players can. Gideon Haigh once wrote about me that I built up business interests as though I 'aspired to leave cricket behind', and I think to a degree I did. As much as I loved it, I didn't want cricket to define me, so there was always a certain restlessness to explore other things.

But the more I explored other things, the more I realised that my heart would always draw me back to cricket. I liked the fact that on the sporting field you knew exactly where you stood at any given time – and you knew what you had to do. If you weren't sure of it, just have a look at the scoreboard. Whereas in business you were making decisions that may not come to fruition for six months, 12 months or even years. There was a far closer parallel between business and selection or talent management than there was with playing the game.

That left me with another question. How was I to make the most of my public profile, gained through cricket, while also stretching myself into areas beyond how to play it, coach or pick teams for it? I'd always had a desire to give service of some kind, having been taught from an early age that there were always people less fortunate than we were. As a young cricketer with South Australia, we were involved with numerous charities, playing cricket with disabled kids in Adelaide, and that helped open my eyes to just what sportspeople could do.

When we came to Queensland we were involved with the Blind Cricket Society. One of the most unusual and enjoyable evenings I ever had was when speaking at the Deaf and Dumb Cricket Society. I'd deliver a couple of sentences, then wait for the translation. Telling a joke involved a longer moment's terror than usual while waiting to see if it would generate any laughs or not! Later after dinner, the society's members danced along, not to the music being played but the vibrations coming through the floor beneath them.

At other times we were involved with the Xavier Children's Hospital. This involved meeting and talking or playing cricket with kids who had suffered from terrible birth defects or subsequent conditions. A lot of them lived in hospital beds. I was also part of a fundraising committee that raised $20 million for the Royal Children's Hospital in Brisbane in 1989, matched dollar for dollar by the state government, which allowed for its rebuild. The Leukaemia Foundation was another organisation I fell in with. That involved some heart-rending visits to the oncology ward early each December for a Christmas party, because many of the kids weren't in good enough shape to make it through to the 25th.

One day I got talking with one of the parents. He was there with his son but also interacting with the other kids, and they were all being jolly in a way that I found extraordinary, given how tough the circumstances were. So I said to him, 'Mate, how do you do it?'

'What do you mean?'

'Knowing what you know, how can you be this upbeat about it all?'

'Greg, I don't have any other choice.'

It really brought home how important the whole thing was.

To also be involved with the Primary Club raising money for the disabled to enjoy physical activity, the Lord's Taverners, likewise raising money for youth and disability sport, and the LBW Trust, which raises money for improving tertiary education opportunities in the developing world, has all been incredibly rewarding. In recent years, the Chappell Foundation for homeless and at risk youth has provided a sense of meaning and wider social benefit that you will never find simply by hitting a cricket ball or raking in the dollars.

Since we first worked together for the LBW Trust, Darshak has been ever present in ensuring that this altruistic streak does not go to waste:

Having seen Greg give his time generously to the international adult education and training charity, The LBW Trust, which I chaired for almost a decade, it was a no-brainer for me to try and persuade him to establish The Chappell Foundation (TCF) in 2017 which, Greg suggested, would work to ameliorate youth homelessness in Australia. We agreed that if we were able to change even one life, it would be worthwhile. TCF has transformed thousands.

Greg has been an absolute rock. He never says NO to our many outrageous requests and can barnstorm the most obdurate doors in Australia. His 'hit' rate is awesome. Not many people say no to him. And, he is absolutely fearless and does not need much convincing. He has graciously and uncomplainingly attended all Chappell Foundation events flying in from Brisbane and boarding/lodging in Sydney, all at his own cost.

What he has helped do with his vision and efforts at TCF is truly inspirational. His charitable work (he has supported a handful of others) over the past fifty years was considered noteworthy enough by the Australian government, who conferred an Officer of the Order of Australia (AO) in January this year, to add to his Member of the British Empire (MBE) honour from over forty-two years ago.

I have seen at close quarters the awe and tremendous respect he elicits from Indian-Australians in particular.

Whether he is at a petrol station, a restaurant or in a social setting, Indians flock to him for a chat, photograph or autograph. So many Indian-Australians want to volunteer, serve and work for The Chappell Foundation, it is embarrassing for me to say no.

If asked what the future holds, I suspect Judy and Greg would want to settle down in Sydney near Ian and Trevor. They have moved around a bit in the past forty years and it would be good if all the Chappells are in the same city in, dare I say it, their twilight years.

From time to time, Judy has challenged me on the point that I do so much of this kind of work, which often means spending time away from her or from family. I do it because it's repaying society for the benefits I've enjoyed from a life in cricket, and because it brings a wider spiritual reward that transcends anything that you can achieve on your own.

We all get a helping hand along the way in life, but we're not always aware of its presence. I have always had the feeling that I owe it to the universe, or to somebody here on earth, to pay that forward.

23

LAST THOUGHTS

WHAT IS CRICKET'S final frontier? For successive generations of Australians involved in the game, it was winning
a Test series in India, something achieved only once in the past
50 years. I have a strong conviction that our final frontier is
actually something deeper than that.

The main reason that I wanted to write this book is to promote
discussion around my belief that the true frontier for cricket is to
conquer the belief that one is best served by hitting thousands of
balls per week in the sterile environment of net practice if one
wants to become a champion with the bat.

My cricket career, and my life, began to change when I realised that I had a superpower within that could help me reach my
potential in a more efficient manner. This superpower is available to us all. It is our power of imagination. The first time I was
introduced to this concept was when I read Dr Maxwell Maltz's
book, *Psycho-Cybernetics*, when I was 21 years old. I made a point

at the time of reading books on methods for success and mental strength – a habit helped perhaps by the frequency of rain in Somerset, where I was playing. Up until that point, I laboured under the false impression that my physical skills were my most important asset.

I started to see the world very differently upon reading these words from Maltz: 'Our self image, strongly held, essentially determines what we become.' This message really hit home after my father sent me an article by Keith Butler from *The Advertiser* in Adelaide. Butler was very critical of my recent form and he accused me of being in danger of wasting my talent. Dad had written a note at the bottom of the article saying, 'I don't believe everything that Keith has to say, but it might be worth thinking about.'

That night, I sat down and thought about every game that I had ever played, from the backyard through school, club, first-class cricket and a handful of Test matches. As I sat reflecting, in the dark of my room at Hadley's Hotel in Hobart, it suddenly struck me that what I thought about, and the attitude that I brought to each day, would be the main determiner of my level of success.

Once I had come to that realisation, I knew that it was my mental skills that I had to focus on perfecting, not my physical skills. What I realised that day was that I had a mental routine which I used on my successful days, but used sparingly on the less successful days. The other realisation was that, up to that point, I had got myself out nine times out of 10. My dismissal might have been contributed to by good bowling and good fielding, but, in the end, it was my mental mistake that had brought about my demise. I knew that if I could manage my mental environment with more discipline, I would delay the inevitable and, ipso facto, I must make more runs.

Having had the epiphany, it became clear to me that my focus from now on had to be to develop my mental routine so that it became a conscious effort leading up to and after each ball, to ensure that I was on top of my inner game. From that day, practice for me became about training my mental routine.

When one realises that the subconscious mind can deal with millions of bits of information per second while the conscious mind can only deal with 40 bits of information per second, it becomes obvious that one needs to facilitate the use of the two parts of the mind to do what they do best. The conscious mind is about creativity and the big picture, while the sole objective for the subconscious is to do the bidding of the conscious mind and run the program.

When we are walking, for instance, the conscious mind focuses on the destination; the role of the subconscious is to activate all the nerves, muscles, ligaments and limbs to get us there as efficiently as possible. It is no different when we are playing cricket. In batting, the main task for the conscious mind is to see the ball, while the subconscious sets about reacting to the information and recruiting the nerves, muscles, ligaments and limbs to execute the appropriate response.

If one tries to run the program with the conscious mind it will be clunky and inefficient. I soon found that my subconscious mind was a much better batsman than I could ever be! From that point, the benchmark for my training sessions became about how well I responded to each delivery rather than how well I hit the ball. Not surprisingly, when my response to each delivery was appropriate, I hit the ball really well. This, allied with putting myself into virtual match scenarios at training, made my practice sessions as game-like as possible.

On top of my physical training sessions, following my revelation at Hadley's Hotel, I began visualising myself batting against the current opposition as I went to sleep each night. These sessions proved to be an extremely efficient way to top up my physical sessions in an era when cricket was a pastime. It was also a great way of preserving my energy for the actual games. What I stumbled upon was the most efficient form of training available to me. This format built a robust method of concentration that stood me in excellent stead to deal with the challenges of the game at the highest level.

It also helped me to deal with the inevitable failures and to come back for the next game with the belief that I had not lost my talent. The length of my lean spells lasted for as long as it took me to realise that my problem was one of thinking rather than execution. Around this time, Russian coaches were already employing visualisation routines for their athletes and sportsmen and -women. This and their revolutionary physical training gave them a huge edge over their Western opponents.

American sportsmen and -women such as Al Oerter (discus) and Billie Jean King (tennis) were using these techniques in the 1960s and '70s to reach the top of their field. Subsequent research has proven the efficacy of these methods over and again.

But cricket is yet to catch on. In fact, the emphasis on coaching in recent times has only served to reinforce the less efficient practice of honing the physical aspects of the game by endless, some would say mindless, net sessions at low intensity that actually limit one's chances of developing into a dynamic, game-changing player. From what I have observed, most coaches are firmly in the camp that believes that batting is primarily about not getting out. Obviously one needs to stay in the middle for extended periods if one wants to make big scores, but if one starts from the premise of playing safe, even if one succeeds, big scores are unlikely to be a regular feature for that player.

Batting is an exercise in risk management. If one wants to make runs, one has to be prepared to play some shots. The quickest way to take the pressure off oneself is to put it back on the bowler by scoring runs. This is particularly so at the highest level. I am firmly of the opinion that cricket approaches batting skill acquisition from the wrong direction.

Rather than start from building a sound defence, I believe that we should be teaching young batters the attacking strokes first, and allow them to develop a sound defence on top of that framework. This can be achieved by encouraging them to explore, from personal experience and robust feedback, which deliveries they can attack and which ones they have to defend or allow to pass. By starting from the defence first approach, I believe we make the learning of batting too difficult for the majority of young players. Once we start them down the path of being told how to do it, we limit just how far they might go by using their own imagination.

One of the benefits I had as a young player was that our father told me what he wanted me to do rather than how to do it. That way, I developed my own style. Had he shown me how he thought I should play a certain shot, that would have put a lid on what I might have come up with, if left to my own devices.

This was reinforced to me when I began coaching young cricketers. Initially, I tried to teach them how to bat. This was frustrating to them as well as to me. Once I began giving them target areas to hit to, and left them to work out how best to do it, I was amazed at how quickly they progressed.

What we know about the champions of each era is that they are best at picking up the cues and clues and they become the best decision-makers. If we want to produce more champions, then we have to include making decisions in real time as part of the learning equation.

This doesn't mean putting on games and just letting them play. It means that coaches have to be educated in how to create learning environments that replicate the needs of the game as much as possible and develop each individual as required. They're all different. This form of training has been proven to develop an individual's mental skills at the same time as they learn the physical game. To me, the challenge of creating these learning habitats is the real art of coaching. If we bring youngsters up in this manner, they will have more fun, plus we will produce more champions than we are currently doing.

The majority of young boys and girls who come to the game will not go on to become state representatives, let alone international stars. It is therefore incumbent on coaches to make sure that youngsters get some memorable experiences so that they enjoy their time as much as possible. It is critical that we teach them the whole game, not just the narrow aspects of batting and bowling.

I believe we will retain youngsters in the game longer by taking this approach and we will more likely develop cricket lovers and future cricket parents along the way. Those who have the desire to play at the highest level will benefit from finding their own way with the assistance of quality mentoring, and be better able to solve problems once they do. This is especially important in an age when the game needs adaptable players rather than adapted ones.

Over the preceding pages I have explored many aspects of my latter-day cricketing life. But most of those moments and lessons come back to the strong belief that the way we teach the game, and how we identify the kinds of young men and women who can go on to long and influential cricket careers, needs a fresh appraisal.

ACKNOWLEDGEMENTS

T HIS IS THE third time I have done a book with Pam Brewster as publisher, and on each occasion, she has done a great job in steering it through to completion. I'm equally grateful for the work of others through Hardie Grant, particularly the sound editing of Michael Epis and Anna Collett.

I could not have put this book together without the assiduous help of my brother Ian, who aided in clarifying some of my thoughts and then gave the manuscript a thorough read-through. Similarly, my 'partner in crime' for the LBW Trust and the Chappell Foundation, Darshak Mehta, looked very closely at the manuscript in its various stages and offered typically wise and worldly counsel.

Extremely helpful, too, was Ben Johnson, who was happy to catch up and talk through his recollections of our work together with Charles Krebs for South Australia, and how the mental side of the game sits as an untapped resource for many cricketers.

There would not have been a book at all without the tireless collaboration of Daniel Brettig, who sat through many hours of interviews and then sculpted my memories into a readable story with an eye for detail.

Lastly, my wife, Judy, has been a constant source of recollection, advice and, I daresay, my favourite chapter of the book itself. It's been a joy to get this far with her, and here's hoping for many more years of shared adventure.